Hispanic American Biographies

Volume 4

Gamboa, Harry, Jr.—Julia, Raul

an imprint of

■SCHOLASTIC

www.scholastic.com/librarypublishing

First published 2006 by Grolier,
an imprint of Scholastic Library Publishing,
Old Sherman Turnpike,
Danbury, Connecticut 06816

© 2006 The Brown Reference Group plc

Set ISBN-13: 978-0-7172-6124-6
Set ISBN-10: 0-7172-6124-7
Volume ISBN-13: 978-0-7172-6128-4
Volume ISBN-10: 0-7172-6128-X

Library of Congress Cataloging-in-Publication Data
Hispanic American biographies.
    v. cm.
  Includes bibliographical references and index.
  Contents: v. 1. Acevedo-Vilá, Aníbal - Bocanegra, Carlos -- v. 2. Bonilla,
Tony - Corretjer, Juan Antonio -- v. 3. Cortés, Carlos - Gálvez, Bernardo
de -- v. 4. Gamboa, Harry, Jr. - Julia, Raul -- v. 5. Juncos, Manuel
Fernández - Montez, Maria -- v. 6. Montoya, Carlos Garcia - Ponce, Mary
Helen -- v. 7. Ponce de León, Juan - Seguín, Juan N. -- v. 8. Selena -
Zúñiga, Martha.
  ISBN-13: 978-0-7172-6124-6 (set : alk. paper) -- ISBN-10: 0-7172-6124-7
(set : alk. paper) -- ISBN-13: 978-0-7172-6125-3 (v. 1 : alk. paper) -- ISBN-
10: 0-7172-6125-5 (v. 1 : alk. paper) -- ISBN-13: 978-0-7172-6126-0 (v. 2 :
alk. paper) -- ISBN-10: 0-7172-6126-3 (v. 2 : alk. paper) -- ISBN-13: 978-0-
7172-6127-7 (v. 3 : alk. paper) -- ISBN-10: 0-7172-6127-1 (v. 3 : alk. paper)
-- ISBN-13: 978-0-7172-6128-4 (v. 4 : alk. paper) -- ISBN-10: 0-7172-6128-
X (v. 4 : alk. paper) -- ISBN-13: 978-0-7172-6129-1 (v. 5 : alk. paper) --
ISBN-10: 0-7172-6129-8 (v. 5 : alk. paper) -- ISBN-13: 978-0-7172-6130-7
(v. 6 : alk. paper) -- ISBN-10: 0-7172-6130-1 (v. 6 : alk. paper) -- ISBN-13:
978-0-7172-6131-4 (v. 7 : alk. paper) -- ISBN-10: 0-7172-6131-X (v. 7 : alk.
paper) -- ISBN-13: 978-0-7172-6132-1 (v. 8 : alk. paper) -- ISBN-10: 0-7172-
6132-8 (v. 8 : alk. paper).
  1. Hispanic Americans--Biography--Encyclopedias--Juvenile literature. I.
Grolier Publishing Company.
E184.S75H5573 2006
973'.046800922--dc22
[B]
                                    2006012294

For information address the publisher:
Grolier, Scholastic Library Publishing,
Old Sherman Turnpike,
Danbury, Connecticut 06816

FOR THE BROWN REFERENCE GROUP PLC

Project Editor: Chris King
Editors: Henry Russell, Aruna Vasudevan,
                                 Tom Jackson, Simon Hall
Design: Q2A Solutions, Seth Grimbly,
                                 Lynne Ross
Picture Researcher: Sharon Southren
Index: Kay Ollerenshaw
Design Manager: Sarah Williams
Production Director: Alastair Gourlay
Senior Managing Editor: Tim Cooke
Editorial Director: Lindsey Lowe

ACADEMIC CONSULTANTS:

Ellen Riojas Clark,   Arnoldo de Leon,
Division of Bicultural Bilingual Department of History,
  Studies,   Angelo State University
University of Texas at San Antonio

Printed and bound in Singapore

ABOUT THIS SET

This is one of a set of eight books chronicling the lives of Hispanic Americans who have helped shape the history of the United States. The set contains biographies of more than 750 people of Hispanic origin. They range from 16th-century explorers to 21st-century musicians and movie stars. Some were born in the United States, while others immigrated there from countries such as Mexico, Cuba, or Puerto Rico. The subjects therefore come from a wide range of cultural backgrounds, historical eras, and areas of achievement.

In addition to the biographical entries, the set includes a number of guidepost articles that provide an overview of a particular aspect of the Hispanic American experience. These guidepost articles cover general areas such as civil rights and religion as well as specific historical topics such as the Treaty of Guadalupe Hidalgo. These articles serve to help place the lives of the subjects of the biographies in a wider context.

Each biographical entry contains a box listing key dates in the subject's life as well as a further reading section that gives details of books and Web sites that the reader may wish to explore. Longer biographies also include a box about the people who inspired the subject, people the subject has influenced in turn, or the legacy that the subject has left behind. Where relevant, entries also contain a "See also" section that directs the reader to related articles elsewhere in the set. A comprehensive set index is included at the end of each volume.

The entries are arranged alphabetically, mostly by surname but also by stage name. In cases where the subject has more than one surname, he or she is alphabetized under the name that is most commonly used. For example, Héctor Pérez García is usually known simply as Hector P. Garcia and is therefore alphabetized under "G." Pedro Albizu Campos, meanwhile, is generally known by his full name and is alphabetized under "A." Both variants are included in the index. Where names are commonly spelled in a variety of ways, the most widespread version is used. Similarly, the use of accents is dictated in each individual case by general usage.

Contributors: Holly Ackerman; Robert Anderson; Kevin Anzzolin; Faisal Azam; Brandee R. Ball; Kelvin Bias; Erica Brodman; John Buentello; Francisco Cabanillas; Irma Cantu Jones; Hector Carbajal; Bec Chalkley; Gerardo Cummings; German Cutz; Anita Dalal; Zilah Deckker; Marcus Embry; Marilyn Fedewa; Héctor Fernández L'Hoeste; José Gamez; Randall Lee Gann; Maryellen Garcia; Conrado Gomez; Leon Gray; Susan Green; José Angel Gutiérrez; Ted Henken; Elizabeth Juárez-Cummings; Nashieli Marcano; Irma Martelango; Danizete Martinez; Fran Meizoso; Rashaan Meneses; Luisa Moncada; Eduardo Moralez; Mark Moreno; Houston Faust Mount; Carlos Ortega; Novia Pagone; Teresa Palomo Acosta; Jill Pinkney Pastrana; Norma Rodriguez; Eliza Rodriguez y Gibson; Henry Russell; Melissa Segura; Angharad Valdivia; Alberto Varon; Santos Vega; Keith Watts; Chris Wiegand; Emma Young.

CONTENTS

Gamboa, Harry, Jr.	4	González, Celedonio	53	Hinojosa, Maria	99
Gamio, Manuel	5	González, Henry B.	54	Hinojosa, Tish	100
Garcia, Andy	6	González, Jovita	56	Hinojosa de Ballí,
García, Clotilde P.	8	Gonzalez, Juan	57	Rosa María	101
Garcia, Cristina	9	González, Juan D.	58	Hinojosa-Smith, Rolando	102
García, Gustavo C.	10	Gonzalez, Kenny "Dope"	59	Hispanic Identity and
García, Héctor P.	11	González, Odilio	60	Popular Culture	104
García, J.D.	12	González, Pedro J.	61	Homar, Lorenzo	110
Garcia, Jeff	13	González, Raúl	63	Hostos, Eugenio María de	111
Garcia, Jerry	14	González, Xavier	64	Huerta, Dolores	113
García, Lionel	16	Gronk	65	Huerta, Jorge A.	115
García, Macario	17	Guadalupe Hidalgo,		Idar, Jovita	116
García, Rupert	18	Treaty of	66	Idar, Nicasio	117
Garciaparra, Nomar	19	Guastavino, Rafael	68	Iglesias, Enrique	118
Garza, Ben	20	Guerra, Manuel	69	Immigration and
Garza, Catarino E.	22	Guerrero, Lalo	70	Immigration Law	119
Garza, Reynaldo	23	Guillermoprieto, Alma	72	Islas, Arturo	125
Garza Falcón, María de la	24	Gutiérrez, José Angel	73	Ithier, Rafael	126
Gaspar de Alba, Alicia	25	Gutiérrez, Luz Bazán	74	Iturbi, José	127
Gavin, John	26	Gutierrez, Theresa	75	Jaramillo, Cleofas M.	128
Gil, Federico	28	Guzmán, Ralph	76	Jaramillo Mari-Luci	129
Gioia, Dana	29	Hayek, Salma	77	Jimenez, Flaco	130
Goizueta, Roberto	30	Hayworth, Rita	79	Jiménez, Luis	131
Goldemberg, Isaac	32	Hernández, Adán	81	Juanes	132
Gómez, Edward	33	Hernández, Antonia	82	Julia, Raul	133
Gomez, José H.	34	Hernandez, Ester	83	
Gomez, Scott	35	Hernández, Joseph Marion	84	Set Index	135
Gomez, Vernon "Lefty"	36	Hernandez, Juan	85	Credits	144
Gomez, Wilfredo	37	Hernandez, Keith	86	
Gómez-Peña, Guillermo	38	Hernández, María Latigo	87	
Gómez-Quiñones, Juan	40	Hernández, Orlando	89	
Gonzales, Alberto	41	Hernández Bros., Los	90	
Gonzales, Boyer	43	Hernández Colón, Rafael	91	
Gonzales, Manuel	44	Hernández Cruz, Victor	92	
Gonzales, Manuel C.	45	Herrera, Carolina	93	
Gonzales, Ricardo	46	Herrera, John J.	94	
Gonzales, Rodolfo "Corky"	48	Herrera, Silvestre	95	
Gonzales-Berry, Erlinda	50	Herrera-Sobek, María	96	
Gonzalez, Alfredo Cantu	51	Hidalgo, Edward	97	
González, Antonio	52	Hijuelos, Oscar	98	

GAMBOA, Harry, Jr.
Artist

The work of Chicano artist Harry Gamboa, Jr., has challenged stereotypes of Mexican Americans, voiced opposition to the mistreatment of minority cultures in the United States, and questioned conventional identity politics within the Chicano community itself.

Early life

Gamboa was born in Los Angeles, California, in 1951 to Harry T. and Carmen Gamboa. He was the first of five children in a working-class Mexican American family. Growing up in East Los Angeles he experienced the social challenges of urban America including poverty, violence, and racial injustice. As a teenager Gamboa was active in local politics and community organizations. In March 1968 he helped organize a series of student protests, known as the "East L.A. Blowouts," in which thousands of young people marched out of six East Los Angeles high schools to draw attention to the inferior conditions and educational imbalances of public schools in poor minority areas of the city. These student protests demonstrated the growing strength of the Chicano civil rights movement. As a result of Gamboa's involvement in civil protests, the Intelligence Division of the Los Angeles Police Department

KEY DATES

1951	Born in Los Angeles, California.
1969	Graduates from Garfield High School in East Los Angeles.
1972	Cofounds the influential Chicano art group Asco, which remains active until 1987.
1978	Cofounds the influential artist-run gallery Los Angeles Contemporary Exhibitions.

(LAPD) focused attention on his activities. In testimony subsequently provided before the U.S. Senate, the LAPD described Gamboa as a militant agitator.

On graduating in 1969 from Garfield High School, Balboa bought a camera and became a self-taught photographer and artist. In 1971, as editor of the Chicano journal *Regeneracíon*, he began collaborating with three of his former classmates, Willie Herrón, Glugio "Gronk" Nicondra, and Patssi Valdez. This group was joined by Humberto Sandoval and developed into the influential avant-garde art group Asco (1972–1987).

Versatile artist

Gamboa has worked in a wide range of media, including fiction, poetry, film, painting (especially murals), photography, and performance art. In each medium he has sought to explore the social forces that have a negative impact on urban Chicano communities. Although he is most commonly associated with Asco, his contribution to Chicano and contemporary art is much broader. Since the late 1980s he has held numerous teaching positions and artistic fellowships. His work has been exhibited internationally, the oral history he compiled has been archived at the Smithsonian Institution in Washington, D.C., and an extensive representative collection of his works has been archived at Stanford University in Palo Alto, California.

▼ *Harry J. Gamboa, Jr., was at the forefront of the Chicano movement in the 1970s and 1980s.*

See also: Gronk

Further reading: Gamboa, Harry, Jr., and Chon A. Noriega. *Urban Exile: Collected Writings of Harry Gamboa, Jr.* Minneapolis, MN: University of Minnesota Press, 1998. http://www.harrygamboajr.com (authorized Web site).

GAMIO, Manuel
Anthropologist

Manuel Gamio is hailed as the father of Mexican anthropology, thanks to his seminal studies of Teotihuacán life and culture. Gamio's later research helped reshape U.S. policies on Mexican immigration.

Gamio was born in the suburbs of Mexico City on March 2, 1883, but little is known about his early life. He graduated from the National Preparatory School of San Ildefonso (now part of the National Autonomous University of Mexico) and was then awarded a doctorate in archaelogy from Columbia University. On his return to Mexico, Gamio took a job as inspector of monuments within Mexico's Ministry of Public Instruction and Fine Arts. In 1917 he became director of the Archaelogical and Ethnographic Studies Office. Gamio himself was instrumental in creating the new department, part of Mexico's Ministry of Agriculture and Development. Under Gamio's direction, the Archaelogical and Ethnographic Studies Office established an ambitious program of study.

Teotihuacán excavations
In 1919 Gamio renamed his department the Anthropology Office and, with the sanction of the secretary for agriculture, embarked on an excavation of the Teotihuacán Valley in central Mexico. Many specialists participated in Gamio's project, including architects, artists, biologists, historians, linguists, and photographers.

▲ **Manuel Gamio influenced the way in which the U.S. government viewed Mexican immigration.**

In the 1920s Gamio relocated his excavations to the highlands of Guatemala near the cities of Quiche, Huehuetenango, and Quetzaltenango. Thanks to his "Think before you dig" methodology, Gamio unearthed numerous complete examples of early pre-Toltec ceramics. He noted similarities between the pottery he found in Guatemala with those buried in ancient lava flows at Mexican sites. Gamio suggested that the early inhabitants of central Mexico moved to escape natural disasters such as earthquakes and volcanoes. He published *La Población del Valle de Teotihuacán* (*The Population of the Valley of Teotihuacán*) in 1922.

Later in his career, Gamio turned his attention to immigration and labor studies of Mexicans migrating to the United States. His research culminated in two important publications: *Mexican Immigration to the United States* (1930) and the acclaimed *The Mexican Immigrant: His Life Story* (1931). In 1942 he became the first director of the Instituto Indigenista Interamericano (III), seeking to establish a Mexican cultural identity based on indigenous ethnic groups. He died in Mexico in 1960.

KEY DATES

1883 Born in Mexico City on March 2.

1917 Becomes director of the newly formed Archaelogical and Ethnographic Studies Office in Mexico.

1919 Conducts detailed excavations of the Teotihuacán Valley in central Mexico until 1921.

1922 Publishes *La Población del Valle de Teotihuacán* (*The Population of the Valley of Teotihuacán*).

1930 Publishes *Mexican Immigration to the United States*.

1931 Publishes the acclaimed *The Mexican Immigrant: His Life Story*.

1942 Becomes the first director of the international Instituto Indigenista Interamericano (III).

1960 Dies in Mexico.

Further reading: Gamio, Manuel. *The Mexican Immigrant: His Life Story*. Chicago, IL: University of Chicago Press, 1931. www.saa.org/publications/oaxaca/chapter2/chapter2-1.html (outlines Gamio's contribution to Mexican anthropology).

GARCIA, Andy
Actor, Filmmaker

Andy Garcia is one of the few Cuban actors to have established a very successful career in Hollywood. Garcia has appeared in more than 40 movies, including *The Untouchables* (1987), *The Godfather: Part III* (1990), *Ocean's Eleven* (2001), and *Ocean's Twelve* (2004). He has produced eight movies and directed four films. Garcia also produced *Master Sessions, Volume 1,* a CD by Cuban music legend Israel "Cachao" Lopez.

Early life
Born in Havana, Cuba, on April 12, 1956, Andrés Arturo García Menéndez was one of the three children of Rene and Amelia Garcia Nunez. When he was five years old, Garcia and his family fled Cuba following Fidel Castro's revolution. They settled in Miami, Florida. Garcia's father, who had been a lawyer, was forced to work in a warehouse. After school, Garcia would help his father sweep the warehouse before going home. A hard-working man, Garcia's father established a fragrance import business; the company eventually became a multimillion-dollar concern. Garcia has frequently said that his greatest influences were his mother and father (*see box on page 7*).

As a young man Garcia was interested in sports, playing for the school basketball team. However, when he was 18, he contracted mononucleosis and hepatitis, which kept him bedridden over the basketball season. During that time his attention turned to acting.

Following a dream
Garcia studied at Florida International University, where he met his future wife, Marivi Lorida Garcia. He acted in regional theater productions before heading to Los Angeles, where he waited tables and loaded trucks to earn a living while he waited for his big break. At the time it was difficult for Hispanic actors to get good roles in Hollywood, and one agent advised Garcia to lose his accent, change his hair, and get his teeth fixed to blend in: Garcia did not follow the advice.

In 1981 Garcia landed his first role, playing a gang member in the popular NBC television series *Hill Street Blues*, after which he began to make regular guest appearances on other TV shows. His breakthrough role was playing a drug dealer in *8 Million Ways to Die* (1986). After seeing Garcia's performance, director

▲ *Andy Garcia was one of the first Hispanic actors to be cast in nonstereotypical roles in Hollywood. He paved the way for other Hispanic Americans to be accepted as major players in the movie industry.*

Brian De Palma cast the young actor in his classic movie *The Untouchables* (1987), opposite Kevin Costner and Sean Connery. Garcia's performance as the agent George Stone was well received. He played another policeman, Detective Charlie Vincent, in his next noteworthy performance in the 1989 Ridley Scott movie *Black Rain*.

Garcia entered Hollywood's major leagues in 1990 with two notable performances—in Mike Figgis's thriller *Internal Affairs* and in Francis Ford Coppola's *The Godfather: Part III*. Coppola had auditioned many of the leading male actors in Hollywood, including Val Kilmer, for the part of Vincent Mancini-Corleone, and he gave the part to Garcia. Although the film received mixed reviews, Garcia's performance garnered him an Oscar nomination for best supporting actor.

Major-league actor
In the 1990s Garcia was offered many leading roles in big-budget movies but he only accepted those he believed in or that he thought had a particular message. His films during this period include *Jennifer Eight* (1992), in which he played John Berlin, a policeman hunting a serial killer, and

INFLUENCES AND INSPIRATION

Actor and producer Andy Garcia has often said that as a Cuban American he has the "benefit of two great cultures and I love both of them." His parents, whom he has said "are the only heroes" in his life, made sure that Garcia knew about his Cuban heritage. Garcia grew up listening to his parents play Cuban music and hearing the stories of his parents and parents' friends, Cubans living in exile.

Garcia has often said that he will not return to Cuba while Fidel Castro is in power, but his interest in the country has not waned. He has worked hard to get films on Cuban-related subjects off the ground. He made the critically acclaimed documentary *Cachao ... Como Su Ritmo No Hay Dos* about the mambo star Israel "Cachao" Lopez. Garcia also helped produce a CD of Lopez's music. Garcia also labored for 10 years to make the movie *The Lost City*. Cowritten with Guillermo Cabrera Infante, the film was set in Havana during the Cuban revolution.

When a Man Loves Woman (1994), in which he played Michael Green, the pilot husband of Meg Ryan's alcoholic character, a role that won him rave reviews.

Wide range

Part of Garcia's success lies in his ability to be convincing in a variety of very different parts, such as the Italian agent George Stone (Giuseppe Petri) in *The Untouchables* (1987), a half-Irish district attorney in Sidney Lumet's *Night Falls on Manhattan* (1997), or the poet Federico Garcia Lorca in *The Disappearance of Garcia Lorca* (1997). In 2000, Garcia appeared in the HBO biopic *For Love or Country: The Arturo Sandoval Story* (2000), about the famous Cuban trumpet player. The performance won Garcia Emmy nominations in the best actor and outstanding made-for-television movie categories. He was also part of Steven Soderbergh's successful cast on *Ocean's Eleven* (2001) and *Ocean's Twelve* (2004), with leading actors George Clooney, Brad Pitt, and Julia Roberts.

In 2001 Garcia produced and starred in the well-received independent feature *The Man from Elysian Fields*, playing a struggling married novelist whose secret life as an escort to wealthy women immerses him in a mysterious and exotic world. His own company, CineSon Productions, developed Garcia's longterm project, *The Lost City* (2005).

Diversification

Not content with acting, Garcia branched out to other areas of the movie business. He produced and directed a 1993 documentary based on Israel "Cachao" Lopez (*see box*), and produced the compilation recording *Master Sessions Volume I* of Cachao's music. Garcia also wrote and produced several songs for *Steal Big Steal Little* (1995).

Political views

Garcia is an outspoken critic of Fidel Castro's regime in Cuba. He has joined fellow critics, such as the late great singer Celia Cruz, musicians Gloria and Emilio Estefan, and broadcaster Cristina Saralegui, to campaign for a democratic Cuba.

KEY DATES

1956 Born in Havana, Cuba, on April 12.

1961 Family moves to Miami Beach, Florida, from Cuba.

1978 Moves to Los Angeles, California, to pursue film career.

1981 Makes TV debut as a gang member in NBC's *Hill Street Blues*.

1983 Makes film debut in *Blue Skies Again*.

1987 Stars as Agent George Stone in Brian De Palma's *The Untouchables*.

1990 Cast as Vincent Mancini-Corleone in *The Godfather: Part III*; receives Oscar nomination.

1993 Produces and directs the documentary, *Cachao ... Como Su Ritmo No Hay Dos*.

1995 Receives a star on the Hollywood Walk of Fame.

2001 Stars as Terry Benedict in Steven Soderbergh's *Ocean's Eleven*, a remake of the Rat Pack's 1960s' heist movie.

2005 Directs, produces, cowrites, and stars as Fico in *The Lost City*.

See also: Cruz, Celia; Estefan, Emilio; Estefan, Gloria; Lopez, Israel "Cachao"; Sandoval, Arturo; Saralegui, Cristina

Further reading: http://www.imdb.com/name/nm0000412/bio (biography and filmography on the International Movie Database site).

GARCÍA, Clotilde P.
Doctor, Teacher

Clotilde Pérez García was an eminent physician, teacher, and advocate of Hispanic genealogy in the United States. Known to patients and colleagues as "Dr. Cleo," García was the sister of the eminent doctor and activist Héctor P. García.

Early life
Born in Ciudad Victoria, Tamaulipas, Mexico, on January 11, 1917, García was one of the seven children of Faustina Pérez and José G. García. In 1918 the Garcías migrated to the United States, where they settled in Mercedes, Texas. Since his qualifications were not recognized in the United States, José and his brother bought a grocery store in Mercedes. The Garcías experienced discrimination at the hands of local people and authorities, however: In 1924 the family store was set on fire by white locals. José and Faustina struggled on, and managed to send their children on to higher education. In all, six of the Garcías graduated as doctors, including Clotilde and her sister, Dalia.

▼ *Clotilde P. García was the only Mexican American student in her year at medical college.*

KEY DATES

1917 Born in Ciudad Victoria, Tamaulipas, Mexico on January 11.

1918 Family moves to Mercedes, Texas.

1954 Receives her medical degree; does an internship at Memorial Medical Center in Corpus Christi in 1955.

1969 Cofounds the Spanish American Genealogical Association with her sister, Dr. Dalia García.

1994 Retires from practice.

2000 Dies on May 27.

Putting a dream on hold
García received a BA and MA from the University of Texas. Accepted into medical school at the same time as her brother, Héctor, García realized that financially it was impossible for both of them to go. She put her career plans on hold and went to work as a teacher, sending part of her modest salary home to help finance her brother's studies. In 1950 García finally enrolled to study medicine, the only Mexican American in her year. A single mother, García made the difficult decision to leave her son at home with her family while she studied at the University of Texas at Galveston. García graduated in 1954.

A dedicated doctor
García is estimated to have delivered more than 10,000 babies during her 40-year career. Known as the "people's doctor," García seldom charged patients the full price for their health care; she often treated patients for free. Despite being a dedicated mother and doctor, García found time to work for charitable and civic organizations. She served with more than 29 such groups in her lifetime, and was nationally honored for her civic engagement. In addition García wrote more than 10 books on South Texas history and the genealogy of Spanish surnames, and helped found a national genealogical association (1969). She retired in 1994 and died in 2000.

See also: García, Hector P.

Further reading: http://www.capitol.state.tx.us/tlo/78R/billtext/SR01017F.HTM (biography).

GARCIA, Cristina
Writer

Cristina Garcia has won several awards for her writing. A former political journalist and *Time* magazine's bureau chief for Florida and the Caribbean, Garcia has also written successful books, including *Dreaming in Cuban*.

Early life
Born in Havana, Cuba, on July 4, 1958, Cristina Garcia was the daughter of Frank and Hope Lois Garcia. Her family immigrated to America in 1961. Garcia attended several Catholic elementary schools, graduating in 1976 from the Dominican Academy in Manhattan. Garcia went on to earn a bachelor's degree from Barnard College, followed by a master's from Johns Hopkins University.

From journalist to novelist
Garcia worked briefly for Procter and Gamble in West Germany before returning to the United States to begin a career as a political journalist. She joined *Time* magazine in 1983, where she worked until 1990.

Garcia then decided to pursue a full-time writing career. She attended the New York State Writers' Institute summer program in 1990, where she studied with Lynn Sharon Schwartz and Russell Banks. With Banks's help,

▼ *Although Cristina Garcia grew up in mainly Jewish communities in the United States, she considers herself to be Cuban, and writes on Cuban and Cuban American issues.*

KEY DATES	
1958	Born in Havana, Cuba, on July 4.
1961	Immigrates with family to the United States.
1979	Receives BA in political science from Barnard College.
1981	Awarded an MA in European and Latin American studies from Johns Hopkins University.
1983	National correspondent for *Time* magazine.
1992	Publishes her first book, *Dreaming in Cuban*.
2004	Awarded the National Endowment for the Arts Literature Fellowship.

Garcia got an agent and published her first novel, *Dreaming in Cuban* (1992). Critically acclaimed and nominated for the National Book Award, the novel examines three generations of a Cuban family living in Havana, Cuba, and Brooklyn, New York.

The Aguero Sisters (1997), Garcia's second book, examines two sisters who were separated before the revolution and reunited as adults. Garcia's characters not only represent the racial diversity and conflict existing in Cuba and Cubans, but intertwine race and gender with politics in a narrative in which Cuban identity is analyzed and understood through family structures and love of women rather than through the political struggles of men.

Garcia's third novel, *Monkey Hunting* (2003), tells the story of Chinese Cubans, descendants of Chinese workers brought to Cuba as forced labor. A love story that spans Cuba, China, and America, this novel is enormous in scope and embraces the United States's great ethnic and racial diversity. Garcia has commented that she hates the attempts made by some commentators to limit what it means to be Cuban. She says: "The point for me is that there is no one Cuban exile. I am out here in California and may not fit in anywhere, but I am Cuban too. I think I am trying to stake out a broader territory [in my writing]."

Further reading: Abney, Lisa, and Susan Disheroon-Green (eds.). *Twenty-first Century American Novelists*. Farmington Hills, MI: Thomson Gale, 2004.
http://www.thelavinagency.com/college/cristinagarcia.html (biography).

GARCÍA, Gustavo C.
Lawyer, Civil Rights Activist

Gustavo "Gus" C. García was an outstanding lawyer who campaigned to improve the education opportunities and working conditions of Mexican Americans. He is famous for his work on the 1954 landmark civil rights case *Hernandez v. Texas*.

Early life

Born in Laredo, Texas, on July 27, 1915, García was the son of Mexican-born Alfredo and Maria Teresa García. García grew up in San Antonio, Texas, where he attended Thomas Jefferson High School. After graduating in 1932, he studied for a BA at the University of Texas, where he gained a reputation as a brilliant public speaker. In 1938 he received his law degree; he passed the bar exam a year later. Before being drafted to serve in World War II (1939–1945), García worked for the Bexar County district attorney and for the assistant city attorney. During the war he was stationed in Japan, where he served in the Army Judge Advocate Corps as an assistant attorney.

"Separate but equal"

In 1945 García returned to San Antonio, where he concentrated on challenging discrimination in Texas. His initial focus was the "separate but equal" policy that led to the segregation of Mexican American children from whites in school. He believed that the educational establishments provided for Mexican American children were inadequate and prepared them only for menial occupations.

García formed an alliance between the League of United Latin American Citizens (LULAC) and the American GI Forum, promising that together they would make a difference. One of his first successes was the case of Hector Flores. García successfully negotiated for Flores and other Mexican Americans to attend a previously all-white elementary school. Some notable professors and attorneys joined García's cause, and despite limited finances, they filed cases against other Texas school districts.

In 1954 García took on the landmark case *Hernandez v. Texas*, with cocounsel Carlos Cardena. An all-white jury had previously convicted migrant worker Pete Hernandez of murder. García argued that the exclusion of Mexican Americans from the jury had denied Hernandez a fair trial. Chief Justice Earl Warren ruled in Hernandez's favor. Although García continued to work on civil rights cases, he later became an alcoholic. He died in June 1964.

▼ *Known for his great public-speaking skill, Gus García was so eloquent that Chief Justice Earl Warren allowed him to speak for an extra 16 minutes in oral argument in* **Hernandez v. Texas (1954).**

See also: Supreme Court

Further reading: Hunter, Miranda. *The Story of Latino Civil Rights: Fighting for Justice.* New York, NY: Mason Crest Publishers, May 2005
www.lulac.org (The League of United Latin American Citizens' site).

KEY DATES	
1915	Born in Texas on July 27.
1936	Graduates with a BA from the University of Texas.
1938	Graduates in law.
1954	Wins appeal at the Supreme Court in the landmark case *Hernandez v. Texas*.
1964	Dies in San Antonio on June 3.

GARCÍA, Héctor P.
Physician, Civil Rights Activist

Dr. Héctor Pérez García was a physician, soldier, and civil rights activist. The founder of the American GI Forum, the largest Hispanic veterans' group in the United States, García was the first Mexican American to receive the presidential medal of freedom.

Early life
Born in Llera, Tamaulipas, Mexico, in 1914, García was the son of José and Faustina García. From the age of three, García was brought up in Mercedes, Texas. García's parents found that their academic qualifications were not recognized in the United States, and they were forced to work in the fields to support their seven children. José García went on to set up a dry-goods store with his brothers. Faustina García became an important figure in the local community. She encouraged her children to help those less fortunate than themselves. The Garcías also emphasized the importance of education to their children: All of them went to college, and six became doctors.

A patriot
After graduating with honors from the University of Texas in 1926, and from the University of Texas Medical School, Galveston, in 1940, García volunteered for military service during World War II (1939–1945). He was quickly promoted to be a combat engineer officer and an officer in the Medical Corps.

In 1946, shortly after his discharge, García married Wanda Fusillo. He began practicing medicine in Corpus Christi, Texas, where many of his patients were Mexican American veterans. García realized that the men were

▲ **Hector García dedicated his life to improving the lives of his fellow Mexican Americans.**

receiving inferior treatment to white veterans: García campaigned to get better rights for the men.

On March 26, 1948, García established the American GI Forum (AGIF). Within months there were AGIF branches all across America. In 1949 the "Felix Longoria Affair" brought the AGIF to national attention. The AGIF learned that the white owner of a mortuary in Texas had denied the Longoria family the right to chapel services for their dead soldier son because he was Mexican American. The AGIF campaigned against this injustice so forcefully that Texas senator Lyndon B. Johnson (who became U.S. president in 1963) arranged for Longoria to be buried with full honors in Arlington National Cemetery. In 1968 García became the first Mexican American to serve on Johnson's U.S. Commission on Civil Rights; he was later made an ambassador to the United Nations. García remained a tireless supporter of the oppressed until his death in 1996.

See also: García, Clotilde P.; Longoria, Felix

Further reading: http://medaloffreedom.com/HectorGarcia.htm (biography).

KEY DATES

1914	Born in Llera, Tamaulipas, on January 17.
1940	Graduates from the University of Texas Medical School, Galveston.
1942	Volunteers for the U.S. Army.
1948	Forms the American GI Forum.
1968	Becomes first Mexican American to serve on the U.S. Commission on Civil Rights.
1996	Dies in Corpus Christi, Texas, on July 26.

GARCÍA, J. D.
Physicist

Award-winning Mexican American theoretical physicist J. D. García has been a professor at the University of Arizona since 1975. Highly acclaimed as both a researcher and a teacher, he says that in his lectures he "uses mathematics to describe the atom and how it works." One of his greatest achievements has been to make the subject accessible to students at all levels.

Early life

José Dolores García was raised in Alcalde, New Mexico, a small, poor, and isolated rural village. On graduating from Saint Michael's High School in Santa Fe he went on to New Mexico State University, where he attended classes for half the year and worked the rest of the time as a laboratory assistant in order to pay for books and other necessary materials. In his sophomore year he won a Fulbright Scholarship that enabled him to study at the University of Göttingen in Germany with some of the world's leading physicists. After completing his undergraduate degree, García took a PhD in physics at the University of Wisconsin–Madison in 1966. He spent the next 10 years in various junior academic teaching posts before being appointed professor of physics at the University of Arizona in 1975.

An important part of García's work as a theoretical physicist involves the use of mathematical models to help develop our understanding of the nature of atomic particles. He has compared such work to trying to figure out a jigsaw puzzle by concentrating on the nature of only a piece or two. His research aims primarily to predict the nature of atoms by analyzing their movements. It examines what happens when atomic particles collide with each other, and hypothesizes about the ways in which they might fit together in the larger universe. The research is

▲ *J. D. Garcia is a distinguished academic physicist who has successfully popularized his subject among a younger generation of scientists.*

painstaking and exact, and the information it yields may enable other scientists to answer such questions as how the universe works, how stars and planets form, and what can happen to matter in various circumstances.

Quantum physics

During the 20th century scientists discovered that the behavior of atomic and subatomic particles is not predictable according to previously accepted physical laws, and can only be speculated. As part of his professorial responsibilities, García conducted extensive research into time-dependent quantum models for collisions. Meanwhile in his administrative role as director of undergraduate studies, he strove to improve education standards for science teachers in high schools and colleges.

KEY DATES

1936   Born in Santa Fe, New Mexico, on January 3.

1966   Receives PhD in Physics from the University of Wisconsin-Madison.

1975   Is appointed professor of physics at the University of Arizona.

1998   Receives the Boucher Award from the American Physics Society.

Further reading: Kalte, Pamela, et al. (eds.). *American Men and Women of Science.* 22nd Edition. Farmington Hills, MI: Thomson-Gale, 2005.
http://www.physics.arizona.edu/physics/personnel/faculty/garcia.html (Department of Physics, University of Arizona).

GARCIA, Jeff
Football Player

Jeff Garcia is one of only six quarterbacks in National Football League (NFL) history to have achieved two back-to-back 30-touchdown passing seasons.

Early life
Born in Gilroy, California, on February 24, 1970, Jeffrey Jason Garcia is of mixed Mexican and Irish American ancestry. He went to Gilory High School, where he showed an early talent in both basketball and football. His early life was marred by tragedy, however. Just before his eighth birthday, two of his young siblings were killed: Garcia's brother drowned, and a year later his sister died in an automobile accident. This early loss made Garcia determined to succeed. He played football at Gavilan College, where he was coached by his father, Bob. He went on to play college football at San Jose State University.

After college Garcia was not drafted by an NFL team, so he joined the Canadian Football League (CFL). He played starting quarterback for the Calgary Stampeders, leading them to the Grey Cup title in 1998.

▼ *Quarterback Jeff Garcia promotes football abroad through his work with NFL international.*

KEY DATES	
1970	Born in Gilroy, California, on February 24.
1994	Signed by the Calgary Stampeders of the Canadian Football League.
1998	Leads the Stampeders to the Grey Cup.
1999	Joins NFL's San Francisco 49ers on February 16.
2005	Signs as a free agent with the Detroit Lions on March 12.

In 1999 Garcia joined the San Francisco 49ers. Under then-49ers coach Steve Mariucci, Garcia became an NFL star. He played in three consecutive Pro Bowls, and threw for a team record of 4,278 yards and 32 touchdowns in 2000. In the following season, Garcia threw for 3,538 yards and 30 touchdowns. In the 2003–2004 season he was a contributing factor in the 49ers beating the New York Giants in the playoffs; in a famous comeback the 49ers recovered from a 24-point deficit to claim victory by a single point. At the end of the 2003–2004 season, however, the 49ers released Garcia.

In March 2004, Garcia signed with the NFL's Cleveland Browns as a free agent. That fall Garcia shared an NFL record for the longest pass completion with a 99-yard throw to Andre Davis against the Cincinnati Bengals. However, Garcia's season ended prematurely when he tore the medial collateral ligament in his left knee. On December 13, Garcia was placed on injured reserve for the remainder of the season. Three months later he was released by the Browns. The Detroit Lions signed him as a free agent on March 12, 2005.

Work for charity
Garcia donates much time to charitable causes. He is a spokesman and fundraiser for the Hispanic Scholarship Fund. He also promotes football in Mexico and other countries through NFL International, which supports grassroots youth football efforts around the globe.

Further reading: Dickey, Glenn. *Glenn Dickey's 49ers: The Rise, Fall, and Rebirth of the NFL's Greatest Dynasty.* New York, NY: Prima Lifestyles, 2000.
http://www.garcianation.com (Garcia site).

GARCIA, Jerry
Musician

Jerry Garcia was the lead singer and guitarist of The Grateful Dead, a rock band whose legendary live shows epitomized the San Francisco hippie movement and helped popularize its philosophy throughout the United States and worldwide. Garcia was a versatile musician who also had multiple solo projects outside rock, ranging from jazz to bluegrass. Garcia maintained a rigorous touring schedule with The Grateful Dead as well as a range of solo projects from 1965 until his death 30 years later.

Early life

Jerome John Garcia was born on August 1, 1942, in San Francisco, California. He was named for composer Jerome Kern (1885–1945). His father, Spanish-born José García, was a talented jazz musician and big band leader; his mother, Ruth, was a pianist and a registered nurse. The family had a vacation home in the Santa Cruz Mountains where they spent many weekends. It was at this mountain retreat that, at age four, Jerry had his right middle finger cut off by his older brother, Tiff, in a woodchopping accident. A year later, in the summer of 1947, the family went camping near Arcata in northern California. Garcia and his father were fishing on the American River when his father slipped into the fast-moving water and drowned. Garcia watched, helpless and terrified, from the riverbank. Overwhelmed by the task of raising and supporting two young boys on her own, Ruth Garcia left her children in the care of her parents in San Francisco's Mission District while she ran a waterfront hotel and bar.

Although Jerry Garcia showed no musical promise after eight years of piano lessons, when he first took up the guitar at age 15 he discovered that his missing finger was not a problem. He knew that he had found his métier, and began performing folk music and rock and roll on street corners with his brother and a cousin. After dropping out of high school in 1959, Garcia had a brief stint in the U.S. Army but left within a matter of months after two courts martial and eight absences without leave. While living in his car near Palo Alto, Garcia met a poet named Robert Hunter (born 1941) and they started playing music together. Their duo did not last long, but Hunter would later become an important lyricist for The Grateful Dead. In the early 1960s Garcia played banjo in bluegrass bands in the San Francisco Bay Area, and eventually joined Mother McCree's Uptown Jug Champions, whose other

▲ *Jerry Garcia played lead guitar for the Grateful Dead. Band followers were known as Deadheads.*

members included Bob Weir and Ron "Pigpen" McKernan. In 1965 the group became The Warlocks and, later that year, The Grateful Dead.

The Dead's lineup changed from time to time, but it remained fundamentally a five-piece band in which Garcia (lead guitar, banjo, and vocals), Weir (guitar and vocals), and McKernan (vocals, keyboards, harmonica, percussion, and guitar) were joined by bass guitarist Phil Lesh and drummer Bill Kreutzmann.

Building a reputation

Over the next five years The Grateful Dead often played in the California mountain home of Ken Kesey (1935–2001) at parties known as "Acid Tests." Kesey was an early proponent of the use of "mind-expanding" psychotropic drugs, and later found fame with his novel *One Flew over the Cuckoo's Nest* (1962). Regular guests, known as "The Merry Pranksters," spread the word about The Grateful Dead, and the band soon became famous for their outstanding live performances, a reputation they maintained throughout their 30-year history. Long free-form sets more reminiscent of jazz than mainstream rock and roll became their stock in trade, and most of their albums were recorded live on stage rather than in the studio.

GARCIA, Jerry

INFLUENCES AND INSPIRATION

Jerry Garcia's musical style began to form when he moved in with his maternal grandparents after the death of his father. His grandmother Nan regularly tuned in to WSM radio's broadcast of the Grand Ole Opry on Saturday nights for a mix of old-time country and bluegrass. It was there Garcia first heard the banjo, an instrument he mastered early in his musical career.

Sometime in the mid-1950s Garcia discovered rock and roll while listening to KWBR, a station in Oakland, and San Francisco's KSAN. The sounds of Bill Haley and The Comets, Little Richard, and Elvis Presley had a strong effect on the young musician, who was captivated by their hybrid of country, blues, and rockabilly. His own guitar style was especially influenced by six-string legends such as Chuck Berry, Bo Diddley, Muddy Waters, and Eddie Cochran. On hearing such musicians play, Garcia asked his mother for a guitar to play the new music himself.

Meanwhile Garcia appeared live and in the studio with several emergent bands from the burgeoning San Francisco music scene, including Jefferson Airplane, Crosby, Stills, Nash and Young, and Big Brother and The Holding Company (Janis Joplin's backing group). He also engaged in various solo projects, touring and recording as The Jerry Garcia Band.

In 1970 The Grateful Dead released two studio albums, *Workingman's Dead* and *American Beauty*, that were closer to their folk and bluegrass roots. Although the albums had a more country feel than their earlier work, the band's live act continued to provide its staple of extended psychedelic jams that seamlessly wove songs together in legendary concerts that often lasted for more than four hours. The Grateful Dead had an extended repertoire that allowed them to perform for such long periods without repeating songs; that, in part, is what helped create their loyal following, whose members were known as "Deadheads." Many fans followed The Grateful Dead from city to city, supporting themselves by selling handmade arts and crafts and food in the parking lots outside the venues. Such areas were known as "Shakedown Street" after one of the band's songs. It was no secret that drugs, specifically psychedelics such as LSD, were an integral part of this scene, and by the early 1980s it also became public knowledge that Garcia was battling his own addiction to heroin.

Decline and revival

For much of the decade Garcia's productivity was restricted by his drug dependency and diabetes: His solo projects diminished. In 1987, however, The Grateful Dead released *In the Dark*, which became its first hit album. Success seemed to breathe new life into Garcia, who returned to touring with both The Grateful Dead and The Jerry Garcia Band. He also released some strong acoustic albums with

KEY DATES

1942	Born in San Francisco, California, on August 1.
1947	Witnesses his father's drowning in a fishing accident.
1959	Drops out of high school during his junior year.
1964	Joins Mother McCree's Uptown Jug Champions.
1965	Mother McCree's becomes The Warlocks and then The Grateful Dead.
1970	Releases *Workingman's Dead* and *American Beauty*.
1994	Inducted into the Rock and Roll Hall of Fame as a member of The Grateful Dead.
1995	Dies in San Francisco on August 9.

mandolinist David Grisman. In the first half of the 1990s Garcia and his fellow band members continued to rank in the top five concert draws in the United States with no sign of faltering in the face of their rigorous tour schedule. However, Garcia continued his battle with heroin. At the end of the 1995 summer tour he checked himself into a San Francisco area drug rehabilitation facility. While attempting to recover, Garcia died of a heart attack in his sleep on August 9, 1995. After several months of reflection, the surviving members of The Grateful Dead announced that they would disband.

A year before his death Jerry Garcia was inducted into the Rock and Roll Hall of Fame. In 2005 an open-air auditorium in McLaren Park in the Excelsior district of San Francisco, where the musician grew up, was renamed the Jerry Garcia Amphitheater.

Further reading: Jackson, Blair. *Garcia: An American Life.* New York, NY: Penguin, 1999.
http://www.jerrygarcia.com (official site).

GARCÍA, Lionel
Author

A child of Mexican American parents, Lionel García is a leading Chicano novelist and short-story writer of the late 20th and early 21st centuries.

Early life
Lionel G. García was born in 1935 in San Diego, Texas, and raised on the ranch where his grandfather worked. He was educated at a local public school and at Texas A&M University. After graduation García went through a long period of uncertainty, during which he worked in a succession of unfulfilling jobs. His time was not wasted, however, for he used it to gather material for his subsequent career as a professional writer by observing the characters and foibles of his friends and family.

▼ *Lionel García was a late starter as a writer, not publishing his first novel until he was nearly 50. Since then, however, he has maintained a steady output of constantly improving work.*

KEY DATES

1935 Born in San Diego, Texas, on August 20.

1984 Publishes his first novel, *Leaving Home*.

1987 Publishes his second novel, *A Shroud in the Family*.

1990 Publishes his third novel, *Hardscrub*.

2001 Publishes short story collection, *The Day They Took My Uncle and Other Stories*.

Although García had written stories since childhood, he did not finally announce himself as an author until 1984, when at age 49 he published *Leaving Home*. The novel described the challenges and difficulties that face Mexican immigrants attempting to adapt to life in the United States. The work received favorable reviews and won the 1984 PEN Southwest Discovery Prize.

Growing reputation
Three years later García consolidated the reputation he had gained from his debut work with *A Shroud in the Family* (1987). His second novel was a modest commercial success, being reprinted three times. The story elaborates on the themes set out in his debut novel, and deals with the culture clash implicit in the term "Mexican American." García's third novel, *Hardscrub* (1990), found an even wider audience, and won both the Texas Literary Award and the Texas Institute of Letters Award for Novel of the Year. Like his other works, it was rooted in personal experience without being autobiographical.

Lionel García is a prolific author of short stories, which have appeared in numerous publications across the United States. A selection was published in book form in 2001 under the title *The Day They Took My Uncle and Other Stories*. García has also written several plays, including *An Acorn on the Moon*, which won the Texas Playwrights Festival Award in 1995, and the libretto for an opera based on part of *A Shroud in the Family*. García is married to Noemi Barrera; the couple has three children.

Further reading: García, Lionel G. *The Day They Took My Uncle, and Other Stories*. Fort Worth, TX: TCU Press, 2001. http://www.lionelgarcia-novelist.com (official Web site).

GARCÍA, Macario
Medal of Honor Recipient

Macario García was awarded the Congressional Medal of Honor for his courage under fire during World War II (1939–1945).

Early life
Born in 1920 in Villa de Castaño, Mexico, García was one of 10 children of Mexican migrant workers Luciano and Josefa García. At age three, he moved with his family to Texas, where they settled in Sugar Land. He picked crops with his family from a very young age.

War hero and victim of discrimination
In 1942 García was drafted into the U.S. Army. He took part in D-Day, the Allied landings in Normandy, France, on June 6, 1944, and was wounded in the fighting. By November, he had recovered sufficiently to rejoin the 22nd Infantry, which by then had advanced into Germany.

García performed the act of conspicuous bravery for which he was awarded the highest U.S. military award on November 27, 1944, on the outskirts of Grosshau, near the border with Luxembourg. As García's unit advanced toward the town, it came under enemy fire. Although García was

▼ Despite holding the highest U.S. military honor, Macario García was still a victim of racism.

KEY DATES	
1920	Born in Villa de Castaño, Mexico, on January 2.
1944	Displays immense courage under fire near Grosshau, Germany, on November 27.
1945	Awarded Medal of Honor on August 23; arrested for assault a month later.
1972	Dies in a car crash on December 24.

hit twice, he managed to crawl to two German machine-gun emplacements and shoot six Wehrmacht soldiers dead, singlehandedly capture another four, and blow up their weapons with hand grenades.

On his return to the United States, García was awarded the Medal of Honor by President Harry S. Truman at a ceremony at the White House in Washington, D.C., on August 23, 1945. He was also honored with a Purple Heart, the Bronze Star, and the Combat Infantryman's Badge. In January 1946, García traveled to Mexico City, where he received the Mérito Militar, Mexico's highest military honor.

García attracted a lot of media attention, but most of it was unfavorable and related to an incident that occurred in Texas in late 1945. Returning home in September 1945, García stopped at a restaurant in Richmond. He was offended when the owner informed him he did not serve Mexicans and a fight broke out between the two men that ended only when the police arrived. García was arrested and charged. Several Hispanic civil rights groups supported him, and the incident was used by the League of United Latin American Citizens (LULAC) to draw attention to both the plight of Hispanic servicemen—heroically serving their country only to be treated as second-class citizens—and discrimination against the Hispanic community in general. In the subsequent trial, the renowned lawyer Gus García helped get García acquitted.

In 1947 García became a U.S. citizen. He remained in the U.S. Army until 1949, when he took a job with the Veterans' Association, where he remained for the rest of his life. He married Alicia Reyes in 1952. He died in 1972.

See also: García, Gustavo C.

Further reading: http://www.army.mil/hispanicamericans/english/timeline/wwii.html (award citation).

GARCÍA, Rupert
Artist, Activist

Since 1968, the Chicano artist Rupert García has created visually bold and intellectually sophisticated art that explores the ways that art and politics intersect. García's political posters, dealing with war, race, and politics, produced between 1967 and 1975, brought him to prominence as an artist. His unique visual style is characterized by bold colors and assertive lines, and his subject matter ranges from images of public protest to personal introspection.

The emergence of a Chicano artist

Born in French Camp, California, in 1941, García grew up in Stockton. Several members of his family were artists and he was exposed to all kinds of art from an early age. García studied at Stockton Junior College before going on to San Francisco State University, where he studied printmaking and silkscreen. While there García became involved in the Chicano student movement. He set up a workshop on campus: The San Francisco Poster Workshop, as it became known, became famous for producing posters that dealt with political, social, and racial issues, such as art supporting student strikes and exposing police brutality.

After graduating with an MA from San Francisco State, García continued to be involved with the workshop. He also produced several attention-grabbing works, including a portrait of Che Guevera featuring the words "Right On!" He also joined Artes 6, a Chicano gallery and collective.

Working for social justice

Throughout the 1970s and 1980s, García's paintings and prints explored advertising and other forms of mass media in order to critique stereotypes and protest injustice both

▲ *The work of Chicano artist Rupert García has often been political in nature.*

in the United States and abroad. For example, he took a famous Lipton tea advertisement featuring a smiling Englishman offering a cup of tea and added the caption "Ceylon Tea—Product of European Exploitation." García's portraits of iconic artists, writers, and political figures, such as Frida Kahlo (five portraits between 1975 and 1990), Che Guevara, Rubén Salazar, and Pablo Picasso pay homage to García's philosophical and artistic influences. García's later works in diptychs (two parts) or triptychs (three parts) allow him to juxtapose seemingly unrelated elements, and it is left to the viewer to make connections. In the past 20 years much of García's focus has turned inward, exploring questions of personal and spiritual identity.

Since 1988 García has been a professor of art at San Jose State University. He has received many awards for his work, including a National Endowment for the Arts individual artist fellowship grant and an honorary doctorate in fine art from the San Francisco Art Institute. Much of García's work is held at the Smithsonian Institution in Washington, D.C.

See also: Salazar, Rubén

Further reading: Albright, Thomas. *Art in the San Francisco Bay Area, 1945–1980*. Berkeley, CA: University of California Press, 1985.
http://www.heartsinsf.com/bio_garcia.htm (brief biography).

KEY DATES
1941 Born in French Camp, California.
1968 Studies at San Francisco State University, where he forms the San Francisco Poster Workshop.
1988 Becomes a professor of art at San Jose State University.
1989 Receives an Individual Artist Fellowship Grant from the National Endowment of the Arts.
1995 Smithsonian Institution archives his papers and holds much of his work.

GARCIAPARRA, Nomar
Baseball Player

When Mexican American Nomar Garciaparra arrived on the major league baseball scene with the Boston Red Sox, he made an immediate impact. After a brief late-season call-up in 1996, in which Garciaparra played just 24 games, in 1997 he returned to record one of the most remarkable rookie seasons in major league history. Garciaparra went on to become a five-time American League (AL) All-Star and win two AL batting titles (1999 and 2000).

The rise to stardom

Anthony Nomar Garciaparra was born on July 23, 1973, in the Los Angeles suburb of Whittier. His father, Ramon Garciaparra, named him "Nomar"—"Ramon" spelled backward. At the Catholic St. John Bosco High School Garciaparra played sports, excelling at soccer and football. Baseball was his favorite game, however, and he went on to help his school team win league titles in 1990 and 1991.

In June 1991 Garciaparra was drafted by the Milwaukee Brewers. Instead of accepting the offer, he chose to attend Georgia Tech University, Atlanta. While there Garciaparra led the Yellow Jackets to their first College World Series. A year later he represented the United States on the 1992 Olympic baseball team in Barcelona, Spain.

Drafted by the Red Sox in June 1994, Garciaparra worked his way through the minors. He made his major league debut in 1996; he had a remarkable 1997 rookie season: Garciaparra hit .306 with 30 home runs, 98 runs batted in, 209 hits, and 22 steals. He was unanimously voted American League Rookie of the Year, making him the second consecutive shortstop after Derek Jeter, who won the title in 1996. Garciaparra's 30 home runs set a new rookie record for shortstops, and his 209 hits broke

▲ *Of Mexican ancestry, Garciaparra was asked to play for Mexico in the World Baseball Classic (2006).*

former Red Sox shortstop Johnny Pesky's 1942 record of 205. Pesky claimed that Garciaparra was the best shortstop in Red Sox history.

In 1998 Garciaparra continued to do well at the plate, hitting .323 with 35 home runs and 122 RBIs. On May 10, 1999, Garciaparra hit three home runs, including two Grand Slams (he was the first Red Sox player to accomplish the feat since Jim Tabor in 1939). Early in 2001 Garciaparra had surgery for tendinitis in his right wrist, causing him to miss all but 21 games that season. By 2002 Garciaparra was back on form: He hit .310, and also achieved three home runs in a single game.

In 2003 Garciaparra married popular U.S. Women's World Cup and Olympic soccer player Mia Hamm in Santa Barbara, California. In July 2004 he was traded to the Chicago Cubs as part of a four-team deal: Four months later the Red Sox went on to win their first World Series since 1918. Conscious of being a role model, Garciaparra works hard to encourage young Hispanics to remain in school.

Further reading: Shalin, Mike. *Nomar Garciaparra: High 5!* Champaign, IL: Sports Publishing, 2002.
http://www.baseballlibrary.com/baseballlibrary/ballplayers/ G/Garciaparra_Nomar.stm (baseball reference site).

KEY DATES	
1973	Born in Whittier, California, on July 23.
1994	Drafted by the Boston Red Sox.
1996	Makes his major league debut with the Red Sox on August 31.
2003	Marries U.S. women's soccer player Mia Hamm on November 22.
2004	Is traded to the Chicago Cubs as part of a four-team trade on July 31.

GARZA, Ben
Activist

Bernardo F. Garza, or Ben Garza, as he was usually known, was the driving force behind the formation of the League of United Latin American Citizens (LULAC), the oldest and most influential Mexican American civil rights organization active in the United States today. He was LULAC's first president (1929–1930), and was active in its early campaigns to combat such issues as school segregation and the systematic exclusion of Hispanic Americans from jury service.

Early life
The son of Bernardo and María de Jesús Flores de la Garza, Bernardo F. Garza was born on June 22, 1892, in the border town and port of Brownsville, Texas. When Garza was a young child, his family moved to Rockport, where Garza was educated at a segregated Mexican school. When Garza was 16, his father died and he left school in order to support his seven brothers and sisters. In 1914 he moved to the nearby city of Corpus Christi, where he worked as a waiter and gained experience in the restaurant trade.

When the United States entered World War I (1914–1918) in 1917, Garza helped the war effort by working in Rockport's shipyards. Shortly after the end of the war, he married Adelaida Carrilles; they settled in Corpus Christi, where they raised a family. In 1919 Garza put his restaurant experience to good use when he joined several of his friends to set up the Metropolitan, an all-night cafe, in downtown Corpus Christi. The cafe soon became a popular meeting place for the city's thriving community of Latino businessmen and later for its civil activists.

The emerging activist
At the start of the 1920s, Mexican Americans living in Texas faced widespread discrimination and racism. Segregation was commonplace in education, housing, and public accommodation, such as hotels and restaurants. The overwhelming majority of Mexican Americans had to live in poverty, in substandard housing, with inadequate health

▼ *Ben Garza (first row, fourth from the right) attended the first LULAC conference in 1929.*

INFLUENCES AND INSPIRATION

Ben Garza was inspired by lawyer, intellectual, educator, and writer José Vasconcelos (1882–1959), one of the most influential figures of the early Mexican American civil rights movement. Vasconcelos served as secretary of education in the Mexican government from 1920 to 1925, and gained a worldwide reputation for his commitment to educational reform. In 1928–1929 Vasconcelos made an unsuccessful bid for the Mexican presidency. Many of his Mexican American supporters set up "Vasconcelos for president" clubs in several cities in Texas and New Mexico. In Corpus Christi, Ben Garza was elected leader of the city's Vasconcelos club and he developed close contacts with the Mexican leader.

Politically Vasconcelos was a moderate, who combined liberal ideas about universal education and equality with a conservative outlook that embraced family values and the Roman Catholic Church. He berated discrimination and racial violence, but was a great admirer of the American way of life. He was one of the few Mexican American leaders respected by the U.S. elite. Although Vasconcelos failed to win the presidency, his attitudes, which bridged both reform and conservatism, were taken up by his Mexican American admirers.

care. Nevertheless, there was also a growing number of professional, middle-class Tejanos, including doctors, teachers, lawyers, and businessmen, who were determined to bring about positive change in their community. From the early 1920s, a number of civic groups were formed across Texas to express solidarity and to lobby local governments on issues such as segregation.

In 1924 Garza joined Council No. 4 of the Order of Sons of America, which had recently been established in Corpus Christi. By 1926 he was the chapter's president. While the Sons of America had some local success in the city, Garza realized that any real gains in Hispanic rights had to come through the efforts of a statewide and unified organization. In 1927 he began to press the Sons of America to merge with other local organizations. The San Antonio chapter resisted, however, and soon after Garza removed his chapter from the organization altogether.

LULAC

On February 17, 1929, 25 delegates from four Mexican American organizations in Texas—the Alice and Corpus Christi chapters of the Sons of America, the San Antonio–based Knights of America, and the Laredo-based Latin American Citizens League—met at the Salón Obreros y Obreras, a Corpus Christi dance hall. With Garza serving as a chairman, the convention formally agreed to merge into a single body that eventually became the League of United Latin American Citizens (LULAC).

At LULAC's first convention, held on May 18 and 19, Garza was appointed the organization's first president general; the prominent San Antonio attorney Manuel C. Gonzales became vice president general. LULAC's motto was "All for one and one for all," emphasizing the movement's new-found unity, while its emblem was a shield, symbolizing LULAC's function to defend its members against racism. By the early 1930s, LULAC had more than 2,000 members in 19 chapters or councils across the state of Texas.

Until his death in 1937, Garza continued to be a leading force in Hispanic activism. In 1930 he appeared before the United States House Committee on Immigration, arguing passionately against restrictions on Mexican immigration to the United States. He also became involved in LULAC's sustained campaign to end school segregation. Hampered by his seriously deteriorating health, caused by tuberculosis, as well as by business worries provoked by the Great Depression, Garza died on February 21, 1937, aged just 44. He was buried in Corpus Christi's Rose Hill Cemetery. A city park was later built in Garza's honor.

KEY DATES	
1892	Born in Brownsville, Texas, on June 22.
1919	Sets up the Metropolitan Café in Corpus Christi, Texas.
1929	Becomes a founding member and first president of the League of United Latin American Citizens (LULAC).
1937	Dies in Corpus Christi on February 21.

See also: Gonzales, Manuel C.; National Organizations

Further reading: Gómez-Quiñones, Juan. *Roots of Chicano Politics, 1600–1940.* Albuquerque, NM: University of New Mexico Press, 1994.
www.lulac.org/about/history.html (LULAC Web site).

GARZA, Catarino E.
Journalist, Revolutionary

Catarino Erasmo Garza was a journalist and revolutionary who challenged the negative representation of Mexican Americans in the press. He frequently wrote about the creation of the border after the U.S.–Mexico War (1846–1848), which had allowed Anglo Americans to dominate land and resources in southern Texas, bringing economic disenfranchisement to many Mexicans. Garza also criticized Mexican president Porfirio Díaz (1876–1911) for encouraging the Anglo American domination of business along the border, and led a revolution against Díaz in 1891. Garza promoted local *sociedades mutualistas* (mutual-aid associations) in order to help create political and economic solidarity among Mexicans and Mexican Americans.

Rebel and folk hero

Born in Matamoros, Mexico, in 1859, Garza grew up in Brownsville, Texas. In the 1860s his family supported the revolutionary Juan Cortina. Schooled at the Gualahuises, Nuevo León, and San Juan College, Garza later served in the National Guard at Port Plaza. Garza also worked at a print office and began working as a journalist. In the 1880s

▼ *Catarino Garza wrote about the cruelty that Mexicans often experienced at Anglo-American hands.*

KEY DATES	
1859	Born in Matamoros, Mexico.
1888	Writes his autobiography.
1890	Travels around Texas reporting as an independent journalist.
1891	Initiates the "Garza War."
1893	Flees to Havana, Cuba; later meets José Martí in Key West, Florida.
1894	Becomes a general in the Costa Rican Army.
1895	Killed at Bocas del Toro, Colombia.

he set up Spanish-language newspapers in Brownsville, Eagle Pass, and Laredo. He became known for his criticisms of both U.S. and Mexican authorities. He wrote about such things as the lynching of Mexicans by Anglo-American law officers.

Garza became increasingly critical of the Díaz regime in Mexico. He managed to band together a group of disgruntled ranchers, peasants, merchants, and others, to revolt against the regime. In 1891 Garza and his men marched from South Texas across the Rio Grande and began attacking government offices. Between 1891 and 1893, Garza led five incursions from Laredo, Texas, into Mexico, a period that became known as the "Garza War." U.S. and Mexican troops worked hard to stop the Garzistas.

In 1892 the government offered a $300,000 reward for Garza's capture. In 1893 Garza fled to Havana, Cuba. He moved on to Key West, where he met José Martí, the revolutionary who hoped to get rid of the last vestiges of Spain's empire in the Caribbean. Before his death in 1895, Garza became a general in Costa Rica's army, and joined anti-imperialist rebels in Colombia, where he was killed in action.

See also: Cortina, Juan; Martí, José

Further reading: Young, Elliott. *Catarino Garza's Revolution on the Texas–Mexico Border.* Durham, NC: Duke University Press, 2004.
http://www.lib.panam.edu/info/speccoll/garzarew.html
(*Harper's Weekly* article from 1892 about Garza).

GARZA, Reynaldo
Judge

In 1961 Reynaldo Guerra Garza became the United States's first Mexican American federal judge. Garza's appointment marked not only the culmination of what was already an impressive legal and civic career but also an historic watershed in the progressive political empowerment of Mexican Americans in the second half of the 20th century.

Early life
A second-generation Mexican American, Garza was born in Brownsville, Texas, on July 7, 1915. His devout Roman Catholic parents had immigrated to Brownsville in 1901. Garza was raised in a highly traditional and conservative household. His parents encouraged him to pursue his early dream of becoming a lawyer; his father, Ygnacio, an accountant in a Brownsville bank, sometimes accompanied Garza on his frequent visits to watch cases at the local courthouse.

Brownsville was predominantly populated by Mexican Americans, and anti-Hispanic discrimination was far less virulent than in most other Texas cities. Garza was able to attend a nonsegregated school; he also mixed freely with the Anglo-American students in his class. After graduation Garza initially went to Brownsville Junior College, but in 1936 he transferred to study law at the University of Texas in Austin. One of only a handful of Mexican American students, Garza graduated in 1939.

A career in law
Despite having assimilated well into the predominantly white U.S. legal profession, Garza chose to return to Brownsville, where he set up a legal practice. His business soon thrived. Garza settled down in Brownsville, married, and raised a family. He also became an active and popular figure in the city's civic affairs.

▲ *Reynaldo G. Garza's fairness and astute application of the law won him many friends, including President Lyndon B. Johnson.*

Garza's career was interrupted by World War II (1939–1945), during which he served in the U.S. Air Force; after his discharge he returned to law. In 1950 he became a partner in Brownsville's largest law firm, where he specialized in civil cases.

Garza was a committed Democrat and frequently helped Texas Democratic candidates during election campaigns. In 1961 the Democratic president John F. Kennedy nominated Garza to the U.S. District Court for the Southern District of Texas. Garza served in the court until 1979, the last 10 years as a chief judge. He gained a reputation for vigorously promoting Mexican American civil rights: In the 1972 case *Medrano v. Allee*, for example, he struck down laws that were being used by the Texas Rangers to break strikes by Mexican American farmworkers.

In 1976 Garza turned down President Jimmy Carter's offer to make him attorney general. Three years later Carter appointed Garza to the United States Court of Appeals for the Fifth Circuit; Garza served on the court until just before his death in 2004.

KEY DATES	
1915	Born in Brownsville, Texas, on July 7.
1961	Becomes first Mexican American federal judge.
1976	Turns down President Jimmy Carter's invitation to become attorney general.
2004	Dies in Brownsville, Texas, in September.

Further reading: Fisch, Louise Ann. *All Rise: Reynaldo G. Garza, the First Mexican American Federal Judge.* College Station, TX: Texas A&M University Press, 1996.
www.utexas.edu/law/news/2004/091604_garza.html (obituary).

GARZA FALCÓN, María de la
Rancher

In the 1750s, María Gertrudis de la Garza Falcón was one of the early Spanish settlers in the Lower Rio Grande Valley. After her husband's death, she became the owner of the Espíritu Santo land grant, 261,275 acres (105,734 ha) of grazing land that sprawled across present-day Cameron County in South Texas. What we know of Garza Falcón's life has been gleaned from legal documents, such as wills, and from the known histories of her close male relatives.

Early life
María Gertrudis de la Garza Falcón was born in 1734 in Cerralvo, Nuevo León, one of the most northerly territories of the Spanish colony of New Spain (Mexico). Her father, Blas María de la Garza Falcón (1712–1767), belonged to one of the leading Spanish Mexican families of neighboring Coahuila and was captain of a presidio (military post) in Nuevo León. Her mother, Catarina Gómez de Castro, died when Garza Falcón and her two brothers were young. The children were brought up by their father's second wife, Josefa de los Santos Coy.

Camargo settlement
In 1748, José de Escandón, governor of Nuevo Santander, was commissioned by the Spanish government to found new settlements along the Lower Rio Grande Valley, which lay to the east of Nuevo León. He sent Blas María de la Garza Falcón to explore the area; Escandón instructed him to establish seven settlements along the river—Revilla, Camargo, Mier, Dolores, Reynosa, Laredo, and Vedoya. The new territory was named Nuevo Santander and its first settlement, Camargo, situated on the river's southern bank (in the present-day Mexican state of Tamaulipas), was founded in 1749 with 40 families. Escandón appointed Garza Falcón's father captain and chief justice of Camargo. In 1750 Garza Falcón and her stepmother and brothers joined him there. Two years later, Blas María de la Garza Falcón founded a ranch, Carnestolendas, on the north side of the river (on what is today Rio Grande City, Texas).

Marriage
In 1754 Garza Falcón married her cousin and fellow settler José Salvador de la Garza, and together they raised three children. Initially, Escandón decreed that the area around the settlement was common land, but in 1767 Salvador de la Garza was finally awarded a large tract of

KEY DATES

1734 Born in Cerralvo, Nuevo León, New Spain.

1750 Moves with her family to Camargo, Nuevo Santander, New Spain.

1754 Marries her cousin José Salvador de la Garza.

1779 Salvador de la Garza is awarded the Espíritu Santo land grant.

1781 Salvador de la Garza officially takes possession of the land; he dies soon after and the land passes to Garza Falcón.

1789 Dies in Nuevo Santander, New Spain.

land on the north bank of the river, where he established a ranch. After three years, however, he sought new grazing lands for his cattle. In 1770 he founded the ranches El Espíritu Santo and El Tanque, which later became known as the Rancho Viejo (situated between Brownsville and Harlingen).

The Espíritu Santo land grant
In 1772 Salvador de la Garza petitioned the Spanish government for ownership of the land. Due to a dispute with José Nicasio Cavazos, who also claimed rights to the land, Salvador de la Garza did not receive the Espíritu Santo land grant, as it became known, until 1779. He took possession of the 261,275 acres of land after paying a $10 fee. Salvador de la Garza died soon after, however. Garza Falcón inherited half of her husband's property, and she and her three children inherited the land.

Garza Falcón died in 1789. She was buried in Camargo. After her death the land stayed in the Garza Falcón family until the mid-19th century, when Feliciana Goseascochea Tijerina sold 500 acres to James Grogan. After that the land gradually fell into the hands of various Anglo settlers and developers.

See also: Escandón, José de

Further reading: Alonzo, Armando C. *Tejano Legacy: Rancheros and Settlers in South Texas, 1734–1900.* Albuquerque, NM: University of New Mexico Press, 1998. http://www.ranchoviejotexas.com/About (article about Garza Falcón, her husband, and their land).

GASPAR DE ALBA, Alicia
Writer, Academic

Mexican American writer Alicia Gaspar de Alba is a leading lesbian Chicana poet, novelist, and academic. Gaspar de Alba's writing often deals with the themes of nationality and sexual identity.

Early life
Born in El Paso, Texas, on July 29, 1958, Gaspar de Alba grew up on the border between Mexico and the United States. As a child she was forbidden to speak English at home, but at school Gaspar de Alba was punished for speaking Spanish, and was forced instead to speak English. This paradoxical background led Gaspar de Alba to examine the idea of "cultural schizophrenia" in her writing.

After graduating from high school, Gaspar de Alba studied for a BA in English at the University of Texas, El Paso. She finished her doctoral thesis in American Studies at the University of New Mexico in 1994. Her dissertation, "Mi casa [no] es su casa—The Cultural Politics of Chicano Art: Resistance and Affirmation," was later published by the University of Texas Press as *Chicano Art: Inside/Outside the Master's House* (1998).

The Chicana writer
Gaspar de Alba believes that the Chicana writer is at the pulse of her language and culture: Through her narratives the Chicana writer not only preserves the values and traditions of the Chicana heritage but she is also able to redefine and reinvent new languages, images, and stories.

▲ *Alicia Gaspar de Alba stands in front of a promotional poster for her book* Desert Blood.

In 1989 Gaspar de Alba published her first collection of poetry, *Beggar on Cordoba Bridge*. Four years later she published her first book of fiction, *The Mystery of Survival and Other Stories*, a collection of short stories that examines the borders and margins of cultural, gender, and sexual identity. Gaspar de Alba's first novel, *Sor Juana's Second Dream*, was published by the University of New Mexico Press in 1999. Based on the life of the 17th-century Mexican nun Sor Juana Inés de la Cruz, regarded by many commentators as the first lesbian writer of the Americas, the book won Gaspar de Alba critical acclaim.

Fact-based fiction
In 2005 Gaspar de Alba published *Desert Blood: The Juárez Murders*. Essentially a mystery novel that examines the suspicious deaths of women found along the Mexico–U.S. border, *Desert Blood* is based on fact. More than 400 poor Mexican American women have been found dead along the border since 1993. Gaspar de Alba began researching these largely overlooked murders in 1998. In 2003 she organized a conference on the subject.

Further reading: Gaspar de Alba, Alicia. *Desert Blood: The Juárez Murders.* Houston, TX: Arte Público Press, 2005. http://voices.cla.umn.edu/vg/Bios/entries/alba_alicia_gaspar_de.html (biography).

KEY DATES

1958   Born in El Paso, Texas, on July 29.

1980   Receives a BA in English from the University of Texas, El Paso.

1989   Publishes *Beggar on Cordoba Bridge* (poetry).

1994   Receives a PhD in American Studies from the University of New Mexico; her dissertation "Mi casa [no] es su casa—The Cultural Politics of Chicano Art: Resistance and Affirmation" wins the Ralph Henry Gabriel Award for best dissertation in American Studies.

1999   Publishes her first novel, *Sor Juana's Second Dream*.

2005   Publishes *Desert Blood: The Juárez Murders*.

GAVIN, John
Actor, Diplomat

John Gavin was a prominent film actor of the late 1950s and early 1960s who later went into politics. He was born John Anthony Golenor in 1928 in Los Angeles, California, and was of Mexican descent through his mother. He grew up bilingual in English and Spanish. On graduating from high school he took a BA degree in economics and politics at Stanford University; in his final year he specialized in Latin American affairs.

From 1952 to 1955 Golenor served in the U.S. Navy, rising quickly through the ranks to become an air intelligence officer. At the end of his service he contemplated a career in business, but the direction of his life took a momentous turn when he went for a screen test. Although he had no particular ambition to be an actor, Universal saw him as the new Rock Hudson (1925–1985) and offered him a film contract.

Screen debut

Golenor's screen debut came in *Raw Edge* (1956), a Western in which he was credited under the name John Gilmore. Later the same year he had a bigger part in *Behind the High Wall*, a jailbreak drama; this was the first film in which he used the name John Gavin. Over the next two years Gavin appeared in three more films: *Four Girls in Town*, *Quantez*, and *A Time to Love and a Time to Die* (also known as *Will o' the Wisp*). In 1959 he won the Golden Globe Award for the Most Promising Male Newcomer.

Gavin's first starring role was in the romantic weepie *Imitation of Life* (1959), in which he played opposite Lana Turner. His next role was in *Psycho* (1960). His performance as Janet Leigh's lover in the classic thriller did not impress the director, Alfred Hitchcock, who referred to Gavin as "the stiff." However, Hitchcock's view of actors was famously uncharitable, and had no apparent detrimental effect on Gavin, who later the same year played Julius Caesar in Stanley Kubrick's epic *Spartacus*.

Gavin was tall and good-looking, and had a large number of devoted female fans. It was partly with them in mind that Universal gave him the romantic lead opposite Susan Hayward in the 1961 remake of Fannie Hurst's

▼ *After a successful career in movies, John Gavin was appointed U.S. ambassador to Mexico by his old friend President Ronald Reagan, another former actor.*

Back Street. Among his subsequent films were *Thoroughly Modern Millie* (1967), *OSS 117 Double Agent* (1968), in which he starred as a secret agent, and *Pussycat, Pussycat I Love You* (1970). In 1970 he was hired to play James Bond in succession to George Lazenby, but lost the job before shooting started when the producers lured back Sean Connery, the original screen 007, to take the starring role in *Diamonds Are Forever* (1971). Gavin also starred in three television series—*Destry* (1964), *Convoy* (1965), and *Doctors' Private Lives* (1979)—and in 1973 made his Broadway debut in *Seesaw*. Gavin was also a board member of the Screen Actors Guild from 1966, and served as its president from 1971 to 1973.

Into politics

Although John Gavin subsequently appeared in occasional roles on screen and television, from the 1970s onward his acting career was subordinated to his business interests: He sat on the board of several U.S. companies, notably investment firms with links to Latin America. He also became increasingly active in politics. The subject had interested him since college, and from 1961 to 1973 he had been a special adviser to the secretary general of the Organization of American States (OAS), a role in which he made full use of his educational and Hispanic background. He also worked for the Department of State and the Executive Office of the President.

KEY DATES	
1928	Born in Los Angeles, California, on April 8.
1956	Appears in his first film, *Raw Edge*.
1971	Is appointed president of the Screen Actors Guild.
1974	Marries Constance Towers.
1981	Is appointed U.S. ambassador to Mexico.
1986	Retires as ambassador.

In March 1981 John Gavin (now sometimes known as Jack) was nominated by President Ronald Reagan, an old friend from their Hollywood days, to serve as U.S. ambassador to Mexico. His appointment in May was criticized by many Mexicans, who suspected that the choice of a Chicano for the post was tokenism. However, even skeptics acknowledged that Gavin responded well to the greatest crisis he faced during his tenure, the 1985 earthquake that devastated Mexico City. The ambassador was widely praised for his decisive and efficient coordination of U.S. relief and rescue efforts in the wake of the natural disaster.

Back to business

After five years at the head of one of the largest U.S. diplomatic missions in the world, Gavin retired as ambassador in June 1986. Although he later became a member of the Congressional Policy Advisory Board, which he advised on defense and foreign policy, he was principally involved in corporate work. He was president of Univisa Satellite Communications, and served on the boards of Apex Mortgage Capital, KKFC Inc., Merrill Lynch Corporation, the UCLA Anderson Graduate School of Management, and Loyola Marymount University. From 1991 to 1994 Gavin was the founding chairman and chief executive officer of the Century Council, an organization dedicated to fighting drunk driving and other forms of alcohol abuse.

John Gavin was twice married. His first wife was Cecily Evans: The couple wed in 1947 and had two daughters. In 1974 he married Constance Mary Towers, who had formerly been an actor on *General Hospital*; they had four children.

Further reading: Sánchez-Thompson, Kimberly. *Nationalism and the Controversial Tenure of U.S. Ambassador John A. Gavin in Mexico*. Cambridge, MA: Harvard University Press, 1987.
http://www.meredy.com/johngavin (John Gavin—So Suave).

GIL, Federico
Educator

Federico Gil was a gifted and popular university professor who pioneered Latin American studies in the United States, and founded one of the country's first centers on the subject at the University of North Carolina.

Early life
Born in 1915 in Havana, Cuba, Federico Guillermo Gil received his early education at Candler College in the island's capital. He went on to study at the Instituto de la Habana, graduating with a BA in 1935. He received two doctorates from the University of Havana in law and political science, in 1940 and 1941 respectively.

Academic distinction
After completing his studies, Gil worked for a short time in Spain before moving to the United States. In 1942, he became an instructor at Louisiana State University. He joined the faculty of the University of North Carolina (UNC) at Chapel Hill in 1943, and remained there for almost 40 years.

In 1955, Gil became a professor at UNC. Four years later, he was asked to set up the university's Institute of Latin American Studies, one of the first foundations of its kind in the United States. He opened the institute in 1959, and served as its director for the next 25 years. During that period, the UNC program was twice voted the best in the United States. It attracted leading scholars and students from all over the world.

KEY DATES

1915	Born in Havana, Cuba, on February 10.
1943	Becomes faculty member at the University of North Carolina (UNC), Chapel Hill.
1957	Publishes *The Governments of Latin America.*
1959	Opens the Institute for Latin American Studies with support from the Carnegie Foundation.
1966	Named Kenan Professor at UNC.
1980	Retires from UNC; appointed an emeritus professor.
1999	Enters full retirement.
2000	Dies in Chapel Hill, North Carolina, on April 22.

In 1966, Gil was appointed Kenan Professor of Political Science at UNC. He made outstanding contributions in the field as a teacher, activist, and scholar.

Gil wrote academic studies in both Spanish and English. His first published book, which he cowrote with fellow Latin American scholar William W. Pierson, was *The Governments of Latin America* (1957). The work became a foundation text throughout the United States, and is still regarded as a classic study.

Authority on Chile
Gil was a leading authority on Chile, and throughout his working life he returned time and again to the modern history and politics of the South American republic. He wrote four books on the subject: *The Genesis and Modernization of Political Parties in Chile* (1962); *The Chilean Presidential Election of September 4, 1964* (1965); *The Political System of Chile* (1966), and *Chile: The Background to Authoritarianism* (1983). He also edited *Chile at the Turning Point: Lessons of the Socialist Years, 1970–1973* (1979).

Gil was man of action as well as an academic. When Augusto Pinochet seized power in Chile in 1973, Gil was instrumental in bringing one of the dictator's leading political opponents, the economist Ricardo Lagos, and his family, to safety at UNC. Lagos returned to Chile in 1983, and in 2000 won election as president, the first socialist to head the state since Salvador Allende, the man toppled by the Pinochet coup.

Other achievements
Gil was involved in several key world organizations, including the United Nations. He helped establish the Latin American Studies Association (LASA), and was its president from 1970 to 1972. He received many awards in the United States, and was named Commander of the Bernardo O'Higgins Order of Merit, the highest honor given by the Chilean government. Federico Gil died in 2000 at age 85.

Further reading: Gil, Federico G., and William W. Pierson. *The Governments of Latin America.* New York, NY: McGraw Hill, 1957.
http://www.unc.edu/depts/ilas/FGilmemoriam.html (memorial site in honor of Federico Gil).

GIOIA, Dana
Poet

Poet, critic, and business leader Dana Gioia was chairman of the National Endowment for the Arts under the administration of President George W. Bush.

Early life
Michael Dana Gioia was born in 1950 in Hawthorne, a suburb of Los Angeles, California. His father, an immigrant from Sicily, Italy, drove a taxi, and his Mexican American mother worked as a telephone operator. He once described his childhood as growing up speaking English and Italian in a Mexican American neighborhood. Gioia became the first member of his family to graduate from college when he completed a BA at Stanford University. He then received an MA in comparative literature at Harvard University before returning to Stanford to complete an MBA.

Commerce and verse
Gioia decided to become a poet during a trip to Vienna, Austria, in his sophomore year in college, although for 15 years he pursued a more practical career in marketing. During that time Gioia's work was published in many literary journals and he completed two small books of poems and a book of translations of Italian poet Eugenio Montale. Gioia came to national attention with the 1991 publication of an article, "Can Poetry Matter?," about the marginalization of poetry in U.S. culture. He expanded the essay into a book of the same title, and was nominated for the National Book Critic's Circle award. After that success, Gioia resigned his position as vice president at General Foods to become a full-time writer. In 1996 he moved with his wife, Mary Hiecke, and their two children to Santa Rosa, near San Francisco.

▲ *Dana Gioia did not become a full-time writer until he was in his early forties.*

For 10 years Gioia lectured widely on poetry and continued to write poems and literary criticism. He believes that the finest expression of poetry is often in handmade books printed using lead type and specially commissioned illustrations. From 1983, Michael Peich, owner of the Aralia Press, published more than 20 of Gioia's chapbooks (small volumes of verse) and broadsides (poems printed on a single sheet).

Gioia's major collections of poems are *Daily Horoscope* (1986), *The Gods of Winter* (1991), and *Interrogations at Noon* (2001), which won the American Book Award. Gioia is part of the "New Formalism" movement, a group of poets that uses traditional poetic forms rather than intensely personal and unstructured free verse.

In 2002 President George W. Bush nominated Gioia as chairman of the National Endowment for the Arts, a federal agency that supports arts groups and artists through grant programs. Following his unanimous confirmation by the U.S. Senate, Gioia successfully lobbied Congress for a larger budget, and focused his efforts on promoting reading and literature.

KEY DATES

1950	Born in Los Angeles, California, on December 24.
1977	Earns MBA from Stanford University.
1992	Publishes *Can Poetry Matter?*; quits his job to write full time.
2002	Poetry collection *Interrogations at Noon* wins American Book Award.
2003	In February, begins work as chairman of the National Endowment for the Arts.

Further reading: Gioia, Dana. *Can Poetry Matter?: Essays on Poetry and American Culture.* 10th Anniversary edition. Saint Paul, MN: Graywolf Press, 2002.
http://www.danagioia.net (author's official Web site).

GOIZUETA, Roberto
Business Leader

Roberto Goizueta was a Cuban American who became head of the Coca-Cola Company, the soft drinks company based in Atlanta, Georgia.

Early life

The son of a wealthy real-estate developer and sugar-mill owner, Roberto Goizueta was born in 1931 in Havana, Cuba. He excelled in his studies at Belén Academy, Cuba's top prep school, and at Yale University in the United States. On completing a degree in chemical engineering, he married his childhood sweetheart, Olga Casteleiro, in June 1953. His father offered him a job in the family business but, preferring to make his own way in life, in 1954 Goizueta started work as a quality-control engineer in the Cuban factory of Coca-Cola. When Fidel Castro seized power in Cuba in 1959, Goizueta and his wife fled the country. They took with them only a weekend suitcase, $200, and 100 shares of Coca-Cola stock, which they never sold. Goizueta remained with Coca-Cola in the United States, and rose through the corporate ranks to become chairman and chief executive officer (CEO) of the firm in 1981.

KEY DATES	
1931	Born in Havana, Cuba, on November 18.
1953	Graduates from Yale University.
1954	Returns to Cuba and works for Coca-Cola as a quality control chemist.
1960	Flees Cuba after Castro takeover.
1974	Becomes one of only two living Coca-Cola executives to know the secret formula for the drink.
1979	Elected vice chairman of Coca-Cola.
1981	Elected chairman & CEO of Coca-Cola worldwide.
1997	Dies in Atlanta, Georgia, on October 18, six weeks after being diagnosed with lung cancer.

Mission statement

Throughout his period in charge, Goizueta's key objectives were to increase the company's profitability and the breadth of appeal of its products, not only in the United States but worldwide. He was fond of quoting pop artist Andy Warhol's remark that: "The President drinks Coke, Liz Taylor drinks Coke and, just think, you can drink Coke, too. A Coke is a Coke and no amount of money can get you a better Coke than the one the bum on the corner is drinking. All the Cokes are the same, and all the Cokes are good." Goizueta ran Coca-Cola for 16 years, during which time the stock market value of the company rose from $4.3 billion to $180 billion, a 3,500 percent increase.

Despite his overall success, Goizueta made mistakes. He tinkered with the secret formula (known only to two living Coca-Cola executives at any time) for making Coke syrup by producing and marketing "New Coke" in 1985. He worked on the modified formula for five years. Within three months of the release of "New Coke," however, he acknowledged his error and brought back "classic Coke." Another setback was the purchase of Columbia Films. When Goizueta realized that Coca-Cola was not equipped to run a movie studio, he turned his

◀ *Roberto Goizueta rose through the ranks to become CEO of Coca Cola in 1981. He worked for the company for 43 years.*

INFLUENCES AND INSPIRATION

The greatest formative influence on Roberto Goizueta was his father, Crispulo, who owned and ran a large sugar refinery in Havana, Cuba. Roberto used and adapted many of the business techniques that he had observed as a child during his own subsequent career with the Coca-Cola Company.

Goizueta also introduced new strategies of his own, and the success of many of them made him a highly respected pundit in the U.S. business community. In addition to his main work at Coca-Cola, he was a board member of other firms anxious to benefit from his wisdom and expertise. They included the Ford Motor Company and Eastman Kodak.

Away from commerce, Goizueta's charity work extended beyond his own Goizueta Family Foundation. He was involved with numerous philanthropic bodies, and a founder of the Points of Light Initiative, an organization that promotes voluntary service.

error around by making a very profitable sale of the company to the Sony Corporation. The readiness to admit mistakes was an essential part of Goizueta's skills. As he said: "The moment avoiding failure becomes your motive, you're on the path of inactivity. You only stumble if you're moving forward."

Problems and solutions

On taking charge of Coca-Cola, Goizueta realized that the company was excessively dependent on the bottlers of its products. There was a constant battle to maintain quality and a struggle to manage price hikes by the glass suppliers. The world's bottlers could hold the beverage company to ransom. Goizueta resolved the problem by entering into partnerships with the bottling firms. He subsidized their growth and modernization in exchange for Coca-Cola holding an interest in their companies. Instead of fighting each other, Goizueta merged the identity and interests of the two parties. The move increased Coca-Cola's profits and gave the company a competitive edge.

Another of Goizueta's strengths was that he did not feel a need to control all the minutiae of the Coca-Cola operation. He delegated wisely, and was known as a calm, supportive boss. Yet he never lost sight of the fact that tranquility could not be achieved without effort. He compared the Coca-Cola Company to a duck on a pond: "On the surface, things look relatively quiet, but below the water line the duck is paddling like hell." As a result of that intense effort, during Goizueta's time as CEO, the Coca-Cola Company was twice voted *Fortune* magazine's Most Admired American Corporation.

Goizueta's management style produced increased profits, and gained him the loyalty and affection of staff and shareholders alike. He became a legend in U.S. industry, and President Jimmy Carter (1977–1980) characterized him as "the corporate leader in modern times who beautifully exemplified the American dream." In the late 1970s, after having spent huge sums on developing plastic containers for Coca-Cola, Goizueta learned that minute quantities of carcinogens (cancer-causing chemicals) were generated when the plastic interacted with the drink. He immediately scrapped the project.

Goizueta never courted publicity, and always refused to discuss his personal life with interviewers. In 1992 he established the Goizueta Family Foundation, the stated purpose of which was to identify prospective investment partners and then work closely with them to achieve their predesignated aims. The earliest main beneficiary of the foundation's work was the Atlanta city community, which received greatly improved educational, social, and cultural resources, together with strategic plans for their long-term future development.

Legacy

Roberto Goizueta died in 1997, a few weeks after having been diagnosed with lung cancer. At the time of his death *Forbes* magazine estimated his personal fortune at $1.3 billion. Since then his widow, Olga, has carried on the work of the foundation, which now helps universities set up scholarships for Hispanic Americans who want careers in business. Although Goizueta was a leading role model for immigrants, he did not regard himself as a member of any particular nation or ethnic group. Trying to define his own identity, he once remarked: "I am not of the Cuban culture. I am not of the American culture. I suppose I am of the Coca-Cola culture."

Further reading: Greising, David. *I'd Like the World to Buy a Coke: The Life and Leadership of Roberto Goizueta*. New York, NY: John Wiley & Sons, 1998.
http://www.goizuetafoundation.org (Web site of the Goizueta Family Foundation).

GOLDEMBERG, Isaac
Writer, Academic

Isaac Goldemberg is considered by some literary critics to be the most important Latin American writer in the United States. Of Peruvian and Jewish ancestry, Goldemberg is the author of *La Vida a Plazos de Jacobo Lerner* (The Fragmented Life of Jacobo Lerner), which in 2001 was selected by the National Yiddish Book Center of the United States as one of the 100 greatest Jewish works of the previous 150 years. Goldemberg is also a respected academic, who has taught at several universities in the United States.

Early life
Goldemberg was born in Chepén, Peru, in 1945. He spent his early years there, living with his mother's family, and was raised as a Catholic. At age eight, he moved to Lima, the capital, where his father lived. In Lima he was confronted by his Jewish heritage for the first time, an issue that would later become central to both his life and work.

Moving on
In 1964, Goldemberg finally settled in New York City, where he attended the City University of New York (CUNY) for his undergraduate degree, after which he studied for an MA at New York University.

Goldemberg began teaching literature in New York; he worked at CUNY for 16 years. He became a key figure in promoting and popularizing Latin American literature. In 1985 he helped set up a Latin American Book Fair in

Washington, D.C., at which 30 leading Latin American writers were present. Two years later, he established the Latin American Writers Institute at CUNY. He became the director of the institute and professor of humanities at Hostos Community College in New York.

An important voice
Goldemberg has established himself as one of the most important representatives of Jewish–Latin American literature. His work often examines the idea of being an outsider in constant search of an identity. Although his themes are clearly inspired by his own experience as a Peruvian, a Jew, and a New Yorker, his treatment of them is often philosophical and reflective, rather than straightforwardly autobiographical.

Goldemberg's work has been translated into several languages, reviewed in academic journals, and published in various magazines and anthologies in Latin America, Europe, and the United States. His work includes: *Tiempo de Silencio* (Time of Silence; poetry, 1970), *Tiempo al Tiempo* (Time to Time; novel, 1984), and *El Nombre del Padre* (The Name of the Father; novel, 2002). He has also published two plays. Goldemberg's critical work includes *El Gran Libro de América Judía* (The Great Book of American Jewry, 1998), an anthology of Jewish–Latin American writings.

Honors
Goldemberg has received several awards for his work, including the Nuestro Award in Fiction (1977), the Nathaniel Judah Jacobson Award (1995), the Lluvia Editores Short Story Award (2000), and the Orden de Don Quijote (2005), awarded by St. John's University, New York, and the Honorary National Hispanic Society Sigma Delta Pi. The award was a recognition of Goldemberg's literary career as both a writer and a scholar. One reflection of Goldemberg's status in modern literature is the growing number of critical studies of his work.

KEY DATES	
1945	Born in Chepén, Peru.
1964	Moves to New York.
1987	Founds the Latin American Writers Institute at the City University of New York (CUNY).
1995	Receives the Nathaniel Judah Jacobson Award.
2000	Receives the Lluvia Editores Short Story Award.
2001	Receives the PEN Club of Peru Poetry Award.
2002	Receives the Luis Alberto Sánchez Award for Literary Essays.
2005	Receives the Orden de Don Quijote.

Further reading: Dolan, Maureen (ed.). *Crossing Cultures in Isaac Goldemberg's Works.* Hanover, NH: Ediciones del Norte, 2003.
http://www.hostos.cuny.edu/oop/Profiles/faculty_Isaac Goldemberg.html (brief biography).

GÓMEZ, Edward
Medal of Honor Recipient

Edward Gómez is one of 40 Latino recipients of the Congressional Medal of Honor, the U.S. military's highest decoration for valor in action. The award was made posthumously after Gómez had given his life in the Korean War (1950–1953).

Early life

Gómez was born in 1932 in Omaha, Nebraska, and attended Omaha High School. Both his parents were Mexican Americans, but, despite his heritage, Gómez had little command of the Spanish language. His friends, however, remembered his love of Mexican music: "Quizá, quizá, quisá" was his favorite song. Physically, Gómez was small but well built; he was a Golden Glove welterweight boxer.

Military service

Gómez enlisted in the U.S. Marine Corps Reserve on August 11, 1949, the day after his 17th birthday. Following induction in San Diego, California, he underwent further training at Camp Pendleton, California, and was then sent to Korea with the 7th Replacement Draft. He was in a company of numerous other young Mexican Americans, many of whom were from the Southwest. Much of what Gómez subsequently accomplished in the military is known through the testimony of his comrade in arms, Oscar "Challo" Franco, from Tucson, Arizona.

Outstanding courage under fire

On September 14, 1951, Gómez's platoon was called forward to reinforce an adjacent company that was being attacked by Chinese forces at Kajon-ni. After setting up their gun positions, the U.S. Marines opened fire. About five minutes later, the enemy started throwing hand grenades. Gómez threw one of them back, but others exploded in the U.S. dugout, killing several men. A further

▲ *Edward Gómez was a U.S. Marine who was killed in action in Korea at age 19.*

grenade then landed by the platoon's gun emplacement. Gómez picked it up, but instead of throwing it back, he pulled it onto his stomach, spun his body away from the gun, and fell on top of the device. The hand grenade exploded, killing Gómez instantly.

For his outstanding heroism in saving the lives of four other Marines, one of whom was Challo, Private First Class Edward Gómez was awarded the Medal of Honor in Korea. He also received a Gold Star in lieu of a second award, the Korean Service Medal with bronze star, and the United Nations Service Medal.

Further reading: http://www.homeofheroes.com/moh/citations_1950_kc/gomez_edward.html (full text of Medal of Honor citation).

KEY DATES	
1932	Born in Omaha, Nebraska, on August 10.
1946	Enrolls at Omaha High School.
1949	Enlists in the U.S. Marine Corps Reserve on August 11.
1951	Killed in action at Kajon-ni, Korea, on September 14.

GÓMEZ, José H.
Archbishop

José Gómez was appointed archbishop of San Antonio, Texas, in 2004. He is a leading member of Opus Dei, a politically conservative and highly controversial organization within the Roman Catholic church.

Early life
José Horacio Gómez was born in 1951, in Monterrey, Mexico, the son of a highly educated and prosperous middle-class family. He originally intended to become a businessman, and received a bachelor's degree in accounting in 1975. By then, however, he was already discovering his true vocation for the church, and he went on to study for a degree in theology at the Rome, Italy, campus of the University of Navarre, an educational foundation of Opus Dei based in Pamplona, Spain.

Gómez graduated in 1978 and was soon afterward ordained as an Opus Dei priest. He continued his theological studies at the University of Navarre, and in 1980 gained a doctoral degree. Much of Gómez's subsequent work was focused on the pastoral care of ordinary Roman Catholics. From 1987 to 1999, he worked in the parish of Our Lady of Grace in San Antonio, the city in which his mother had been born and raised. Meanwhile he also established a wider role, becoming president of the National Association of Hispanic Priests in 1996.

In 2001, Pope John Paul II appointed Gómez auxiliary bishop of Denver, Colorado—the first Hispanic to hold the rank of bishop within the diocese. Like all auxiliary bishops, he was also ordained as a titular bishop and given the title of Titular Bishop of Belali, a former diocese in Tunisia, North Africa. In 2004 he was appointed to his current position as archbishop of San Antonio, in succession to Patrick Flores. Archbishop Gómez was installed in San Fernando Cathedral on February 15, 2005.

▲ *José Gomez has spent much of his life working in San Antonio, Texas. He was appointed the city's archbishop in 2004.*

Work as archbishop
Since his installation, Archbishop Gómez has emphasized the important role he believes Hispanic Roman Catholics will play in shaping the future of the United States. Immigrant Hispanics, he argues, often have values that are deeply rooted in faith and family life, and their strong ethical code will counter the powerful secular (nonreligious) and materialistic forces that he believes predominate in the country today. Among other initiatives, the bishop has headed an important project that aims to translate the Bible into a Spanish version that is readily comprehensible to North American Hispanics—most Spanish Bibles currently available in the United States are Latin American in origin. José Gómez is currently regarded as a leading candidate for appointment to the office of cardinal, the highest rank in the Roman Catholic church after the Pope.

See also: Flores, Patrick

Further reading: "Bienvenido, Archbishop-Designate José H. Gómez!" *Today's Catholic*, January 21, 2005. www.catholic-hierarchy.org/bishop/bgomezj.html (official resumé of Gómez's church career).

KEY DATES	
1951	Born in Monterrey, Mexico, on December 26.
1978	Becomes a priest within Opus Dei.
2001	Appointed auxiliary bishop of Denver, Colorado.
2004	Appointed archbishop of San Antonio, Texas (ordained 2005).

GOMEZ, Scott
Ice Hockey Player

A leading professional ice hockey player, Scott Gomez was the first Latino ever to be drafted into the National Hockey League (NHL).

Early life

Born in Anchorage, Alaska, on December 23, 1979, Scott Carlos Gomez was the son of a Mexican American father and a Colombian American mother. Aged 18, he began playing for the Tri-City Americans, a Western Hockey League (WHL) team based in Kennewick, Washington. He soon made his mark there as a left-handed center, and at the end of his first season he was named in the WHL All-Rookie Team.

In 1998 Gomez was drafted by the New Jersey Devils, who made him their 27th pick in the first round. He remained with the Americans for a further season, scoring 108 points in 58 games, and winning a place on the WHL All-Star team. He made the move to East Rutherford in time for the start of the 1999–2000 season. Once on the

KEY DATES	
1979	Born in Anchorage, Alaska, on December 23.
1997	Joins Tri-City Americans of the WHL.
1998	Drafted by the New Jersey Devils.
1999	Debuts for Devils in the NHL.
2005	Wins Devils' Most Valuable Player award; returns to Anchorage during NHL lockout to play for the Alaska Aces.

Devils team, he lost no time in making his presence felt, scoring 70 points and making 51 assists in the league, and scoring 10 points in the 2000 playoffs as the Devils won the Stanley Cup. In recognition of his feats, Gomez was honored with the Calder Trophy, awarded annually to the NHL's leading rookie; he was also chosen for the NHL All-Star game.

Maturing player

Gomez scored 63 points in his second season, during which the Devils promised great things but were ultimately disappointing. They again reached the finals of the Stanley Cup, but lost to the Colorado Avalanche.

In the 2001–2002 NHL season, Gomez's third, both he and the Devils failed to build on the foundations of the two previous years. The player, hampered by injury, scored only 48 points and 10 goals, and his team lost to the Carolina Hurricanes in the first round of the playoffs.

That year's poor results turned out to be a blip rather than a crisis. In 2002–2003, Gomez and the Devils reasserted themselves as Gomez's 55 points made a major contribution to another Stanley Cup triumph. He also scored 12 points in the playoffs. The following season, Gomez scored 70 points and tied for the highest number of assists (56). The Devils, however, fell short of the mark, losing in the playoffs to the Philadelphia Flyers.

When the 2004–2005 NHL season was canceled owing to a dispute between players and the league, Gomez returned to his native Anchorage to play for the Alaska Aces of the East Coast Hockey League. He was voted his new team's Most Valuable Player.

▼ *Scott Gomez of the New Jersey Devils looks for a way around the Atlanta Thrashers' Brad Larsen.*

Further reading: http://sports.espn.go.com/nhl/players/profile?statsId=1844 (career statistics).

GOMEZ, Vernon "Lefty"
Baseball Player

Born Vernon Louis Gomez in 1908 in Rodeo, California, Lefty Gomez was a leading baseball pitcher of the 1930s. Throughout his career he dominated the mound, and his extrovert personality and evident sense of humor made him a favorite with fans and sports reporters, who referred to him as "The Gay Caballero" and "El Goofy."

Rising star

Gomez first played for the San Francisco Seals, but in 1929 the 20-year-old was scouted by the Yankees, and the New York team bought out his contract for $35,000. He made his Major League debut for the Yankees on April 19, 1930. Over the next two years he helped his team to 21 victories. His left-handed fastball made him one of the two key pitchers for the Yankees. The other was Red Ruffing, a right-handed pitcher. They were a formidable pairing.

▼ *New York Yankees pitcher Vernon Gomez was one of the most popular baseball stars of the 1930s.*

KEY DATES

1908	Born in Rodeo, California, on November 26.
1930	Makes Major League debut for New York Yankees.
1934	Wins Baseball's Triple Crown for wins, strikeouts, and ERA.
1972	Inducted into National Baseball Hall of Fame.
1989	Dies in Greenbrae, California, on February 17.

In 1934 Gomez led the Major Leagues in seven categories. He had the most wins with 26, the most strikeouts with 158, and his earned run average (ERA) was 2.33. In 1937 he led the league again in three categories. Gomez made his name as a notoriously fast pitcher. Later in his career he slowed down, partly through injury, but he compensated for his loss of speed with guile: Where he had once beaten batters with his speed, he now outwitted them.

World Series

Lefty Gomez played in the 1932 World Series and in the World Series for 1936, 1937, 1938, and 1939. He set a World Series record by winning six games without a single loss. He was an All Star seven times in a row, from 1933 to 1939. He led the league twice in wins, and led the league in shutouts in 1934 and 1937. Gomez also helped the New York Yankees win five American League pennants and five World Championships.

Lasting reputation

After his retirement from baseball in 1943, Gomez worked as a goodwill ambassador for the Wilson Sporting Goods Company. He was always a comic and never disappointed his fans. In 1972 he became only the second Latino to be inducted into the National Baseball Hall of Fame (the first was Roberto Clemente).

See also: Clemente, Roberto

Further reading: *The Baseball Encyclopedia*. New York, NY: Macmillan, 1990.
http://www.baseballhalloffame.org/hofers_and_honorees/hofer bios/gomez_lefty.htm (National Baseball Hall of Fame).

GOMEZ, Wilfredo
Boxer

Wilfredo Gomez was a boxing champion who won three world titles in different weight categories. Of his 44 wins, 42 were achieved by knockout.

Emerging talent

The son of a taxi driver, Wilfredo Gomez was born in 1956 in Las Monjas, a poor area of San Juan, Puerto Rico. Nicknamed "Bazooka" as a child, he learned to fight by defending himself from bullies, and saw boxing as an opportunity to escape poverty.

In 1974 Gomez won the world amateur championship in Havana, Cuba, and decided to turn professional to alleviate his family's financial problems. His first professional fight in the super bantamweight (or junior featherweight) class ended in a six-round draw against Jacinto Fuentes of Panama, but he won his next 33 fights by knockout, one of the longest streaks in boxing history.

In 1977 Gomez won his first world championship by knocking out Dong-Kyun Yun of South Korea. Gomez then set a record by successfully defending the title 17 times before being beaten in 1983.

In August 1981, Gomez took on Salvador Sanchez of Mexico, the world featherweight champion. He lost in eight rounds, and later admitted that he had underestimated his opponent. A rematch was planned, but never took place: Sanchez was killed in a car crash in the following year.

Gomez won the world featherweight title against fellow Puerto Rican Juan LaPorte in 1982. He lost his title on his first defense, succumbing to Azumah Nelson of Ghana in the 11th round. Gomez reacted to defeat by changing weight class once more. In 1985 he beat American Rocky Lockridge to win the world junior lightweight crown.

▲ **Wilfredo Gomez (facing) prepares to hit Lupe Pintor during their 1982 world title fight.**

Again, however, he failed in his first defense, losing in 1986 to Alfredo Layne of Panama. The disappointment prompted Gomez to retire, although he made a fleeting return in 1988 and 1989, winning two more bouts.

Cautionary tale

After retirement, Gomez found life very difficult, suffering from drug problems, and serving a jail sentence in Venezuela. He also had several broken marriages. A disorder affecting his speech and short-term memory was a further unwanted legacy of his boxing career.

He later returned to Puerto Rico, where he was reconciled with one of his ex-wives and became a full-time boxing coach. His life has been the subject of a documentary film, *Bazooka: The Battles of Wilfredo Gomez* (2003), which he regards as a cautionary tale. He has said: "I want the film to be a lesson for Latino youth … I want them to see how you can reach the highest highs but also fall to the lowest lows."

KEY DATES	
1956	Born in San Juan, Puerto Rico, on October 29.
1974	Becomes world amateur boxing champion; turns pro.
1977	Wins world junior featherweight title.
1982	Wins world featherweight title.
1985	Wins world junior lightweight crown.
1986	Retires.
2003	Is subject of documentary *Bazooka*.

Further reading: Fleischer, Nat, and Sam Andre. *An Illustrated History of Boxing.* New York, NY: Citadel Press, 2001. http://www.ibhof.com/gomez.htm (International Boxing Hall of Fame Web site).

GÓMEZ-PEÑA, Guillermo
Actor, Writer

Guillermo Gómez-Peña is a Mexican American actor, filmmaker, singer, poet, playwright, and critic. He first found fame in the early 1980s, and became best known as a performance artist.

Early life
Gómez-Peña was born in 1955 in Mexico City, Mexico, and studied linguistics at the city's Universidad Nacional Autónoma de México (UNAM). As a student, he developed a taste for experimental art, and on graduation in 1978, he traveled to the United States to pursue his interest. He settled in Los Angeles, California, and joined the California Institute of Arts.

In 1981, Gómez-Peña was one of the founders of Poyesis Genetica, a performance troupe that combined Mexican *carpa* (a form of popular theater) with traditional Japanese Kabuki drama and modern electronic special effects. The group spent two years touring the U.S.–Mexico border in and around San Diego and Tijuana in order, as Gómez-Peña put it, "to embrace the urban Chicano experience." The project spawned the Border Arts Workshop/Taller de Arte Frontizero, which was established in 1985 in San Diego. The stated purpose of the enterprise was to "deconstruct" the *mestizaje* (mixed) Mexican heritage: in other words, to break up the confusing entity that it had become into its original Spanish and Indian parts.

Challenging stage performances
On stage, Gómez-Peña appeared in numerous personas. One of his most famous creations was the Mexterminator, a machete-toting karate expert on a one-man mission to reconquer the U.S. Southwest. The character spoke and sang in an inimitable combination of English, Spanish, and Spanglish. Much of Gómez-Peña's work at the time was superficially comical, but had a serious underlying purpose. It aimed to subvert lazy notions about ethnicity and culture, and particularly to demonstrate that Mexican people are so diverse that generalizations about them are meaningless.

His act, which was created and honed on the U.S.–Mexico border, was soon in demand throughout the United States. Gómez-Peña toured extensively in the late 1980s, and made memorable appearances at a variety of venues, including the Whitney Museum of American Art, New York, the Smithsonian Institution in Washington, D.C., and the Art Institute in Chicago, Illinois.

Explaining and informing
Gómez-Peña complements his performance art with a wide range of written work in which he explains the intellectual foundation of his stage acts. His key publication is *Mi Otro Yo* (My Other Self; 1988), a collection of interviews with the leading Chicano and Chicana artists Judy Baca, Harry Gamboa, Jr., José Montoya, and Luis Valdez.

Gómez-Peña is also an accomplished poet and critic. Among his best-known works are *Border Brujo* (1990), *Warrior for Gringostroika: Essays, Performance Texts, and Poetry* (1994), *The New World Border* (1996), *Temple of Confessions: Mexican Beasts and Living Santos* (1997), *Friendly Cannibals* (1996), *Dangerous Border Crossers: The Artist Talks Back* (2000), and *Codex Espangliensis* (2000). As a journalist, he has contributed to a range of publications, including *The Drama Review*. In 1986, Gómez-Peña cofounded *La Linéa Quebrada (The Broken*

◄ *Performance artist Guillermo Gómez-Peña first found fame in the early 1980s. Although his work is often humorous in its approach, it tackles serious issues such as racism.*

INFLUENCES AND INSPIRATION

Guillermo Gómez-Peña works in numerous media, but nearly all his performances and writings are unified by a single impulse: the determination to break down received ideas about Chicanos and Chicanas. As he wrote in *The New World Border*, modern Mexican

Americans are "denationalized, de-Mexicanized, transchicanized, and pseudo-internationalized … divided (better yet, trapped) by multiple borders." In that case, he argues, how can any generalization about them not be false?

The versatility and originality of Gómez-Peña have inspired a generation of performance artists in the United States. Part of his achievement is that he has influenced not only fellow Latinos but also Anglo- and African Americans.

Line), a cultural journal in Spanish and English. He has also been a regular contributor to *All Things Considered*, a National Public Radio program.

Gómez-Peña has worked in film and video on both sides of the camera. He played himself in two movies about cultural stereotyping and relations between Mexican and Anglo Americans: *Frontierland* (1995) and *The Couple in the Cage* (1997).

Countering bigotry

In 1997, Gómez-Peña set up on the Internet a radical interactive Web site in which he and his longtime collaborator, Roberto Sifuentes, encouraged surfers to express their racial prejudices. The idea was to confront ignorance, and to overcome irrationality with reasoned argument. When asked in a 1998 interview to explain his

motives for undertaking the project, Gómez-Peña replied: "Currently there is a national denial about the state of race relations and racism in the United States. In fact there is a backlash, and people are unwilling to discuss these issues in public forums, and that is one of the reasons why we decide to bring the darkest zones of the subconscious to these Internet questionnaires, where people are as free as possible and linguistically unpoliced, and they can be as sincere or insensitive or direct as they want to be."

Awards and honors

Gómez-Peña has received widespread acclaim for his work in numerous media. In 1989, he won the Prix de la Parole—an award made by the International Theatre of the Americas in Montreal, Canada—for his stage performances. In the same year, he took the New York Bessie award for the best children's educational software.

In 1991, the movie version of *Border Brujo* took first prize at both the National Latino Film and Video Festival in Chicago and the Cine Festival in San Antonio, Texas. In the same year, Gómez-Peña became the first Mexican-born recipient of a MacArthur Fellowship. The years 1996 and 1998 brought further triumphs for his videos at the San Antonio festival, first with *El Naftazteca: Cyber Aztec TV for 2000 AD*, and then for *Temple of Confessions*. In 1997, he received the American Book Award for *The New World Border*. Four years later, *Borderstasis*, a film of his one-man show, won the prize for the best performance video at the Vancouver Video Poetry Festival.

KEY DATES

1955	Born in Mexico City, Mexico.
1978	Moves to the United States.
1981	Cofounds performance troupe Poyesis Genetica.
1985	Helps establish the Border Arts Workshop/Taller de Arte Frontizero in San Diego, California.
1986	Cofounds cultural journal *La Linéa Quebrada* (*The Broken Line*).
1988	Publishes *Mi Otro Yo* (*My Other Self*).
1990	Publishes *Border Brujo*.
1995	Appears in the movie *Frontierland*.
1996	Publishes *The New World Border*.
1997	Appears in the movie *The Couple in the Cage*.
2000	Publishes *Dangerous Border Crossings: The Artist Talks Back*.

See also: Baca, Judy; Gamboa, Harry, Jr.; Montoya, José; Valdez, Luis M.

Further reading: Gómez-Peña, Guillermo. *Ethno-Techno: Writings on Performance, Activism, and Pedagogy*. New York, NY: Routledge, 2005.
http://www.levity.com/corduroy/pena.htm (Bohemian Ink Web site dedicated to experimental literature).

GÓMEZ-QUIÑONES, Juan
Academic

Juan Gómez-Quiñones is a leading Chicano scholar and a community activist. Gómez-Quiñones specializes in political and labor history. He has contributed greatly to the development of Chicano studies in the United States, both as an academic and as the author of several influential books and articles.

Early life
Born in Parral, Chihuahua, Mexico, Gómez-Quiñones moved to Los Angeles as a child, where he attended Cantwell High School before going on to study for a BA in literature at the University of California at Los Angeles (UCLA). He received a master's degree in Latin American studies and a doctorate in history from UCLA. In 1965 Gómez-Quiñones began teaching at UCLA.

Chicano studies
In 1969 Gómez-Quiñones contributed to one of the most influential documents in Chicano studies and MEChA (Movimiento Estudiantil Chicano de Aztlán) history, El Plan de Santa Barbara. He also cofounded the leading journal in the field, *Aztlán: Chicano Journal of the Social Sciences and Arts* (later subtitled the *International Journal of Chicano Studies Research*). *Aztlán* was named after the legendary spiritual home of the Aztecs. The combination of scholarship and activism modeled by Gómez-Quiñones in his work can be seen in *Aztlán*'s mission statement, which stated that the journal existed to "promote an active quest for solutions to the problems of the barrios of America." Gómez-Quiñones promoted the fundamental notion that Chicano studies was different from other academic disciplines because its focus lay in scholars working to improve society. In the early 1970s, Gómez-Quiñones also promoted the importance of Chicano history, arguing that it was key to the present and future of the Mexican American community.

Activism
As a prominent scholar and recognized activist, Gómez-Quiñones supported several contemporary political struggles. In the early 1990s he protested the proposed politically charged changes to the El Pueblo Historic Park in Los Angeles (Olvera Street), which would have reduced the involvement of Mexicans in favor of other ethnic American groups. In 1993 he also mediated the historic dispute at UCLA over the transition of Chicano studies from a center to a department.

Career
Gómez-Quiñones has authored several articles and books, including *Mexican American Labor, 1790–1990, The Roots of Chicano Politics, 1600–1940,* and *Chicano Politics, 1940–1990*. The works are considered "classics" in Chicano studies, and frequently used in college classes. Gómez-Quiñones also sat on the boards of MALDEF (the Mexican American Legal Defense and Education Fund) and California State University.

Recognition
Gomez-Quinones's contribution to education was recognized in 1990, when he was given the National Association for Chicana and Chicano Studies (NACCS) Scholar of the Year Award. He was also awarded the Rosenfield Distinguished Community Partnership Prize (2003–2004) for his substantial grant-writing and curricula development contributions to the Latino Museum of History, Art, and Culture.

KEY DATES

1940 Born in Parral, Chihuahua, Mexico, about this time.

1969 Contributes to El Plan de Santa Barbara.

1972 Wins the National Endowment for the Humanities Fellowship.

1975 Trains at Newberry Library in Chicago.

1990 Receives the National Association for Chicana and Chicano Studies (NACCS) Scholar of the Year Award.

2003 Receives the UCLA Rosenfield Distinguished Community Partnership Prize.

See also: Activism; Political Movements

Further reading: Gómez-Quiñones, Juan. *Mexican American Labor, 1790–1990*. Albuquerque, NM: University of New Mexico Press 1994.
http://www.sscnet.ucla.edu/history/gomez-quinones (Gomez-Quiñones's biography on the UCLA site).

GONZALES, Alberto
Attorney General

Alberto Gonzales rose from humble beginnings to become a close confidant of President George W. Bush and the first Latino to serve as attorney general of the United States. Despite his outstanding success, his career has been dogged by controversy.

Early life

Alberto Gonzales was born in 1955 in San Antonio, Texas, to Pablo and Maria Gonzales. His father, a construction worker, and his mother were second-generation Mexican Americans who had less than a high-school education. Gonzales was the second of eight children and the only one of his siblings to graduate from college. He was an honors student at MacArthur High School in Houston, after which he served for two years in the U.S. Air Force. In 1975 he was accepted to the Air Force Academy, and in 1977 transferred to Rice University, where he majored in political science. Gonzales then earned his juris doctor (JD) degree from Harvard Law School in 1982. During his time at Harvard he married Diane Clemens, but the couple divorced in 1985. Soon after he married Rebecca Turner, with whom he has three children.

From 1982 to 1994, Alberto Gonzales worked as an attorney in private practice with Vinson and Elkins, a Houston-based law firm representing the oil and gas

▲ *Attorney general Alberto Gonzales is a close political ally of George W. Bush.*

industries. During the period Gonzales was also active as a board director of the United Way, an administrative group that raises funds for a coalition of charities, and served as president of Leadership Houston, an organization that supports the development of leadership skills in the Greater Houston community. Gonzales was also chair of the Commission for District Decentralization of the Houston Independent School District, and a member of Rice University's committee on undergraduate admissions.

Contact with Bush

In 1994, after becoming a partner at Vinson and Elkins, Gonzales was named general counsel to George W. Bush, who was then governor of Texas. In the same year the Texas branch of the U.S. Junior Chamber (the Jaycees) chose him as one of its Five Outstanding Young Texans. In 1995 and 1996 Gonzales served on delegations sent by the American Council of Young Political Leaders to Mexico and China. In 1997 he was appointed by Bush as Texas

KEY DATES	
1955	Born in San Antonio, Texas, on August 4.
1973	Joins the U.S. Air Force, where he serves for two years before being accepted to the Air Force Academy.
1982	Graduates from Harvard Law School and joins Houston-based law firm Vinson and Elkins.
1994	Appointed chief legal counsel to Texas governor George W. Bush.
1997	Appointed Texas secretary of state by Governor George W. Bush.
1999	Appointed to the Texas Supreme Court by George W. Bush.
2001	Appointed as White House legal counsel by President George W. Bush.
2005	Appointed as U.S. attorney general by President George W. Bush on February 3.

Alberto Gonzales made up his mind at an early age that he would escape the poverty trap that had ensnared his Mexican American parents. Fortunately for him, he was an academically gifted child who found his way out through a college education and law school.

After qualifying as an attorney Alberto Gonzales was most strongly influenced by George W. Bush, and his fortunes became inextricably linked with those of the Texas governor who, in 2001, became the 43rd president of the United States. Bush was a major catalyzing force in the career of

Gonzales, whom he promoted from the rank of an attorney in private practice to the nation's chief law enforcement officer. Gonzales has been ardently loyal to Bush, who has, in turn, rewarded him by appointing him to high government positions five times in 10 years.

secretary of state, and received the Presidential Citation from the Texas bar for his work in addressing the basic legal needs of the poor. Two years later George W. Bush appointed him as a justice to the Texas supreme court.

When Bush became president of the United States in January 2001, he commissioned Alberto Gonzales to serve as White House counsel. In 2005 Gonzales became the 80th attorney general of the United States.

Controversial figure

In the wake of his success, Gonzales has attracted much bad publicity. As counsel to Bush, he intervened to secure the governor's exemption from jury duty after he had been called to serve in a 1996 drunk driving case in Travis County. During the 2000 presidential campaign it emerged that Bush's answers to the juror questionnaire had not disclosed that he had himself been convicted of a misdemeanor for drunk driving in 1976. Gonzales's argument—that Bush be excused from jury duty because of the possibility that, as governor of Texas, he might be called on to pardon the accused—was derided by critics.

Gonzales also played a key role in the unusually large number of inmates executed in Texas during Bush's governorship. A 2003 article in *The Atlantic Monthly* alleged that Gonzales, whose job as chief legal counsel for Bush required him to conduct thorough reviews of all clemency cases, had provided the governor with "negligent counsel" and "only the most cursory briefings on the issues in dispute." The execution of Terry Washington—a severely mentally handicapped 33-year-old man—was cited as an instance where valid claims for clemency based on legal and material facts were ignored by Gonzales, and subsequently by Bush.

Other causes of criticism were Gonzales's links with the energy industry. While serving as an elected member of the Texas supreme court, Gonzales accepted $35,450 in contributions from the energy giant Enron, in addition to

more than $100,000 from other energy industry sources. The payments brought Gonzales under suspicion of partiality. The most serious charge against him came while he was White House legal counsel, when he was alleged to have helped conceal the details of secret energy task force meetings that Vice President Dick Cheney held with various energy company executives, thereby adding to a perception that the Bush administration allowed national policy to be determined by partisan corporate executives.

Human rights abuses

Alberto Gonzales became involved in further controversy during the U.S. response to the terrorist attacks on New York and Washington, D.C., on September 11, 2001. In 2002, as legal counsel for the White House, Gonzales drafted a memo in which he argued that "the war against terrorism is a new kind of war" that "renders obsolete the Geneva Convention's strict limitations on questioning of enemy prisoners and renders quaint some of its provisions." While he recognized that these views could "undermine U.S. military culture which emphasizes maintaining the highest standards of conduct in combat," Gonzales nonetheless advocated that prisoners held in Guantanamo Bay, Cuba, and elsewhere need not be subject to the Convention's rules. Gonzales's critics have charged that this counsel was interpreted by some members of the U.S. military as a justification for the abuse of Arab prisoners in what became known worldwide as the Abu Ghraib prison torture scandal.

Further reading: Minutaglio, Bill. *The President's Counselor SPA: The Rise to Power of Alberto Gonzales.* New York, NY: Rayo, 2006.
http://www.americanprogress.org/site/pp.asp?c=biJRJ8OVF&b=2 58608 (Web site with links to information about Alberto Gonzales compiled on the eve of his nomination as U.S. attorney general).

GONZALES, Boyer
Artist

Boyer Gonzales was a critically acclaimed marine and landscape artist of the late-19th and early-20th century. He was the first Mexican American painter to have his work recognized in the United States.

Early life

Boyer Gonzales was born in 1864 in Houston, Texas. All four of his grandparents were Spaniards who came to Mexico between 1810 and 1821 while the country was seeking independence from Spain. One of his grandfathers, Victor, practiced medicine in Mexico for 20 years. Boyer's own father, Tomas Gonzales, was born in Tampico, Mexico, in 1829. His family subsequently immigrated to the United States when the disruptions caused by the independence struggle made normal life in Mexico too difficult to sustain.

Artistic development

Gonzales's recognition as an artist was gradual, and came over a long period of preparation and guidance from masters such as Winslow Homer, under whom Boyer Gonzales studied in the 1880s. Among the other painters who influenced the work of Gonzales were the Dutch artist Hendrik Willem Mesdag and the American watercolorist William J. Whittemore, with whom Gonzales worked in 1894.

◀ *Boyer Gonzales's work was inspired by that of his friend Winslow Homer.*

The following year, 1895, Gonzales went to Mexico. There he began creating watercolor scenes inspired by the sea, harbors, ships, and indigenous waterfowl. Some of his earliest works were derivative, but gradually he developed his talent and created a unique and distinctive artistic world. Although Gonzales subsequently painted the mountains around Taos, New Mexico, and other landscapes elsewhere, it is his Mexican seascapes that are generally regarded as his finest works of art.

Maturity

In 1907 Gonzales married Nell Hertford in New York City. They spent their honeymoon in Woodstock, New York, where Gonzales studied watercolor with painter Birge Harrison at an art colony sponsored by the Art Students League of New York. Previously Gonzales had painted in his spare time away from his day job as a cotton broker, but henceforth he became a full-time artist and, by the end of his life, one of the most acclaimed landscapists in the United States.

Boyer Gonzales died in 1934 at age 69. His posthumous reputation has grown steadily. Today many public and private collections in the United States and Europe house his oil paintings and watercolors. Some of the finest examples of his work are in the Modern Art Museum of Fort Worth, Texas, and the Vanderpoel Art Association in Chicago, Illinois. In 1980 a large number of his oil paintings and watercolors were bequeathed to the Rosenberg Library in Galveston by his son, Boyer Gonzales, Jr.

KEY DATES	
1864	Born in Houston, Texas, on September 22.
1894	Collaborates with American watercolorist William J. Whittemore.
1895	Visits Mexico; paints extensive series of landscapes and seascapes.
1907	Marries Nell Hertford; becomes a full-time painter.
1934	Dies in Galveston, Texas, on February 14.

Further reading: Simmen, Edward. *With Bold Strokes, Boyer Gonzales, 1864–1934.* College Station, TX: Texas A&M University Press, 1997.
http://www.tsha.utexas.edu/handbook/online/articles/GG/fgo71.html (Handbook of Texas Online).

GONZALES, Manuel
Cartoonist

Spanish-born illustrator Manuel Gonzales worked as an artist for Walt Disney for more than 40 years. He is best known for his Sunday Mickey Mouse comic strips. He had a particular fondness for the good-natured dog Goofy, and was responsible for introducing the mynah bird Ellsworth, Goofy's mischievous pet, to the strip. Gonzales's professionalism, craftsmanship, and surreal sense of humor have made his work particularly popular among collectors of Disney art work and memorabilia.

Early life
Manuel Gonzales was born on March 3, 1913, in Spain. After graduating from school, he trained as a fine artist. In the early 1930s, Gonzales decided to immigrate to the United States. In 1936 he began working in the publicity department of Walt Disney Productions.

Tribute
Within two years Gonzales's talent as an illustrator had brought him to the notice of the management at Disney. In 1938 he took over the illustration of the Sunday editions of the Mickey Mouse comic strips from fellow cartoonist Floyd Gottfredson (1905–1986). The Mickey Mouse cartoon strips, which had made their first appearance in U.S. newspapers in 1930, were a great success and were popular with U.S. readers: Gonzales's appointment to the project was a tribute to the high regard in which he was held.

Gonzales's association with Disney was a long and fruitful one. Apart from serving in the military for three years in World War II (1939–1945), Gonzales continued to pencil (provide the drawings for) the cartoon strip until his retirement.

Collaborators
During his long association with the cartoon, Gonzales partnered with several writers who produced the scripts for the strip. His most successful collaboration was with Bill Walsh (1913–1975), who worked on the strip from 1946 to 1963. In Gonzales's and Walsh's hands, the cartoons focused on Mickey Mouse and his ordinary everyday tasks and chores in a gentle satire of American suburban life. Gonzales specialized in drawing Mickey Mouse's dog, Goofy. Gonzales and Walsh introduced the character Ellsworth into the strip in 1949; Ellsworth

> **KEY DATES**
>
> **1913** Born in Spain on March 3.
>
> **1936** Hired as an illustrator at Disney.
>
> **1938** Takes over from Floyd Gottfredson to illustrate the syndicated Sunday Mickey Mouse cartoons.
>
> **1942** Performs military service during World War II.
>
> **1946** Begins working with writer Bill Walsh.
>
> **1949** Introduces the character of Ellsworth to the strip.
>
> **1950** Illustrates other Disney characters, including Cinderella and Lady and the Tramp.
>
> **1981** Retires from Disney.
>
> **1993** Dies in Van Nuys, California, on March 31.

featured predominantly in the strip for more than 10 years. Over time a host of Mickey Mouse's eccentric relatives also joined the Sunday editions.

In the first half of the 1950s, Gonzales also illustrated other Disney characters, including Cinderella, Lady and the Tramp, and Alice in Wonderland. He also inked (the penciler produces the original drawings, while the inker applies colored inks to the drawings) several of Al Taliaferro's Donald Duck dailies in the mid-1950s. Taliaferro (1905–1969) had worked with Gottfredson on the Mickey Mouse cartoons. Donald Duck went on to become one of the most popular Disney cartoons.

An all-round professional
Throughout his career in cartoons, Gonzales worked as an inker as well as a penciler. His most notable work in this capacity was for the daily "Scamp" cartoon strips, which he helped produce from 1956 to 1981. He also illustrated several Disney books and annuals, such as *Come Play with Mickey Mouse*. Gonzales died of cancer on March 31, 1993, in Van Nuys, California, aged 80.

Further reading: Smith, David. *Disney A to Z: The Updated Official Enyclopedia.* Los Angeles, CA: Disney Editions, 1998.
www.lambiek.net/artists/g/gonzales_manuel.htm (biography).

GONZALES, Manuel C.
Attorney, Civil Rights Activist

During the 1920s and 1930s, Manuel C. Gonzales was an influential figure in the early Mexican American struggle for civil rights in Texas. Prominent in several civic organizations, including the League of United Latin American Citizens (LULAC), Gonzales challenged the widespread racial discrimination and injustice faced by Tejanos. Like many other activists of his generation, Gonzales was a Democrat and a moderate, believing that change would come peacefully and gradually through the judicial process and political lobbying.

Early life
Manuel C. Gonzales was born on October 22, 1900, in Hidalgo County, Texas. His grandfather was José María Jésus Carbajal (died 1874), a Tejano hero of the Texas Revolution (1835–1836). Aged 10, Gonzales moved with his family to San Antonio, where he studied in local schools while working at the drugstore of Francisco A. Chapa, an influential local politician.

▼ *Manuel C. Gonzales was a respected civil rights lawyer: He highlighted the problem of Mexican American segregation in schools.*

KEY DATES	
1900	Born in Hidalgo County, Texas, on October 22.
1910	Moves with family to San Antonio, Texas.
1924	Graduates from the University of Texas School of Law at Austin.
1929	Founding member of LULAC.
1930	Wins public recognition for *Salvatierra v. Del Rio ISD*.
1986	Dies in San Antonio, Texas.

Gonzales enrolled at Nixon Clay College in Austin, after which he worked as a law clerk. From 1918 to 1919, he went to Europe to work at the U.S. embassies in Spain and France. Following his return to the United States, he studied for a bachelor's degree in law first at Saint Louis University, Missouri, and later at the University of Texas School of Law, Austin, from which he graduated in 1924.

A civil rights lawyer
Gonzales soon gained a reputation for being a formidable champion of Mexican American rights. He played a key role in several important civic organizations, including the San Antonio–based Orden Caballeros de America (Order of Knights of America), as well as the Mexican Chamber of Commerce. Gonzales's most significant contribution, however, was to the League of United Latin American Citizens (LULAC), of which he was one of the founding members (1929); he was elected president general two years later. Through LULAC, Gonzales campaigned tirelessly on issues such as school desegregation: He also ran for the state legislature in 1930. Gonzales challenged discrimination in the courts in such cases as *Salvatierra v. Del Rio Independent School District*, the first legal challenge to segregated schools for Mexican Americans.

See also: Chapa, Francisco A.; Supreme Court

Further reading: Kaplowitz, Craig A. *LULAC, Mexican Americans, and National Policy.* College Station, TX: Texas A&M University Press, 2005.
www.tsha.utexas.edu/handbook/online/articles/GG/fgo57.html (biography).

GONZALES, Ricardo
Tennis Player

Ricardo "Pancho" Gonzales (also Gonzalez) was the first Latino to win a Grand Slam tennis tournament. Known for his bad temper on court, Gonzales took the tennis world by storm in the late 1940s. He is considered to be one of the all-time great tennis stars, despite the fact that he never had a formal lesson. Known as Richard to his friends and "Gorgo" (short for Gorgonzola or "Big Cheese") to some of his colleagues, Gonzales influenced many leading tennis players, including Jimmy Connors. His decision to turn professional in 1949 meant that Gonzales could not compete in traditional tournaments until 1968, when the age of open competition began. As a result, Gonzales's considerable contribution to tennis is sometimes overlooked by commentators.

Early life
Born in Los Angeles, California, on May 9, 1928, to Mexican parents Manuel Antonio Gonzales and Carmen Alire Gonzales, Gonzales was known as "Pancho" to his six younger brothers and sisters. He began playing tennis after his mother gave him a tennis racket instead of

▼ *The actor and director Robert Redford claimed that playing tennis as a child with Ricardo "Pancho" Gonzales ranked among the greatest moments of his life.*

the bicycle that he desperately wanted for his 12th birthday. After entering and winning a few boys' tournaments, Gonzales came to the attention of Perry T. Jones, president of the Southern California Tennis Association. Jones banned Gonzales from competing because he skipped school.

In love with tennis
At the end of World War II (1939–1945), Gonzales served in the U.S. Navy. His ban ended when he reached age 18, and after his discharge from the Navy in 1946, he began to play in tennis tournaments once again.

In 1947 Gonzales played his first senior tennis tournament at the Southern California Championships at the Los Angeles Tennis Club. He beat the British player Derek Barton before losing to Gar Mulloy, the fourth seed. His later successes against Jaroslav Drobny, Frank Parker, and Bob Falkenberg helped him to end the year ranking number 17 in the United States.

Champion in the making
In 1948 Gonzales continued to build on the success of the previous year, winning the U.S. clay court championships. At Long Island he beat Budge Patty, but lost to Gar Mulloy in New Jersey.

He was seeded eight for the U.S. Championships at Forest Hills. Gonzales went on to beat Ladislav Hecht in the second round and Gus Ganzenmuller in his third round. He had a tougher time winning against Art Larsen in his next match. He struggled to begin with, but rallied in the fourth and fifth sets to take the match. In the semifinals Gonzales played the second seed, Grobny. He won and went on to meet Eric Sturgess in the final, which he won 6–3, 6–3, 14–12. Sturgess, however, got his revenge several weeks later in the semifinals of the Pan American championships, held in Mexico City.

Gonzales was known for his sheer determination and drive. His strong, almost unreturnable serve, sometimes compared to that of modern-day great Pete Sampras, helped him win many of his matches. He was driven by a need to prove to the mainstream white tennis establishment that a Chicano player could reach the top if he tried hard enough. Gonzales even played when injured: In one match against Ted Schroeder, Gonzales continued to play despite having a broken nose.

INFLUENCES AND INSPIRATION

One of the top tennis stars of the 20th century, Ricardo "Pancho" Gonzales was one of the most influential Latino athletes in history. Through sheer determination, talent, and hard work, Gonzales managed to smash through racial barriers to become a leading personality in an area that often discouraged ethnic minorities. Howard Cosell, the respected sports broadcaster, once claimed that, next to the African American baseball legend Jackie Robinson, "Pancho Gonzales was the most competitive athlete I've ever known."

Long before the famous outbursts of John McEnroe, Gonzales became renowned for losing his temper on court and abusing anyone who got in his way, but he was also known for his style. Jimmy Connors said that watching Gonzales play was "like looking into the flame of a fire … you couldn't take your eyes off him because you never knew what he would do next."

In 2005 the U.S. Tennis Association (USTA) announced that Gonzales's win against Eric Sturgess at the 1948 U.S. Championships, when Gonzales became the first Hispanic man to win a Grand Slam championship, was the top accomplishment in Hispanic tennis history.

Building on his success

Gonzales began 1949 with a win at the National Indoor Championships in New York. He played his first international tournament at the French Open. Gonzales reached the semifinals, but lost to Budge Patty. He also got knocked out when he played Geoff Brown in the fourth round of the prestigious Wimbledon championship in Great Britain. Back in the United States, Gonzales was a key member of the victorious 1949 U.S. Davis Cup team, which beat Australia in New York. He also successfully defended his U.S. Championship title against Ted Schroeder in a grueling and gripping final.

Turning professional

The desire to earn more money led Gonzales to turn professional in 1949. This was initially a distrastrous decision. In 1950 he took part in a professional tour against the top professional player Jack Kramer. Gonzales ended up losing 96 matches and winning just 27. His career went into decline for several years after his run-in with Kramer.

In 1954, however, Kramer retired and Gonzales made a stunning comeback. He beat Frank Sedgman, Don Budge, and Pancho Segura on tour. For a decade Gonzales was the world professional champion. He also set a record by winning the U.S. Professional Singles title eight times.

In 1968, professional players were allowed for the first time to compete in Grand Slam tournaments. Aged 40, Gonzales knocked out the second seed, Tony Roche, to reach the quarter-finals of the U.S. Open. In 1969 Gonzales, now a grandfather, beat Charlie Pasarel in a Wimbledon match of 112 games that lasted more than

five hours. He was defeated by Arthur Ashe in the fourth round, but reached number six in the world rankings that year. Three years later he became the oldest player ever to win a professional tournament, at the 1972 Des Moines Open. Gonzales retired two years later.

Gonzales was married six times. His last wife was Rita Agassi, the sister of the tennis star Andre Agassi. When Gonzales died penniless in 1995, his brother-in-law paid for the funeral.

KEY DATES

1928	Born in Los Angeles, California, on May 9.
1946	Starts to compete on the senior circuit.
1948	Wins the U.S. Singles Championship; becomes the first Hispanic to win a Grand Slam championship.
1949	Turns professional.
1954	Wins U.S. professional singles title for the first of eight times.
1969	Beats Charlie Pasarel in Wimbledon's longest-ever singles match.
1974	Retires from the main tennis circuit.
1995	Dies in Las Vegas, Nevada, on July 3.

Further reading: Gonzales, Doreen. *Ricardo "Pancho" Gonzales: Tennis Champion*. Berkley Heights, NJ: Enslow Publishers, 1998.
http://www.tennisfame.org/enshrinees/pancho_gonzales.html (essay on Gonzales).

GONZALES, Rodolfo "Corky"
Boxer, Activist

As a young man, Rodolfo "Corky" Gonzales made his name as a professional boxer. He later became better known as an author and one of the prime activists in the Chicano movement that swept the western United States during the late 1960s and early 1970s.

Early life

The youngest of eight children, Gonzales was born in 1928 in Denver, Colorado. His father, a migrant worker, had been a soldier in the Mexican Revolution of 1910, and the stories of his exploits filled Corky with an abiding sense of cultural pride that would later help inspire his political activism. Before that, however, Corky Gonzales found fame as a featherweight boxer.

After graduating from high school, Gonzales won a national amateur boxing title in 1947; he turned professional the following year. At his peak he was ranked third in the world by *The Ring* magazine and topped the ratings of the National Boxing Association. Perhaps surprisingly, in view of his career record—65 victories,

KEY DATES	
1928	Born in Denver, Colorado, on July 18.
1948	Becomes a professional boxer.
1955	Retires from boxing.
1957	Works for Democratic Party in Denver.
1966	Founds Cruzada para Justicia.
1969	Sponsors the first National Chicano Youth Liberation Conference.
2001	*Message to Aztlán* (his collected works) is published.
2005	Dies on April 12.

nine defeats, and one draw—he never got a shot at a world title. Gonzales retired from boxing in 1955, and the same year entered politics, making an unsuccessful bid for a seat on the Denver city council. He then took a series of laboring jobs, working at various times in a packing house, as a lumberjack, and as a farmworker.

Political rise

In 1957, at age 29, Gonzales became the first Mexican American to be appointed as a Democratic district captain in Denver. Over the next few years, Gonzales went into business as a bail bondsman and owner of an automobile insurance agency; he also financed *Viva*, a Latino-oriented newspaper. In 1960 he acted as the Colorado coordinator of the Viva Kennedy campaign that mobilized Democratic voters and helped secure the election of John F. Kennedy as U.S. president.

In 1964 Gonzales was appointed director of the Neighborhood Youth Corps (NYC), part of the "Great Society" social program sponsored by the administration of President Lyndon B. Johnson. Two years later, Gonzales suffered a setback when a newspaper alleged that he was favoring Latinos in NYC job services. His Democratic patrons did not support him, and Gonzales grew disenchanted with traditional politics. On March 28,

◀ *Corky Gonzales developed "El plan espiritual de Aztlán" (The Spiritual Plan of Aztlán) with the poet and activist Alurista.*

1966, Gonzales and several dozen others walked out of an Equal Employment Opportunity Commission meeting in Albuquerque, New Mexico. They were angered that not a single member of the commission was Mexican American. Gonzales then resigned from his NYC post. Soon afterward, on April 29, 1966, he founded the Cruzada para la Justicia (Crusade for Justice), a movement that advocated Mexican American empowerment through grass-roots community efforts. At about the same time, young Mexican Americans in the Western states began calling themselves Chicanos, a previously derogatory term for Mexican immigrants. The move symbolized their political awakening in reaction to racial discrimination.

"I am Joaquin"

Gonzales and his organization soon moved to the forefront of the new Chicano movement. In 1967 he published "Yo Soy Joaquin" ("I am Joaquin"), a poem that declared a new awareness of Latinos "caught up in a whirl of gringo society." An increasing number of Mexican American college students became politically active. Their agitation and demands for social justice coincided with the rise of the United Farm Workers Union under César Chávez, and with the anti-Vietnam war and Black Power movements.

Through the pages of his newspaper, *El Gallo: La Voz de la Justicia*, Gonzales advocated Chicano self-determination through individual self-governing communities. The Crusade for Justice building in Denver was expanded to include a bookstore, a boxing gym, a large auditorium, and a new school for the children of the urban barrios. La Escuela Tlatelolco, named after an ancient Mexican center of learning, taught students at elementary, high school, and undergraduate college levels, and at one point enrolled 300 students. Gonzales was also instrumental in organizing three National Chicano Youth Liberation conferences from 1969 to 1971. Out of them came "El plan espiritual de Aztlán (The Spiritual Plan of Aztlán), developed with the poet and activist Alurista. Based on a concept that called for Chicano autonomy and self-determination within the United States, Aztlán was the name given to the mythical northern home of the Aztec people.

Gonzales became a sought-after public speaker, addressing audiences on the plight of Mexican Americans and promulgating his ideas on how to remedy their problems. He was also Colorado state chairman of La Raza Unida, a political party that flourished briefly in the late 1960s but disintegrated in the early 1970s after infighting between Gonzales and other Chicano leaders.

Later years

In 1978 Gonzales suffered a heart attack while driving his car and sustained permanent head injuries in the ensuing crash. Thereafter he rarely appeared in public. In 2001 a collection of his poetry, plays, and commentary was published in a volume entitled *Message to Aztlán*. In early 2005, Gonzales was hospitalized for congestive heart failure; he died peacefully at home that April at age 76. He left behind a large family that included his wife of more than 50 years, Geraldine Romero Gonzales, eight grown children, and 22 grandchildren. A week after Gonzales's death, a public march in his honor brought out 2,000 people, including several Colorado luminaries, some of whom were Mexican Americans whose entry into politics he had inspired. The school he founded, La Escuela Tlatelolco, still survives, and his works are prescribed in Chicano studies courses throughout the United States.

See also: Alurista; Chávez, César

Further reading: Gonzales, Rodolfo. *Message to Aztlán: Selected Writings of Rodolfo "Corky" Gonzales*. Houston, TX: Arte Público Press, 2001.
http://escuelatlatelolco.org/website/corky_bio.html (Escuela Tlatelolco obituary notice).

GONZALES-BERRY, Erlinda
Educator

Erlinda Gonzales-Berry is chair of the ethnic studies department at Oregon State University. A respected academic, Gonzales-Berry has published many articles on Chicano/a and Nuevomexicano literature and culture.

Early life
Born in Roy, New Mexico, in 1942, Gonzales-Berry was one of the five daughters of a rancher and a schoolteacher. Gonzales-Berry grew up in the Llano Estacado, the famous staked plain of eastern New Mexico and western Texas, which Rudolfo Anaya made famous in *Bless Me, Ultima*. The history of the land is of migrant people—plains American Indians, Spaniards, Mexicans, and European immigrants—determined to dry-land farm the area. This landscape influenced Gonzales-Berry's writing and research in later life. After studying at El Rito High School, Gonzales-Berry studied at the College of Education at the University of New Mexico (UNM). In 1970 she became a teaching assistant at UNM while working to get a masters (1971). In 1978 she received a PhD from UNM.

Academia
Working her way up through the tenure-track and tenure ranks at UNM, Gonzales-Berry published the book *Paso por Aqui: Critical Essays on the New Mexican Literary Tradition* (1989), which opened the door for many non-Hispanics to study a rich Chicana/o literary heritage. Together with Teresa Marquez and Tey Diana Rebolledo, Gonzales-Berry

▲ **Erlinda Gonzales-Berry has written extensively on Chicano/a literature and immigration. She was a leading force in creating Chicano studies programs.**

hosted conferences, trained graduate students, and presented scholarship of such a high level that they established UNM as a leading center in Chicano studies.

In 1997 Gonzales-Berry accepted the chair of ethnic studies at Oregon State University and moved to the Pacific Northwest. Her work at Oregon reflects the growing interest in Latino studies throughout the United States.

Writing
Gonzales-Berry's academic work includes: *Recovering the U.S. Hispanic Literary Tradition II* (1996), *The Contested Homeland: A Chicano History of New Mexico* (2000), *Herencia: The Anthology of the Hispanic Literary Heritage* (2001), and *En Otra Voz: Antologia de Literatura Hispana en Los Estados Unidos* (2002). Gonzales-Berry has also published a novella, *Paletitas de Guayaba* (1991).

See also: Anaya, Rudolfo

Further reading: Garcia, Nasario. *Conversations with Hispanic Writers of New Mexico.* Austin, TX: Texas Tech University Press, 2000.
http://oregonstate.edu/cla/ethnic_studies/faculty/gonzales-berry.php (biography).

KEY DATES	
1942	Born in Roy, New Mexico.
1978	Receives PhD from the University of New Mexico.
1984	Teacher of Year Award, University of New Mexico.
1990	Receives a Fulbright Fellowship to teach Latino literature in Germany.
1992	Begins working on *Paso por Aqui* for the University of New Mexico Press.
1997	Associate editor, *Voces: A Journal of Chicana/ Latina Studies.*
1997	Becomes professor and chair of ethnic studies at Oregon State University.

GONZALEZ, Alfredo Cantu
Medal of Honor Recipient

Alfredo (Freddy) Cantu Gonzalez was a Mexican American who was killed in action during the Vietnam War (1964–1975). He was posthumously awarded the Congressional Medal of Honor, the highest U.S. military decoration, which is given for "conspicuous gallantry and intrepidity at the risk of life, above and beyond the call of duty."

Early life
The son of Mexican immigrants Andrés Cantu and Dolia Gonzalez, Freddy Cantu Gonzalez was born in 1946 in Edinburg, Texas. He was educated at the local high school, where he excelled at sports, particularly football. During summer vacations he worked with his mother in the cotton fields. On graduating in 1965, he enlisted in the U.S. Marine Corps Reserve in San Antonio. After completing basic recruit training and individual combat training, he served as a rifleman with the First Marine Division until January 1966, when he was promoted to private first class and sent to join the U.S. forces in Vietnam. In October he was promoted to lance corporal, and in December to corporal. Gonzalez returned to the United States in January 1967 and spent the spring at Camp Lejeune, North Carolina.

Second tour
Gonzalez did not have to return to the war, but when he learned that some of his old comrades in arms had been killed after his departure, he decided that it was his duty to undertake a second tour. His friends tried to dissuade him, but he would not take their advice. Having made his intentions known to his commanding officer, in May 1967 he was ordered to Camp Pendleton, California, to await transfer back to Southeast Asia. On July 1, 1967, Gonzalez

was promoted to sergeant. Later that month he was airlifted to Vietnam and almost immediately saw action against the Vietcong near Thua Thein.

Heroic death
On January 31, 1968, a platoon under Gonzalez's command moved to help relieve pressure on the beleaguered city of Hue. As the truck convoy neared the village of Lang Van Lrong on Route No. 1, the U.S. soldiers came under heavy enemy fire. Gonzalez maneuvered his troops quickly and decisively, and they scattered the snipers by throwing hand grenades into their positions. During the encounter, one U.S. Marine on top of a tank was wounded and fell to the ground. Gonzalez ran though heavy fire and rescued his comrade, despite being wounded himself in the process. On February 3, Gonzalez was hit again, but refused medical treatment. The platoon entered Hue, and, on February 4, came under renewed Vietcong attack from the grounds of St. Joan of Arc Catholic church in the downtown area. Gonzalez knocked out a rocket position and suppressed much of the enemy fire before taking a direct hit from a Vietcong missile. He fell dead beneath a statue of St. Joan of Arc.

Home to rest
The body of Freddy Gonzalez was returned to the United States and buried at Hillcrest Cemetery in Edinburg. He was awarded the Medal of Honor, which was presented to his mother in 1969 by Vice President Spiro T. Agnew. Gonzalez was one of only 13 Hispanic Americans to win the award, and the only U.S. soldier to win it during the battle for Hue. He was also the posthumous recipient of the Purple Heart, the Presidential Unit Citation, the National Defense Service Medal, the Vietnamese Cross of Gallantry with Star, the Vietnamese Cross of Gallantry with Palm, the Military Merit Medal, and the Republic of Vietnam Campaign Medal.

More recently various buildings and a street in Edinburg have been named for Gonzalez. In 1996 the battleship USS *Alfredo Gonzalez* entered service with the U.S. Navy at Corpus Christi. It was the first ship to be named for a Hispanic Texan soldier.

KEY DATES	
1946	Born in Edinburg, Texas, on May 23.
1965	Enlists in Marine Corps Reserve.
1966	First tour in Vietnam War.
1967	Promoted to sergeant and makes second tour in Vietnam War.
1968	Killed in action in Hue, Vietnam, on February 4.
1969	Posthumously awarded Medal of Honor.

Further reading: http://www.tsha.utexas.edu/handbook/online/articles/GG/fgoqp.html (Handbook of Texas Online).

GONZÁLEZ, Antonio
Activist

Antonio González is director of the Southwest Voter Registration Education Project (SVREP), a national nonprofit, nonpartisan organization that seeks to increase voter participation among Latinos and other minority groups in U.S. elections at both the national and statewide levels. In González's hands the SVREP has played a key role in making the Latino vote an important force in modern American politics, one that neither Republicans nor Democrats can afford to ignore. In 2005 *Time* magazine named González one of the 25 most influential Hispanics in America.

Early life
Antonio González was born into a Mexican American working-class family in Los Angeles, California, in about 1957. After graduating from high school, he enrolled at the University of California at San Diego, later transferring to the University of Texas, San Antonio. He graduated with a degree in U.S. history in 1981. In the following year González studied for a master's degree in Latin American history at the University of California at Berkeley.

Making a difference
In 1984 González joined the SVREP. Founded in 1974 by the charismatic Chicano activist William ("Willie") C. Velásquez, the SVREP seeks to increase voter registration and election turnout among Hispanic Americans through the setting up of community-based education programs. On joining the organization, González initially worked on registration drives for the 1984 presidential election campaign between incumbent president Ronald Reagan and Democrat Walter Mondale; he then went on to work on a number of special projects. In 1991 he became a

▲ **Antonio González expanded SVREP's activities. Today the organization operates in 16 U.S. states.**

director of SVREP's sister organization, the Southwest Voter Research Institute (SVRI), which Valásquez had set up to conduct research into Latino voting behaviors.

Increasing the Hispanic vote
Valásquez, who was an important influence on González, died in 1988. His close collaborator Andy Hernández succeeded him as director of SVREP. In 1994 Hernández resigned and González became director of both SVREP and SVRI, which was subsequently renamed the William C. Velásquez Institute. González soon proved himself an able and energetic administrator, massively expanding both SVREP's budget and voter recruitment programs, as well as strengthening its media profile: Between 2000 and 2004, the numbers of Hispanics registered to vote increased from 7.6 million to 9.3 million.

See also: National Organizations; Velásquez, Willie

Further reading: Roosevelt, Margo. "Antonio González: The Get-Out-the-Vote Guy." *Time*, August 22, 2005. www.svrep.org (Web site of SVREP, including González's biography).

KEY DATES	
1957	Born in about this year.
1984	Joins the Southwest Voter Registration Education Project (SVREP)
1994	Becomes director of SVREP
2004	Hispanic voter registration reaches 9.3 million
2005	Named by *Time* magazine as one of the top 25 most influential Hispanics in the United States.

GONZÁLEZ, Celedonio
Writer

The novelist and short-story writer Celedonio González was influential in creating a new direction for Cuban literature in the United States in the last quarter of the 20th century. He is best known for works that concentrate on the Cuban diaspora—the people who were exiled from the Caribbean island after the revolution led by Fidel Castro in 1959—and their ultimately unrealistic longing to return home. His work examines the difficulties and successes not only of the Cuban refugees but also of their children born in the United States.

Early life
Celedonio González was born in 1923, in the small town of La Esperanza in central Cuba. He was educated at a Catholic school in the neighboring town of Santa Clara before graduating from a Protestant high school in Cárdenas. On returning to La Esperanza, he started work on his father's sugar plantation. He eventually took over the family business.

As a young man González opposed the right-wing dictatorship of Fulgencio Batista. Following the Cuban Revolution he was initially a strong supporter of the new leader, Castro, but within a year he had become disillusioned with the government, which was growing more overtly communist in its policies. González was imprisoned for two months on charges of conspiring against the government.

Writing debut
On his release from jail in 1961, González emigrated with his family to the United States, where they settled in Miami, Florida. There he took a succession of odd jobs until 1965, when the family relocated to Chicago, Illinois, in search of a better standard of living. While living in Chicago, González started to write. It was not until 1971, when the family moved back to Miami, that he completed his first successful novel, *Los Primos* (The Cousins). The book was a literary landmark: one of the first novels to explore the Cuban experience in the United States rather than in Cuba. Later the same year, González also published *La soledad es una amiga que vendrá* (Solitude Is a Friend Who Will Come), a collection of short stories that described the loneliness of life for the Cuban exile in the United States. His second novel, *Los cuatro embajadores* (The Four Ambassadors), published in 1973, was a critical look at capitalism and what he saw as the dehumanization of U.S. life.

Mature work
El espesor del pellejo de un gato ya cadáver (The Thickness of Skin of a Dead Cat) is widely regarded as one of González's best novels. Published in 1978, it advised American Cubans to give up the dream of one day returning to Cuba, and to concentrate instead on making the best of life in their new home. González did not publish anything else for the next 10 years, finally breaking his long silence with *Que veinte años no es nada* (That Twenty Years Are Nothing; 1987). His next novel, *Fontainebleau Park*, appeared in 1998. The work, like all his other publications, was written in Spanish and published by Ediciones Universal, a firm that specializes in Cuban exile literature.

Other activities
Among Cuban Americans, Celedonio González has acquired a reputation as *"el cronista de la diáspora"* (the chronicler of the diaspora). He is both a spokesman for his own generation and an inspiration to the next. In addition to writing fiction, González has worked as a scriptwriter for Radio Martí, an anti-Castro radio and television station based in Miami and financed by the U.S. government's Broadcasting Board of Governors. He is also a regular columnist for *Diario Las Américas*, a Miami-based Spanish-language newspaper. González has been honored with awards by the city of Oviedo, Spain, and the Voice of America radio station.

Further reading: González, Celedonio. *Fontainebleau Park*. Miami, FL: Ediciones Universal, 1998.
www.bibliocuba.org/articulos (Spanish-language overview of Cuban literature).

KEY DATES	
1923	Born in La Esperanza, Cuba, on September 9.
1961	Emigrates to the United States.
1971	Publishes first novel, *Los Primos* (The Cousins).
1998	Publishes *Fontainebleau Park*.

GONZÁLEZ, Henry B.
Politician

Henry B. González was a liberal Democrat who became the first Mexican American to win election from Texas to the U.S. Congress, where he served 18 consecutive terms from 1961.

Early life

Henry Enrique Barbosa González was born in 1916 in San Antonio, Texas, to Leonides González and Genevieve Barbosa González. His father, a former mayor of Mapimi, Durango, Mexico, fled his homeland during the 1910 Mexican Revolution and arrived with his wife and family in San Antonio the following year. Once settled in the United States he became general manager for *La Prensa*, a Spanish-language newspaper. The González home was a popular meeting place for local Mexican American politicians, landowners, intellectuals, and artists seeking the latest news from their ancestral homeland.

As a child Henry González experienced racism at first hand when he was refused entry to local swimming pools and restaurants because he was Hispanic. He was studious, and spent much of his time in the local library, where he read books on a wide range of subjects, particularly history, law, philosophy, and poetry. Through his passion for works in English, French, and Spanish he developed a broad range of knowledge that would serve him well in his subsequent career.

After graduating from high school González briefly attended the University of Texas at Austin, before enrolling at St. Mary's University Law School. While studying there he met Bertha Cuellar and married her in 1940. González finished law school but never took the bar.

After graduating González spent some time as a probation officer, and also worked for the San Antonio Housing Authority. In those roles he frequently witnessed racism, discrimination, and violations of human rights. The victims were predominantly Mexican Americans and African Americans. His desire to help combat such injustices inspired him to run for election to the San Antonio City Council. His father advised him not to, but he would not be deflected: He won a seat in 1953.

During his three years on the council González returned to the Housing Authority as deputy director, a role that first brought him into contact with rising Massachusetts congressman and future U.S. president John F. Kennedy. In 1956 González became the first

▲ **Henry B. González was a member of the U.S. House of Representatives for 36 years, longer than any other Hispanic served in Congress.**

Mexican American to be elected to the Texas Senate. There he earned the admiration and respect of fellow politicians by speaking continuously for 36 hours in order to filibuster a range of segregationist bills put forward by Governor Price Daniel.

National politics

In 1961 González was nominated by the Democratic Party to run for the U.S. Congress, representing the 20th District in Texas. Although González subsequently spent much of his time in Washington, D.C., he always remembered where he came from and remained true to his roots. He returned to his home in Texas every weekend, and the sign he had placed on the door of his room in the Capitol building bore the legend "This

INFLUENCES AND INSPIRATION

Henry B. González entered the U.S. Congress in the same year that John F. Kennedy took office as the 35th president of the United States. The two Democrats worked closely together throughout the administration, and González was in the motorcade when Kennedy was assassinated in Dallas, Texas, in 1963. Their association was recalled 31 years later, when González won the 1994 John F.

Kennedy Profiles in Courage Award for his outspokenness on controversial issues.

When González decided in 1998 not to seek reelection to the House of Representatives, it was generally regarded as the end of an era. However, the voters of Bexar County (the 20th Congressional District, Texas) elected his son, Charles A. (Charlie) González, to succeed him. It soon became apparent

that the young man had inherited much of his father's political acumen, and that he was both well qualified and temperamentally disposed to continue along the same populist path. The young González has maintained and matched his father's devotion to the interests of his Texas constituents. He has also served since 1999 as chair of the Hispanic Caucus Civil Rights Task Force.

office belongs to the people of the 20th Congressional District, Texas."

Record in Congress

During his 18 terms in the U.S. Congress, González became renowned for not backing down from fights and for steadfastly standing up for less fortunate Americans, regardless of their ethnicity. A populist champion of the poor, women, and the elderly, he campaigned vigorously for increased openness in government and full disclosure by financial institutions. He was an energetic and effective chair of the House Banking, Finance, and Urban Affairs Committee and the subcommittee on housing and community development. He also enhanced his reputation for epic-length speeches.

Most of González's work in Congress was undertaken in the interests of the people of San Antonio—protecting their civil rights, and improving their economic and educational opportunities—yet the legislation he helped enact had nationwide benefits. For example, the Financial Institutions Reform, Recovery, and Enforcement Act of 1989, which he helped draft, paved the way for the

Federal Deposit Insurance Corporation Improvement Act. González's efforts to increase the availability of safe, cheap accommodation in his native city led to the National Affordable Housing Act of 1990. Also known as the Cranston-González Act, the law makes provision for low-income families and individuals with disabilities to receive subsidies in the form of rental assistance, and for the rehabilitation of public housing, the construction of new homes, and assistance for first-time home owners.

Final years

In his eighties González developed heart trouble and his health deteriorated. Some fellow Democrats began to regard him as a liability, but when they tried to oust him from the House Banking Committee in 1996 he routed them with a speech that demonstrated that he had lost none of his former power. Nevertheless, the following year he thought about retiring, but decided to stay on until his term ended in 1998, partly to spare the people of Texas the inconvenience and expense of a special election.

When Henry B. González finally stood down after 37 years he was succeeded in the U.S. Congress by Charlie, one of his eight children. He spent his final years in retirement in San Antonio, where he died aged 84 in November 2000.

KEY DATES

1916	Born in San Antonio, Texas, on May 3.
1953	Elected to San Antonio City Council.
1956	Becomes first Mexican American to win election to Texas Senate.
1961	Elected to U.S. Congress; serves 18 terms.
2000	Dies in San Antonio, Texas, on November 28.

Further reading: Sloane, Todd A. *González of Texas: A Congressman for the People (Contemporary Profiles and Policy Series for the Younger Reader).* Evanston, IL: John Gordon Burke Publishing, 1996.
http://bioguide.congress.gov/scripts/biodisplay.pl?index=G000272 (biographical information).

GONZÁLEZ, Jovita
Writer

Jovita González was a 20th-century novelist and short-story writer writer whose work drew on the history and folklore of her Mexican American heritage. Virtually unknown in her lifetime, she was discovered in the 1990s.

González was born in Roma, Texas, in 1903. She grew up on her grandparents' ranch until age seven, when the family moved to San Antonio, where she graduated from high school. She then completed her first year at the University of Texas at Austin before being forced to drop out through lack of funds. Back in San Antonio she won a scholarship to Our Lady of the Lake College, where she completed an undergraduate degree in Spanish in 1927.

González spent her summers in Austin, and there in 1925 she met J. Frank Dobie (1888–1964), a folklorist and chronicler of Texas and Southwestern culture. They quickly became friends, and under Dobie's guidance González

▼ *Jovita González was a folklorist who achieved posthumous fame with a novel.*

began to collect stories from the Texas–Mexico border. In 1930 González completed an MA in history at the University of Texas. In 1934, again with Dobie's assistance, González was awarded a Rockefeller grant, which enabled her to continue writing.

Productive period

In 1935 González married Edmundo E. Mireles, and in 1939 the couple moved to Corpus Christi, where they both took teaching jobs. Throughout the 1940s Jovita González de Mireles, as she was now known, collaborated with Eve Raleigh—the pen name of Margaret Eimer (died 1978)—on *Caballero*, a historical novel about a family adjusting to the effects of the Mexican–American War (1846–1848). It failed to find a publisher, however, and it was not until 1993, 10 years after González's death, that the manuscript was rediscovered by Professor José E. Limón of the University of Texas at Austin. The first printed edition of the work finally appeared in 1996.

Caballero was a milestone in Mexican American literature. Its belated publication inspired widespread interest in the rest of González's output: several studies of local history and legend, and *Dew on the Thorn*, an early work that is billed as a novel but is really a loosely connected collection of folktales set in a fictional town in southern Texas. The stories show an author in transition from folklorist to fully fledged creative writer, and reveal a growing awareness of the complex relations between Mexicans and Americans in the southern United States.

KEY DATES	
1903	Born in Roma, Texas, on January 18.
1925	Begins professional association with J. Frank Dobie.
1983	Dies in Corpus Christi, Texas.
1996	*Caballero*, the novel she completed with Eve Raleigh in the 1940s, is finally published 13 years after her death.

Further reading: King, Rosemary A. *Border Confluences: Border Narratives from the Mexican War to the Present.* Tucson: University of Arizona Press, 2004.
http://www.tsha.utexas.edu/handbook/online/articles/GG/fgo34.html (Handbook of Texas Online).

GONZALEZ, Juan
Baseball player

Juan "Igor" Gonzalez was one of the most prolific hitters in baseball's American League (AL). He led the AL in home runs (HRs) in 1992 and 1993, and was named the AL's Most Valuable Player (MVP) in 1996 and 1998. In 17 major league seasons through 2005, Gonzalez hit 434 HRs, had 1,404 runs batted in (RBIs), and batted .295.

Rapid rise

The son of a high-school math teacher, Juan Gonzalez was born in 1969 in Alto de Cuba, a poor part of the Vega Baja region of Puerto Rico with a high crime rate. In 1982 the family moved to a safer area, and there Gonzalez began to excel at baseball. In May 1986 he signed as a free agent with the Texas Rangers. After three years in the minor leagues, he was a late-season callup in 1989. In 1992, the muscular righthander led the AL in HRs (43). The next year "Igor"—a childhood nickname taken from his favorite wrestler, Mighty Igor—hit .310 and smashed a league-best 46 HRs.

Adversity and triumph

Gonzalez's career was not without setbacks, however. His progress was slowed when the 1994 Major League Baseball season was cut short by a strike, and in 1995 he herniated a disk in his back and played in just 90 games. In 1996 Gonzalez returned from his layoff fitter and slimmer and turned in one of his finest seasons. He had 47 home runs, batted in 144 runs, hit .314, and was named the AL MVP for the first time. He suffered torn ligaments in his left thumb early in the 1997 season, but still managed to drive in 131 runs in 133 games.

▲ *Juan Gonzalez took his nickname "Igor" from his favorite wrestler, Mighty Igor.*

Miraculous season

Gonzalez's greatest achievements came in the 1998 season, during which he became only the second player in baseball history to exceed 100 RBIs by the All-Star break. By the end of the season he had notched a total of 157 RBIs, the highest number in the AL since 1949. Gonzalez batted .318 and had 45 HRs as the Rangers won the AL West title, and he easily won his second AL MVP award that year. In November 1999, Gonzalez was traded to the Detroit Tigers. Over the next six seasons he also played for the Cleveland Indians, the Kansas City Royals, and again for the Rangers.

Further reading: http://www.baseballlibrary.com/
baseballlibrary/ballplayers/G/Gonzalez_Juan.stm
(reference Web site).

KEY DATES	
1969	Born in Vega Baja, Puerto Rico, on October 16.
1986	Signs with the Texas Rangers as an amateur free agent.
1989	Makes his major league debut on September 1.
1993	Leads the American League in home runs for the second straight year.
1996	Wins his first AL MVP award.
1998	Wins AL MVP award for the second time.
2005	Signs with the Cleveland Indians in January.

GONZÁLEZ, Juan D.
Journalist, Activist

Award-winning journalist Juan D. González is best known for his work as a columnist on the *New York Daily News* and as co-host of the independent morning news radio program *Democracy Now!* His forthright antiestablishment views have won him admirers and detractors all over the United States. Through organizations such as the National Association of Hispanic Journalists and UNITY: Journalists of Color, González also works to strengthen Hispanic involvement and representation in the media.

KEY DATES

1947 Born in Ponce, Puerto Rico.

1968 Graduates from Columbia University, New York.

1988 Joins the *New York Daily News*.

2000 Publishes *Harvest of Empire: The History of Latinos in America*.

2002 Publishes *Fallout: The Environmental Consequences of the World Trade Center Collapse*.

Early life

Juan D. González was born in 1947 in Ponce, Puerto Rico. At the time thousands of Puerto Ricans were leaving their homeland in the hope of finding better prospects in the United States, and in 1948 González's parents, Pepe and Florinda Gonzáles, joined Pepe's brother in New York City. They initially settled in El Barrio, the Puerto Rican neighborhood of East Harlem, but later moved to a New York City housing project.

Although González did not learn to speak English until he went to school, he nonetheless did well in his studies and eventually won a place at Columbia University, from where he graduated in 1968. While at Columbia he became involved in militant left-wing politics and was an active member of Students for a Democratic Society (SDS), a moving force behind the anti-Vietnam and civil rights movements. In 1968 and 1969 he helped form the New York branch of the Young Lords, a militant Puerto Rican group that protested poverty and discriminatory health care in U.S. urban ghettos.

Investigative journalist

In the decades that followed, González established a reputation as an investigative journalist. During the early 1980s he worked for the *Philadelphia Inquirer and Daily News*. In 1988 he began to work for the *New York Daily News*, where he led a 1990–1991 strike at the paper. He also worked as the Belle Zeller Visiting Professor in Public Policy and Administration at the Brooklyn College of the City University of New York.

In 2000 González published *Harvest of Empire: The History of Latinos in America*, a book in which he attacked the United States's longstanding exploitative immigration policy toward Hispanics and called for an independent Puerto Rico. In *Fallout: The Environmental Consequences of the World Trade Center Collapse* (2002), he argued that the Environmental Protection Agency had systematically attempted to cover up health hazards at Ground Zero in New York after the terrorist attacks of September 11, 2001.

◀ *Juan González has won many honors, including the George Polk Award in 1998 and a Hispanic Heritage Award in 1998.*

Further reading: González, Juan. *Fallout: The Environmental Consequences of the World Trade Center Collapse*. New York, NY: New Press, 2002.

GONZALEZ, Kenny "Dope"
Musician, Record Producer

Kenny "Dope" Gonzalez is a prolific record producer, remixer, and solo artist. He has long collaborated with "Little" Louie Vega as Masters At Work (MAW): The two men are widely credited with revitalizing dance music. MAW fuses house music, hip-hop, Latin, jazz, and soul, and its trademark sound is a combination of live instruments with sampled beats, as typified by the *NuYorican Soul* album. MAW has produced some of the most innovative dance remixes of recent times.

Early life
Born in Brooklyn, New York, in 1970, Kenny Gonzalez grew up in Sunset Park. As a boy he listened to the street music played in his neighborhood. In the early 1980s he discovered hip-hop at neighborhood parties, where he watched DJs mixing, and learned about "breaks" and "beats." By 1985 Gonzalez was working in his local music shop, the WNR Music Center, where he eventually became the music buyer.

Gonzalez learned a lot from watching the working methods of his friend, Mike Delgado. Delgado edited records for the renowned DJ Todd Terry. When Gonzalez helped Delgado organize a series of local parties, he called

▼ *Regarded as house-music royalty, Kenny "Dope" Gonzalez is an innovative producer and DJ.*

himself Masters at Work (MAW). Terry later borrowed the name to record two club hits.

In 1989 Gonzalez launched the independent label Dope Wax. He had several underground hits, including "Salsa House," a track particularly admired by DJ "Little" Louie Vega. Terry introduced Gonzalez to Vega in 1990, and they became friends. They released their first remix, Debbie Gibson's "One Step Ahead," under the name MAW. The track became an underground success, as did MAW's "The Ha Dance." Gonzalez and Vega's remix of Tito Puente's "Ran Kan Kan" successfully combined house music and mambo, and their distinctive remix of Saint Etienne's "Only Love Can Break Your Heart" was extremely popular with fans.

Solo stardom
Gonzalez's breakthrough as a solo artist came with his 1995 Bucketheads' track "The Bomb! (These Sounds Fall into My Mind)," which was a major hit in America and Europe. In 1997 MAW recorded the Grammy-nominated album *NuYorican Soul,* which was credited with changing the direction of dance music. Gonzalez and Vega also began to produce such artists as La India. In 2001 MAW released the successful *Our Time Is Coming.* Gonzalez continues to DJ worldwide; he also records as a solo artist.

KEY DATES	
1970	Born in Brookyln, New York City.
1990	Meets "Little" Louie Vega.
1995	Solo breakthrough with the Bucketheads' "The Bomb! (These Sounds Fall into My Mind)."
1997	MAW's *NuYorican Soul* album is nominated for a Grammy.
2001	MAW releases *Our Time Is Coming.*

See also: La India; Vega, "Little" Louie

Further reading: Fikentscher, Kai. *You Better Work! Underground Dance Music in New York.* Middletown, CT: Wesleyan University Press, 2000.
http://www.mastersatworkinc.com (Masters at Work official Web site).

GONZÁLEZ, Odilio
Musician, Composer

Acclaimed Puerto Rican musician Odilio González first won fame on his native island as a composer and singer of *décimas*, the traditional romantic ballads that played an important role in Puerto Rico's Jíbaro (rural inland mountain) culture. Later, in New York City, González sang in a wide variety of styles, including bolero, and became an internationally respected Latino star. Throughout his career, González sang in the same distinctive high yet rugged voice that had so enchanted audiences during his adolescence in Puerto Rico.

Early life
Odilio González Arce was born on March 5, 1937, in Lares, a small inland town in Puerto Rico and a strong center of Jíbaro culture. Jíbaro refers to the culture of the mountain people who lived inland in the heart of Puerto Rico. Jíbaros become poets, singers, composers, and storytellers, and music is a large part of their culture.

A singer of bitter-sweet songs
Like other young Jíbaros, González began singing and composing *décimas* while still a boy. He showed great talent, and as a teenager became a local celebrity, known for his distinctive voice. In 1950 González's family moved to the large seaport town of Arecibo, and he was invited to perform on WCMN radio.

González's adolescent voice combined with the bittersweet lyrics of his songs soon attracted fans, and he became well known across the island. González recorded his first single in 1956, releasing his debut album, *Cantando en el Campo* (*Singing in the Countryside*), in the following year to critical acclaim.

El Jibarito de Lares
In 1958 the Puerto Rican impresario and bolero singer Pedro "Piquito" Marcano invited González to join a group of Puerto Rican musicians that he was taking to New York City to perform at the popular Teatro Puerto Rico. For the performances, González was billed as "El Jibarito de Lares," or the "Folk Singer from Lares," a sobriquet (nickname) that would remain with him throughout his career.

González's music soon became popular among New York City's burgeoning Puerto Rican community. González's slightly wistful Jíbaro style made them nostalgic for their native island.

Songs of nostalgia
From the 1960s onward, González recorded a series of popular albums, most notably on the BMC label, such as *Odilio Gonzalez: The Jíbarito de Lares*. González's hits of the period included "Penitencia" (Penitence), "Hablame" (Let's Talk), "Mano de Dios" (Hand of God), and "Una Tercera Persona" (A Third Person). They appealed to audiences throughout Latin America, as well as in the United States. Perhaps González's best-loved song, however, was the Christmas song "Yo Tenia una Luz" (I Had a Light).

González's faster-paced songs were influential in the development of the guitar-based dance music known as bachata, which became popular in the early 1960s and 1970s.

Honors
The recipient of many honors, González's achievements in music were honored by the House of Representatives of the 92nd General Assembly of the State of Illinois (2001–2002).

See also: Music

Further reading: Flores, Juan. *Divided Borders: Essays on Puerto Rican Identity*. Houston, TX: Arte Publico Press, 1993.
www.prpop.org/biografias/o_bios/odilio_gonzalez.shtml (short biography in Spanish).

KEY DATES	
1937	Born in Lares, Puerto Rico, on March 5.
1956	Records his first single.
1957	Records debut album, *Cantando en el Campo* (*Singing in the Countryside*).
1958	Moves to New York City, where he launches a successful recording and performing career.
1963	Releases *Odilio González: The Jíbarito de Lares*.
2001	Honored by the House of the Representatives of the 92nd General Assembly of the State of Illinois for his outstanding music career.

GONZÁLEZ, Pedro J.
Musician, Broadcaster

Pedro J. González was one of the most important Mexican American broadcasters of the 1930s. Playing with the band Los Madrugadores, he became a leading Latino musician in California. González was also an outspoken critic of the way in which Mexican Americans were treated by the U.S. government (*see box on page 62*), and he gained a reputation for defending the civil liberties of the Hispanic community.

Early life
Born in about 1894 in Chihuahua, Mexico, Pedro Javier González left school as a young boy to become an apprentice telegraph operator. He went to work for the revolutionary leader Pancho Villa following the outbreak of the Mexican Revolution in 1910. For the next seven years, he carried messages and gathered intelligence for Villa. González was eventually captured by enemy troops and sentenced to death, but a group of schoolchildren intervened and stopped his execution. He later married Maria Salcido, one of his rescuers.

Going to the United States
In the 1920s, González and his wife moved to the United States, where he initially worked as a laborer. His luck changed, however, after he answered a newspaper advertisement looking for Spanish-speaking singers. González found himself recording songs for several major record labels of the day, including Columbia and Victor, which were anxious to break into the Latino market.

González worked hard. Realizing the importance of radio to the local community, he determined to break into broadcasting. In 1928, he became the first Spanish-speaking broadcaster in Los Angeles. By the following year, he was the host of the first Spanish-language radio program on the West Coast. Each morning, thousands of Mexican Americans tuned in between 4:00 AM and 6:00 AM to listen to his live broadcasts from the Hidalgo Theater.

The show—a mixture of commentaries, advertisements, and live music often played by González and Los Madrugadores, which formed in 1930—turned González into a star almost overnight. His programs were popular with Hispanic audiences tired of attempts by authorities to Americanize them and discourage their culture and language. González's Spanish-language show also opened the door for other similar Hispanic broadcasters to follow.

▲ *Pedro J. González (back row, center) is pictured with his band Los Madrugadores.*

KEY DATES	
1894	Born in Chihuahua, Mexico, about this time.
1910	Works as a telegrapher for Mexican revolutionary leader Pancho Villa.
1920	Immigrates to the United States at about this time.
1923	Moves to Los Angeles, California.
1929	Begins broadcasting Spanish-language radio programs.
1930	Begins recording with Los Madrugadores, which becomes a leading Latino band.
1934	Accused of rape; convicted, and sentenced to 150 years in jail.
1940	Paroled, and immediately deported to Mexico
1970	Returns to the United States.
1983	Subject of documentary, *Ballad of an Unsung Hero*.
1995	Dies aged between 99 and 101.

INFLUENCES AND INSPIRATION

Pedro J. González used his position as the leading Spanish-language broadcaster of the 1930s to highlight injustices against the Latino community, particularly the forced repatriation of Mexicans that had been authorized by President Herbert Hoover. More than two million people were deported from the United States to Mexico in order to free up jobs for "real" Americans during the Great Depression. About 60 percent of those expelled had either been born in the United States or had legitimate U.S. citizenship. González drew attention to the abuses by discussing them on his radio show. Some of his radical comments were regarded as subversive, and it is possible that his subsequent arrest on a charge of rape was an effort by the authorities to silence one of their most influential critics.

After González had spent six years in a U.S. jail, and another 30 years in exile in Mexico, he returned to the United States in 1970. In 1983, a radio documentary about him revived public interest in the injustices of the 1930s, and prompted the Mexican American Legal Defense and Education Fund (MALDEF) to file a class action suit on behalf of the survivors of the deportations. In 2003, Democratic California senator Joe Dunn sponsored a state senate hearing into the deportations, and in 2005 California passed Senate Bill 670, in which the state apologized for "the fundamental violations of basic civil liberties and constitutional rights during the period of illegal deportation and coerced emigration." However, Governor Arnold Schwarzenegger vetoed the companion act, Senate Bill 645, which would have created a commission to make financial reparations to victims.

In 1930, González set up the Club Ideal-Circulo Artisto de Radio for his fans. Thousands of his listeners sent in 25 cents per month, and in return received photographs, dedication requests, and songbooks from González. From the early 1930s, González began to perform with Jesús and Victor Sanchez, and singer Fernando Linares: The quartet formed the core lineup of Los Madrugadores. They sang and recorded contemporary compositions and traditional Mexican songs. While González sometimes sang with these musicians on singles, many of Los Madrugadores's recordings from the decade feature other singers, such as Josefina Caldera. González also used the Madrugadores' name to sponsor ingredients for Mexican cooking, coffee, and spices.

Increasing controversy

Although extremely popular, not just with Spanish-speaking audiences but also with city officials, González also made many enemies. His frank commentaries on the U.S. treatment of Hispanics brought him censure. As the Great Depression of the 1930s began to bite, there was an upsurge in discrimination against Mexicans and Mexican Americans, who were resented for taking what Anglos regarded as "American" jobs. Officials became increasingly uncomfortable with the number of Hispanics in their cities, and the United States began deporting Mexicans, many of whom were documented U.S. citizens. When González discussed the issue on his program, critics expressed their concern at his opinions, and also at his growing influence on the Hispanic community.

In 1934, one of González's fans accused the broadcaster of rape. The subsequent trial became a media sensation, and González became the focus of much anti-Mexican sentiment. Although González strenuously denied the charge, and was supported by many civil rights activists, he was convicted and sentenced to 150 years in jail. After González had spent eight months in San Quentin prison, the alleged victim admitted that she had been coerced into lying under oath; despite the revelation, González served six years in jail. While there, he fought for better conditions in prison, organizing hunger strikes among the inmates.

Exile and return

González was paroled in 1940, but immediately on his release he was deported to Mexico. He spent the next 30 years in Tijuana, where he continued to work in radio. He used his program on station XEAU to highlight political corruption and other injustices in the region.

In 1970, González was finally allowed to return to the United States. Ten years later, he became the subject of a KPBS documentary, *Ballad of an Unsung Hero*, which later provided the material for the TV film, *Break of Dawn* (1988).

Further reading: http://www.arhoolie.com/titles/7035.shtml (brief article on González and Los Madrugadores).

GONZÁLEZ, Raúl
Texas Supreme Court Justice

During the 1980s and 1990s, Mexican American Raúl González became one of the most highly respected jurists in the state of Texas. His trailblazing career as a Texas Supreme Court justice served as an inspiration to generations of Hispanic American leaders. González is counsel in the well-known Texas law firm Locke, Liddell, and Sapp, where he specializes in the area of state and federal appellate law (the law relating to appeals).

Early life
González was born in Weslaco, South Texas, in 1941. He attended Weslaco High School, from which he graduated in 1959. He went on to study at the University of Texas, Austin, where he earned a bachelor's degree in 1963. He then went on to study at the University of Houston School of Law. He was admitted to practice as an attorney before the Texas bar in 1966. In 1968 he gained his LLM (master of laws) from the prestigious University of Virginia Law School in Charlottesville.

Building a legal career
González soon established a successful legal career that straddled both private and public sectors. From 1969 to 1973 he worked as an assistant United States attorney in

▼ **Raul González was the first Latino to be elected to a state office in Texas.**

KEY DATES	
1941	Born in Weslaco, Texas, in about this year.
1978	Appointed state district judge, Brownsville, Texas.
1984	Appointed to the Texas Supreme Court.
1986	Elected as a Texas Supreme Court justice.
1998	Retires as Texas Supreme Court justice in December.

the Southern District of Texas, serving as the chief of the Brownsville Division, Brownsville, Texas. In 1973 he helped establish the civil and criminal practice Gonzalez and Hamilton in the same city. A committed Christian, during this time González also served as attorney to the Brownsville Catholic Diocese.

To the Texan Supreme Court
In 1978 González was appointed a state district judge in Brownsville. In 1981, Texas governor Bill Clements appointed him a justice on the 13th Court of Appeal in Corpus Christi, and only three years later, Clements's successor, Mark White, appointed González as a justice on the Texas Supreme Court, the state's highest court, which has its seat in Austin. In 1986 González ran for the position and became the first Hispanic to be elected to a state office in Texas.

During his career, González has been widely honored. In 1987–1988 he was named an outstanding alumnus by the University of Houston Law School, and in 1989 he was the recipient of the Rosewood Gavel Award from St. Mary's University School of Law, San Antonio.

González has always played an important civic role in his home state. In 1998 he stepped down from the Texas Supreme Court before the end of his term of office, and was replaced by Alberto R. Gonzales, a future U.S. attorney general.

See also: Gonzales, Alberto

Further reading: Who's Who in American Law, 2000–2001. New Providence, NJ: Marquis Who's Who, 1999.
www.mcca.com/site/data/lawfirms/Platinum/locke/llsgonzalez.htm (biography).

GONZÁLEZ, Xavier
Artist

Xavier González was a Spanish-born painter and sculptor who lived in the United States. González was a very versatile artist; his work includes both figurative and abstract styles, naturalistic landscapes, and strongly colored modernist images.

Early life
Born in Almería, Spain, on February 15, 1898, González moved with his family to Puebla, Mexico, when he was eight. For most of González's childhood his father worked abroad as an agricultural engineer, and González lived in Argentina and Mexico, where he later trained to be a mechanical engineer. A talented artist, González also studied art at the San Carlos Academy in Mexico City.

Becoming an artist
In the early 1920s, González traveled to San Antonio, Texas, to stay with his uncle, the painter José Arpa (1858–1952). During this time González began to draw and paint, specializing mainly in landscapes.

In 1922 González traveled to the United States to study at the Art Institute of Chicago. On his return to Mexico, he taught art in public schools, before deciding to move permanently to San Antonio, Texas, in 1925. He joined his uncle there to help run the Arpa School of Painting, the art school that Arpa had founded in 1923. In 1936 the school was incorporated into the newly founded Witte Memorial Museum. González had a solo exhibition there in 1928. Three years later González moved to New Orleans, Louisiana, to teach at the H. Sophie Newcomb Memorial College. In 1935 he married one of his students, the acclaimed artist Ethel Edwards (1914–1999).

Making a name for himself
During the 1930s, González traveled around Europe. In Paris, France, he met several influential artists, including the renowned Spanish artist Pablo Picasso (1881–1973), with whom he had many discussions about art. González's work thereafter displays both the influence of his uncle in his naturalistic landscape paintings and that of a more modernist approach in his murals.

In 1933 González was commissioned to paint his first mural by the Civil Works Administration, part of the New Deal art program. González's mural, created for the Municipal Auditorium in San Antonio, featured images of an upraised fist and a bleeding palm. It was considered too radical and was removed in 1935.

One of González's best known murals features contemporary jazz musicians at Dixie's Bar of Music in New Orleans, Louisiana (1938–1941). The piece was commissioned by owners Dixie and Irma Fasnacht; it includes 66 jazz luminaries, including Lena Horne and Benny Goodman.

During World War II (1939–1945), González designed posters and drew maps for the Naval Department. After the war he moved to New York, where he settled permanently.

Artist and teacher
González led an active life both as an artist and teacher. In the 1960s he was one of 40 leading artists, including Ethel Edwards, commissioned by the Bureau of Reclamation to paint a series of murals on the organization's water development sites. He taught at several schools, including the Art Students League of New York from 1976. The recipient of several awards, González had his work featured in the collections of several major national museums. He died in New York on January 9, 1993.

Further reading: Steinfeldt, Cecilia. *Art for History's Sake: The Texas Collection of the Witte Museum.* San Antonio, TX: The Texas State Historical Association, 1993.
http://www.tsha.utexas.edu/handbook/online/articles/GG/fgo65.html (biography).

KEY DATES	
1898	Born in Almería, Spain, on February 15.
1922	Begins studying at the Art Insitute of Chicago.
1925	Moves to San Antonio, Texas.
1933	Creates mural for Municipal Auditorium, San Antonio.
1935	Marries Ethel Edwards.
1939	Designs posters and draws maps for the Naval Department during World War II (1939–1945).
1941	Completes mural in Dixie's Bar of Music, New Orleans, Louisiana.
1993	Dies in New York on January 9.

GRONK
Artist

The internationally acclaimed multimedia artist known as Gronk was born Glugio Gronk Nicandro. Of Mexican ancestry, Gronk chose to be known by his middle name, a Brazilian Indian word meaning "to fly." An award-winning artist, Gronk has built up a reputation based on his wide-ranging body of work, which includes paintings, murals, sculpture, performance pieces, set design, and digital animations.

Early life
Born in Los Angeles, California, in 1954, Gronk was brought up in a single-parent household by his mother. He was influenced by television, particularly by programs that featured space ships. He began re-creating some of these images on paper. Gronk also loved reading—both art and books were a way of escaping the reality of the poverty in which he and his mother lived. At Stevenson High School, Gronk began making African masks and burying them in time capsules all over Los Angeles. His ceramics teacher, Betty LeDuc, encouraged him to talk about art.

Becoming Gronk
Aged 16, Gronk dropped out of school. In 1972, he was a founding member of the East Los Angeles-based Chicano art group Asco, which took its name from the Spanish word for "nausea." The group included three now well-known Chicano artists: Harry Gamboa, Jr., Willie Herrón,

▲ *Although he is best known as a muralist, the artist Gronk has worked in various media. This 2005 painting is entitled* **The Garden.**

and Patssi Valdez. Asco became an influential avant-garde, or experimental, collaborative art group. Its works were among the first within the Chicano art scene to incorporate political activism into its representational practices.

Later work
Influenced by surrealist and German expressionist art, and concerned with his own heritage, Gronk initally focused on issues confronting the Mexican and Mexican American communities of East Los Angeles. Since then his work has developed to address a broad range of cultural and artistic themes. Gronk is probably best known as a muralist and for his provocative approach to artistic practice, much of which has resulted in temporary installations. His site-specific paintings are often executed at the scale of an entire gallery floor, or are accompanied by a music performance in the presence of a live audience. The interaction between artist, gallery space, and audience results in a performance that puts on display the act of painting, an act typically done out of public view. The artist and the creative process are thus demystified.

See also: Gamboa, Harry, Jr.; Marin, Cheech

Further reading: http://www.mexicanmuseum.org/collection/collection.asp?key=233&language=english (site of the Mexican Museum in San Francisco's collection of Chicano art).

<table>
<tr><td colspan="2">KEY DATES</td></tr>
<tr><td>1954</td><td>Born in Los Angeles, California.</td></tr>
<tr><td>1972</td><td>Cofounds the influential Chicano art group Asco, which operates until 1987.</td></tr>
<tr><td>1977</td><td>Named Artist of the Year by the Mexican American Fine Art Association.</td></tr>
<tr><td>1990</td><td>Asco's work is featured in "Chicano Art/Resistance and Affirmation, 1965–1985," the first major nationally traveling retrospective of Chicano art (1990–1993).</td></tr>
<tr><td>1994</td><td>Presents "Living Survey," a traveling solo exhibition held at the Mexican Museum in San Francisco, the Los Angeles County Museum of Art, and the El Paso Museum of Art.</td></tr>
<tr><td>2002</td><td>His work is included in "Chicano Visions: American Painters on the Verge," a national exhibition of Cheech Marin's private collection of Chicano Art (2002–2007).</td></tr>
</table>

The Treaty of Guadalupe Hidalgo brought a formal end to the Mexican-American War (1846–1848). It was signed at Guadalupe Hidalgo, near Mexico City, on February 2, 1848, and proclaimed on July 4.

Under the terms of the treaty, the defeated Mexico ceded more than half of its territory to the victorious United States. The lands included the whole of the future states of California, Nevada, and Utah, as well as significant parts of Arizona, Colorado, New Mexico, and Wyoming. The agreement also obliged the United States to pay Mexico $15 million, and to take over all the claims of U.S. citizens against Mexico. Mexicans remaining in the newly defined U.S. territory were permitted to become U.S. citizens, and were guaranteed their constitutional rights.

Original demands

The talks that culminated in the treaty began when U.S. forces under General Winfield Scott (1786–1866) occupied Mexico City on September 14, 1847. U.S. president James K. Polk (*see box on page 67*) sent Nicholas P. Trist as his commissioner to Mexico. Trist's instructions were to push for the cession of the whole of California (including the present Mexican state of Baja California) as well as New Mexico in exchange for a $15 million payment, less $3 million in damages owed by Mexico to U.S. citizens. In addition, Mexico would be required to recognize the Rio Grande as the

border of Texas, rather than the Nueces River to the north, which it had previously claimed as the frontier.

The Mexicans did not welcome Trist's proposals, but with their capital city in U.S. hands, they were in no position to dictate terms. Yet, just as Trist appeared close to a deal, Polk became concerned that the United States might be selling itself short. The president ordered Trist to break off negotiations and return home. Fearful that the opportunity for peace might pass, Trist defied his instructions and continued talks with the Mexican leadership. Trist's insubordination angered Polk, but the president turned a blind eye as his delegate concluded an agreement with Mexico.

The terms of the treaty were similar to those of Trist's original demands, although he did make some significant concessions.

This contemporary map shows the area affected by the Treaty of Guadalupe Hidalgo.

Mexico ceded New Mexico and California, and recognized the Rio Grande as the border of Texas. It retained Baja California, however. The United States agreed to pay $15 million to Mexico, and to take over the damages claimed by U.S. citizens against Mexico, amounting to $3,250,000.

Critical points

Article IX of the Treaty of Guadalupe Hidalgo contained assurances that the civil and property rights of former Mexican citizens would be protected. Article X protected Mexicans holding land grants. Article XI made the United States responsible for controlling Native American raids into Mexico from the U.S. side of the border.

JAMES KNOX POLK

James Knox Polk (1795–1849) was the 11th president of the United States and the man most responsible for the war with Mexico. A Jacksonian Democrat and advocate of national expansion, Polk was a plantation owner who served in the Tennessee legislature before entering the U.S. Congress in

1825. He served as speaker of the house from 1835 to 1839. Polk was then elected governor of Tennessee, where he served a single term. He emerged as the dark-horse Democratic candidate for the presidency in 1844. Polk's election victory was interpreted as a mandate for expansion. In addition to provoking war with

Mexico, he pressed for the acquisition of territory in the Pacific Northwest. To that end, he concluded an agreement with Britain in 1846 that extended U.S. control over much of the region. Polk did not run for a second term, and died soon after leaving office in 1849.

After nearly five months' wrangling, representatives of the United States and Mexico signed the Treaty of Guadalupe Hidalgo on February 2, 1848. However, the content of the treaty was substantially altered by the U.S. Congress during ratification.

Polk commended the treaty to Congress, but qualified his approval with a request that Article X be deleted. Congress readily agreed to Polk's recommendations, and further altered the agreement by replacing the explicit protections of Article IX with a more ambiguous statement that nonetheless reaffirmed U.S. commitment to protecting Mexican Americans' individual liberty, property, and freedom of worship. The Senate eventually

ratified the modified version of the treaty on March 10, 1848.

Polk then sent two commissioners to Mexico City to convince the Mexican government that the changes were mere details and did not substantially alter the spirit of the agreement. Their contentions were later embodied in a statement known as the Protocol of Querétaro. Despite concerns over the altered treaty, the Mexican Congress accepted the document and the nations exchanged ratifications on May 30, 1848.

Legacy
The Treaty of Guadalupe Hidalgo has remained binding ever since. However, it has never been fully honored. The most flagrant violations occurred with respect

to the terms that guaranteed Mexicans who stayed in the ceded territories the rights to their lands. Neither the civil nor the property rights of Mexican Americans were respected after the signing of the treaty. Over the years, Spanish and Mexican land grants were invalidated by the U.S. Congress and courts. Anglo-American ranchers, businessmen, and railroad tycoons appropriated the lands of Mexican Americans, as did the U.S. Department of the Interior and the Department of Agriculture. In two generations, some 4 million acres (1.6 million hectares) were lost by Mexican Americans to private owners, and some 15 million acres (6 million hectares) to state and federal authorities. Such violations became a rallying point for the Chicano movement that emerged in the 1960s.

KEY DATES

1844	James K. Polk elected president of the United States.
1845	United States annexes Texas.
1846	Polk dispatches U.S. forces to the Rio Grande, provoking hostilities and leading to a declaration of war on Mexico on May 13.
1847	General Winfield Scott captures Mexico City on September 14.
1848	Treaty of Guadalupe Hidalgo signed on February 2; ratified by the United States on March 10, and by Mexico on May 30; proclaimed on July 4.

Further reading: Porterfield, Jason. *The Treaty of Guadalupe-Hidalgo, 1848: A Primary Source Examination of the Treaty That Ended the Mexican-American War.* New York, NY: Rosen Central Primary Source, 2006. http://www.loc.gov/rr/hispanic/ghtreaty/ (Library of Congress Treaty of Guadalupe Hidalgo exhibit page).

GUASTAVINO, Rafael
Architect

Rafael Guastavino was an enterprising Spanish-born architect and engineer. He settled in the United States at the end of the 19th century and worked with some of the leading architects of the time. Guastavino was an architectural innovator; he helped develop a system of fireproof-tile construction widely used in public buildings.

Establishing a career as an architect

Born in Valencia, Spain, on March 1, 1842, Guastavino trained as a builder and architect in Barcelona. In the 1860s he profited from the great urban expansion in the city. Guastavino revived the traditional *boveda catalan* (Catalan vault), a fireproof method of construction that used tiles and mortar. By 1873 he was an established architect with commissions for factories and private houses across the country. In 1876 Guastavino's designs were presented at the Philadelphia Centennial as part of the exhibit "Improving the Healthfulness of Industrial Towns." He received a medal of merit.

The United States

In 1881 Guastavino decided to immigrate to New York with his nine-year-old son, Rafael, Jr. Guastavino patented his construction methods: Between 1885 and his death he took out more than 24 patents for construction systems.

Guastavino worked with some of the leading U.S. architects. His collaboration with McKim, Mead, and White on the vault of the Boston Public Library (1887–1895) helped establish his career in the United States. The project received critical acclaim from the architectural press. As a result, Guastavino was invited to lecture at the Society of Arts at the Massachusetts Institute of Technology in October 1889: The lecture was later published as *Essay on Theory and History of Cohesive Construction, Applied Especially to the Timbrel Vault*.

In 1889 he founded the Guastavino Fireproof Construction Company, which was responsible for the building of vaults, staircases, domes, and arches in about 1,000 U.S. buildings. Most were situated in New York, such as St. Paul's Chapel, Columbia University (1907), the Cathedral of St. John the Divine (1907), City Hall Subway Station (1904), and the Western Union Building (1929).

After the company closed in 1969, the Guastavino archive was acquired by Professor George R. Collins. Since 1988 it has been held in the Avery Architectural and Fine Art Library at Columbia University. In the 1990s several of Guastavino's buildings were restored, bringing renewed interest in his construction systems. In 1996 an exhibition of Guastavino's work was held at the Wallach Art Gallery, Columbia University.

▲ *Rafael Guastavino (right) supervises the construction of the Boston Public Library in 1889.*

Further reading: Parks, Janet, and Alan G. Neumann. *The Old World Builds the New: The Guastavino Company and the Technology of the Catalan Vault, 1885–1962.* New York, NY: Columbia University 1996.
http://www.guastavino.net (site about Guastavino).

KEY DATES	
1842	Born in Valencia, Spain, on March 1.
1881	Immigrates to the United States from Spain.
1889	Founds the Guastavino Fireproof Construction Company.
1908	Dies in Asheville, North Carolina, on February 2.

GUERRA, Manuel
Politician

Politician Manuel Guerra came from an old and distinguished landowning family in South Texas. In 1767 the King of Spain gave Guerra's grandfather, Don José Alejandro Guerra, two land grants in the area. A banker, rancher, and the Democratic leader of Starr County, Manuel Guerra practically controlled the county's political and business affairs from 1894 to 1906.

Early life

Born in what is now Mier, Mexico, across from Rio Grande City, Texas, in 1856, Guerra was the son of Jesús Guerra Barrera. Guerra was home schooled by his mother until the age of 14, after which he was sent to Corpus Christi, Texas, where he learned about business and studied English. Aged 21, Guerra moved to Roma, Texas, to run the family ranch lands and open his first mercantile store.

A political career

In 1894 Guerra ran for the position of county commissioner of Starr County Court and won. He established strong ties with Sheriff W. W. Shely and with another area political boss, James B. Wells, Jr., in the adjacent area near Brownsville, Texas.

Guerra almost owned the Democratic Party machine in his county. He appointed his brother, son, and a cousin to three important Starr County positions as sheriff, treasurer, and tax collector. His time in power was one of turbulence, violence, and corruption, however. His position was challenged by Edward C. Lasater, who represented Anglo farmers and businessmen in the northern sector of Starr County. Lasater was a wealthy landowner who had amassed more than 380,000 acres (153,780 ha) of land and 30,000 head of cattle. He was also a Republican and owned a newspaper, *Falfurrias Facts*. Lasater also began a dairy and founded the still famous Falfurrias brand butter sold in stores in the United States.

▲ **This building in Roma, Texas, was the location of the store opened by Guerra in 1887; he lived for a time in the upper story.**

Both Lasater and Guerra were supported by large forces of armed men who made sure that their patrons' wishes were carried out. In 1906 matters came to a head when rioting broke out between Lasater's and Guerra's men just before the county election. In early 1907 Guerra's cousin, Deodoro, who was also the sheriff, was involved in the murder of a customs inspector. Both Manuel and Deodoro Guerra were indicted for conspiring to murder a federal official, but they were subsequently acquitted.

After countless skirmishes with Lasater, Guerra accepted a truce brokered by James B. Wells, Jr. In 1911 Starr County was split into two. Lasater named his area Brooks County in honor of the Texas Ranger Captain John Brooks. Guerra died on June 9, 1915.

Further reading: Anders, Evan. *Boss Rule in South Texas: The Progressive Era.* Austin. TX: University of Texas Press, 1982. http://www.tsha.utexas.edu/handbook/online/articles/GG/fgu14.html (biography).

KEY DATES	
1856	Born in Mier, Mexico.
1894	Elected as county commissioner of Starr County Court.
1915	Dies on June 9.

GUERRERO, Lalo
Musician

Father of Chicano music Lalo Guerrero was a Mexican American singer, songwriter, and nightclub performer. Recording in English and Spanish, Guerrero crossed over to appeal to mainstream U.S. music audiences at a time of great discrimination against the Mexican and Mexican American community. Guerrero performed at special engagements well into his 80s.

Early life
Eduardo (Lalo) Guerrero was born in a barrio in Tucson, Arizona, on December 24, 1916. He was one of 24 children, of whom only eight survived to adulthood. Guerrero grew up in a musical household (*see box on page 71*). His mother was a skilled musician who taught him to play the guitar. He began composing songs as a teenager, writing in both English and Spanish. During this time he wrote "Canción Mexicana," a song that many people consider to be the unofficial Mexican anthem.

A special kind of music
In the 1930s Guerrero started earning money to help support his family by playing and singing at parties and fiestas. He and some friends formed the quartet Los Carlistas; they played engagements in Tucson and Los Angeles. Guerrero mostly played traditional music in Spanish, but American swing music and rhythm and blues also appealed to him. He had a sharp ear, and his songs captured the speech of the Pachucos, the young men who expressed their Mexican American identity in sharp "zoot suits" and by using a special slang called *caló*. Guerrero began to incorporate *caló*, a mixture of Spanish and English, made up of clever rhymes, invented words, and hidden meanings, into his songs: "Las Chicas Patas Boogie," "Vamos a Bailar," "Los Chucos Suaves," and "Marijuana Boogie" all use this slang.

A reputation in the making
In the 1940s Guerrero moved to Los Angeles, where he took a few uncredited roles in movies. He formed the Trio Imperial and recorded with Imperial Records. He also sang regularly at La Bamba, a popular club frequented by celebrities, including actor Rita Hayworth. Guerrero formed his own orchestra, Lalo y Sus Cinco Lobos, which toured in the Southwest. During World War II (1939–1945), the band played at military camps and hospitals.

▲ *Lalo Guerrero was one of the first Chicano musicians to appeal to both mainstream American and Latino audiences.*

In the 1950s Guerrero brought the Mexican American experience to the masses through his parodies of popular U.S. mainstream songs of the day. These tunes were broadcast over the radio and became hits in record stores. One of his most popular songs of the era was "Pancho López," sung to the theme tune of the popular Disney movie and television series *Davy Crockett*. Guerrero's song narrates the story of the fictional title character, who flees the Mexican Revolution to open up a taco stand on Olvera Street in Los Angeles. It sold more than 500,000 copies. Other parodies recorded in both English and Spanish were "Pancho Claus," "Elvis Perez," and the more serious "Mama, Don't Let Your Babies Grow Up to Be Busboys," a comment on discrimination.

New ventures
In the 1960s Guerrero opened a nightclub in Los Angeles named Lalo's. A popular spot, the club showcased Guerrero's music and that of other leading musicians.

INFLUENCES AND INSPIRATION

Father of Chicano music Lalo Guerrero influenced generations of musicians. In 1980 the Smithsonian Institution named him "a national folk treasure." Guerrero, who died in 2005, always acknowledged the influence that his parents had on him. They instilled in him a great love of music. His mother, Concepción, was a skilled guitarist and singer. She taught the young Guerrero about music from an early age. His father, Eduardo, taught Guerrero to respect and honor his Mexican heritage and culture, attitudes that are often reflected in his music.

Guerrero was one of the first artists to record in Spanish and English. He used Mexican Spanish and slang in his lyrics, merging it with elements of American swing, as heard in such songs as "Marijuana Boogie" and "Vamos a Bailar." Throughout his long career, Guerrero used his music to promote Mexican culture. The classic song "Canción Mexicana," composed when Guerrero was just a teenager, became the unofficial anthem of Mexico. In 1941 it became a hit when it was recorded by the respected musician Lucha Reyes.

During this period Guerrero invented "Las Ardillitas," a group of fictional squirrels that parodied "The Chipmunks," a popular mainstream recording by Ross Bagdasarian. Their creation opened up a new audience for Guerrero: Spanish-speaking children who delighted in the funny lyrics of the high-pitched voices on the records.

Guerrero's music also touched on serious themes, however. He penned protest songs such as "El Corrido de Delano" in support of the California farmworkers led by the activist César Chávez in the 1960s, and "La Tragedia del 29 de Agosto," commemorating the death of journalist Ruben Salazar in 1970. Chávez later said that Guerrero chronicled Hispanic events in the United States "a lot better than anyone else."

In 1972 Guerrero closed his club. Although he seriously contemplated moving back to Tucson to retire, he got as far as Palm Springs, California, a desert community about 90 miles (144km) from Los Angeles.

Guerrero's "retirement" was anything but conventional, however: It consisted of his becoming lead singer of another band in a new Mexican restaurant on the town's main street, a gig that lasted for 24 years. He also played in a band with Mark, his son, who in his teens had provided some of the backing music on several of Guerrero's popular songs.

In 1996 Guerrero finally retired. He carried on living in southern California. He stayed active by performing on television, at schools, in retirement homes, for charity functions, and at other special events. Guerrero wrote his autobiography, *Lalo: My Life and Music*, before his death in 2005 from prostate cancer.

Lifetime honors

Guerrero's life was long and fruitful. He made a major contribution to Mexican American arts through his legacy of English- and Spanish-language songs. His influence on Mexican American and U.S. culture can be seen in the play and movie *Zoot Suit* by Luis Valdez and in the musical play *Chavez Ravine* by Ry Cooder. Guerrero received many awards and honors during his career, including the Golden Eagle Award in 1989, the presidential National Medal of Arts in 1996, and the National Heritage Fellowship from the National Endowment for the Arts in 1991.

See also: Chávez, César; Salazar, Ruben; Valdez, Luis M.

Further reading: Meece Mentes, Sherilyn, and Lalo Guerrero, *Lalo: My Life and Music.* Tucson, AZ: University of Arizona Press, 2002.
http://markguerrero.net/8.php (biography on his son Mark Guerrero's Web site).

KEY DATES

1916	Born in Tucson, Arizona, on December 24.
1941	Lucha Reyes has a hit with Guerrero's song "Canción Mexicana."
1949	Has hits with "Chicas Patas Boogie," "Vamos a Bailar," and "Los Chucos Suaves."
1977	Luis Valdez uses Guerrero's music in his successful musical *Zoot Suit.*
1989	Receives the prestigious Golden Eagle Award.
1996	Wins National Medal of the Arts.
2005	Dies in Palm Springs, California, on March 17.

GUILLERMOPRIETO, Alma
Journalist

Alma Guillermoprieto is a Mexican journalist who has specialized in Latin American affairs. Her work is well known in the Spanish-speaking world and has appeared in a wide range of U.S. newspapers and periodicals, including *The New Yorker* and *The New York Review of Books*.

From dance to journalism

Alma Guillermoprieto was born in 1949 in Mexico City. As a child she was an excellent dancer, and was a member of the Ballet Nacional de México. At age 16 she moved to the United States, where she studied modern dance in New York under Martha Graham, Merce Cunningham, and Twyla Tharp. She performed professionally from 1962 to 1973.

In 1978 Guillermoprieto began a new phase of her life when she became Central American correspondent for the British daily newspaper *The Guardian*. Her first major assignment was to cover that year's Sandinista revolution in Nicaragua. Throughout the 1980s she worked for the *Washington Post*. In 1982 Guillermoprieto collaborated with Raymond Bonner of the *New York Times* to break the story of the El Mozote massacre. In December 1981 some 900 villagers at El Mozote, El Salvador, had been murdered by the U.S.-backed Salvadoran army. The revelations had serious repercussions for the administration of U.S. president Ronald Reagan, which had previously tried to dismiss rumors of the atrocity as propaganda.

In the 1990s Guillermoprieto was South America bureau chief for *Newsweek*. She diversified as a freelance writer, publishing her first books: *Samba* (1990), which combined her passions for dance and social justice, and *The Heart That Bleeds* (1994), considered a masterpiece of Latin American reporting. Also in 1994 she won a National Magazine Award for her work on Peru's Shining Path guerrillas. The following year she was awarded a MacArthur Fellowship and, at the invitation of the novelist Gabriel García Márquez, one of the most prominent

▲ *Alma Guillermoprieto is a campaigning author whose work has highlighted several major injustices in Latin America.*

admirers of her work, taught at the inaugural workshop of the Fundación para un Nuevo Periodismo Iberoamericano in Cartagena, Colombia.

From dance to journalism

Guillermoprieto has since published two further volumes: *Looking for History* (2001), a collection of essays on life and politics in Colombia, Cuba, and Mexico, and *Dancing with Cuba* (2004), a memoir of her experiences in 1970 as a dance teacher at the National Schools of Art in Havana, Cuba. The latter work was originally written in Spanish. Alma Guillermoprieto lives in Mexico City.

Further reading: Guillermoprieto, Alma. *Looking for History: Dispatches from Latin America*. New York, NY: Pantheon Books, 2001.
http://www.fnpi.org (listed under "Maestros" at the Fundación para un Nuevo Periodismo Iberoamericano Web site).

KEY DATES	
1949	Born in Mexico City, Mexico, on May 27.
1978	Becomes correspondent for *The Guardian*.
1982	Breaks story of El Mozote massacre in El Salvador.
1995	Is awarded a MacArthur Fellowship.

GUTIÉRREZ, José Angel
Academic, Activist

José Angel Gutiérrez is an activist, politician, and educator. Considered to be one of the fathers of the Chicano civil rights movement, Gutiérrez organized and educated Chicanos about the political process in the United States. His work as an activist led the FBI and CIA to keep Gutiérrez under surveillance for several decades. In 2000 *Latino Monthly* named Gutiérrez one of the "100 Outstanding Latino Texans of the 20th Century."

The emergence of a civil rights activist

Born in rural south Texas in 1944, Gutiérrez was aware of discrimination at an early age. He studied at Crystal City High School, graduating in 1962. At Texas A&I University in Kingsville, where he received his bachelor's degree in 1966, Gutiérrez began organizing students. He formed the Mexican American Youth Organization (MAYO) at St. Mary's College in San Antonio in 1967. Gutiérrez and other MAYO members helped found La Raza Unida Party (the United People's Party or LRUP). Both MAYO and LRUP were Chicano-centric and focused on economic and political self-determination, as well as Chicano nationalism.

Gutiérrez held many political offices. He was president of the Crystal City School Board (1973–1974), Crystal City Urban Renewal Commissioner (1970–1972), county judge for Zavala County, Texas (1974–1981), commissioner for the Oregon Commission on International Trade (1983–1985), City of Dallas administrative law judge (1990–1992), and a member of the City of Dallas Ethics Commission (1999–2000). Gutiérrez made an unsuccessful bid to become an Oregon state representative in 1984.

▲ *José Angel Gutiérrez's complaint about the heavy Hispanic casualties in the Vietnam War brought him condemnation from Héctor P. García, head of the American GI Forum.*

Gutiérrez has taught at several colleges and universities, including the University of Texas in Arlington and Colegio César Chávez in Mt. Angel, Oregon. In 1993 he founded the Center for Mexican American Studies (CMAS) at the University of Texas, Arlington, to assist Latino faculty, staff, students and community. Gutiérrez has also authored several books, such as *The Making of a Chicano Militant: Lessons from Cristal* (1998), *A Gringo Manual on How to Handle Mexicans* (2001), and *A Chicano Manual on How to Handle Gringos* (2003) on the Chicano civil rights movement. He has received many honors, including a distinguished faculty award from the Texas Association of Chicanos in Higher Education (1995).

See also: García, Hector P.; Gutiérrez, Luz Bazán; National Organizations; Political Movements

Further reading: Gutiérrez, José Angel. *The Making of a Chicano Militant: Lessons from Cristal.* Madison, WI: University of Wisconsin Press, 1999.
http://libraries.uta.edu/tejanovoices/gutierrez.asp (Tejano Voices site biography of José Angel Gutiérrez).

KEY DATES

1944 Born in Crystal City, Texas.

1967 Organizes the Mexican America Youth Organization (MAYO).

1973 Becomes the school board president for Crystal City Independent School District.

1976 Receives a PhD from University of Texas at Austin.

1988 Awarded a JD from the University of Houston, Bates College of Law.

1993 Founds the Center for Mexican American Studies (CMAS) at the University of Texas at Arlington.

GUTIÉRREZ, Luz Bazán
Activist

Luz Bazán Gutiérrez was a leading advocate of Mexican American rights and equal opportunities in Texas in the 1960s and 1970s.

One of four children, Gutiérrez was born in 1945 in Texas, and raised on a dairy farm. After graduating from high school she attended colleges at Kingsville and Edinburg, where she completed a teaching qualification. In 1967 she took her first job, at Kelly Elementary in San Antonio, and married José Angel Gutiérrez. The couple had four children between 1968 and 1980: Adrian, Tozi Aide, Olin Roldán, and Avina Cristal. While continuing to work during the 1970s, Luz Gutiérrez also took a graduate degree in sociolinguistics and public health.

In 1967 Gutiérrez was one of the prime movers in the formation of the Mexican American Youth Organization (MAYO). She contributed financially to the fledgling movement, and provided administrative backup while her husband and other MAYO leaders traveled the state encouraging young Hispanics to protest discrimination against them in schools.

Raza Unida Party

In the summer of 1969 Luz and José Gutiérrez became the lead organizers of MAYO's Winter Garden Project, a three-county initiative in southwest Texas that culminated in the historic boycott of schools in Crystal City. The following year the couple was largely responsible for the formation of the Raza Unida Party (RUP), a new political grouping devoted to achieving economic and social self-determination for Mexican Americans. By 1974 the RUP had majority seats on all governmental units in Zavala County, and some in other counties.

▲ *Chicana activist Luz Gutiérrez (center) is pictured at the 1972 national convention of the Raza Unida Party.*

Later, however, the RUP factionalized after internal differences over policy. Some activists wanted to expand the party, but others (including José Gutiérrez) wanted to concentrate on local issues.

In the 1980s Luz Gutiérrez turned her attention to the poverty and poor health care suffered by Mexican American migrant workers in south Texas. She proposed a community-based health clinic in Zavala County, and when it was completed she became its first executive director. In 1984 Gutiérrez relocated to Oregon, where she became the director of Woodburn's Medical Health Clinic. Five years later she became a regional director for the Department of Social and Health Services in Yakima, Washington. There she established the Center for Latino Farmers and became president of the Rural Community Resource Center. She also trades real estate and heads a stockbroker dealership.

See also: Gutiérrez, José Angel

Further reading: http://www.leagueofruralvoters.org/headlines.cfm?refID=76404 (official Web site for the League of Rural Voters).

KEY DATES

1945   Born in Brooks County, Texas.

1967   Helps in the formation of the Mexican American Youth Organization (MAYO).

1970   Cofounder with her husband of the Raza Unida Party (RUP).

1995   Is named among "100 People of Influence," *Pacific Magazine, The Seattle Times*, June 9.

2003   Receives the Peace and Justice Award of the Congregation of Humility of Mary.

GUTIERREZ, Theresa
Journalist

During the 1970s Theresa Gutierrez was among the first Latinas to break into television journalism. Today she retains a high profile within an industry in which Hispanic Americans—especially Hispanic American women—are still critically underrepresented. Gutierrez works as a general assignment reporter and as public-affairs program host on the ABC-owned and operated Chicago television station WLS-TV, also known as ABC 7. Her regular appearances on the station's news bulletins, as well as on *Ñ Beat*, a series of special programs celebrating Latino achievements, have helped make Gutierrez a popular and influential figure among Chicago's Hispanic community of 1.6 million.

A media pioneer
After graduating with a BA from Indiana University in Bloomington, Theresa Gutierrez began her career in television in 1971, when she was given a job as a production assistant with the Chicago station WMAQ—also known as NBC 5. In the following year, Gutierrez joined NBC 5's rival, ABC 7. She also began to make her name in radio, working as a moderator on such groundbreaking programs as *Ms. Understood*, which focused on women's issues, and *Hispano*, which sought to address issues relevant to Chicago's rapidly growing—and largely Mexican American—Hispanic population.

At this time the Hispanic community was largely overlooked in radio and television programs across the United States. This was in part a reflection of the very small number of Latinos working in media. Gutierrez was able to carve out a pioneering career, eventually hosting and producing television talk shows for ABC 7, such as *The Feminine Franchise, Weekend Edition, Weekend*, and *Sunday in Chicago with Theresa Gutierrez*.

KEY DATES
1971   Appointed production assistant with the Chicago station WMAQ—NBC5.
1972   Joins ABC 7 in Chicago.
1986   Appointed general assignment reporter for ABC 7 News.
1999   Named as one of the 100 women "making a difference" by *Today's Chicago Woman Magazine*.

▲ *Theresa Gutierrez has won several awards and honors: She was named one of six outstanding U.S. broadcasters by* **Hispanic USA** *magazine.*

In 1986 she broke into the male-dominated bastion of news journalism after she was appointed as a reporter for ABC 7 News.

Serving the community
Throughout her career, Gutierrez has been an active figure in Chicago's civic life, and has served on the boards of such organizations as the Vernon Jarrett Educational Foundation and the Kids International Surgical Services (KISS). Her achievements have won her wide recognition and honors, including the Woman of the Year Award, given by the Indiana Hispanic Chamber of Commerce. In 1999 *Today's Chicago Woman Magazine* named Gutierrez as one of the 100 women "making a difference" in the United States.

Further reading: Browne, Donald R., Charles M. Firestone, and Ellen Mickiewicz. *Television/Radio News and Minorities.* Washington, D.C.: Aspen Institute, 1994.
http://www.abclocal.go.com/wls/story?section=bios&id=3397125 (ABC 7 staff biography).

GUZMÁN, Ralph
Scholar, Activist

Respected academic Rafael "Ralph" Cortéz Guzmán was an influential civil rights activist. He wrote about and campaigned for better rights for Mexican Americans.

Early life

Born in Moroleón, Guanajuato, Mexico, in 1924, Guzmán moved with his family to the United States during the Great Depression of the 1930s. Working in the agricultural fields of the Southwest and finally settling in Los Angeles, Guzmán learned English. He also became known as Ralph. One of the relatively few Mexican Americans to graduate from high school in East Los Angeles, Guzmán joined the Merchant Marine and U.S. Navy during World War II (1939–1945). On his return to the United States, he began a long and illustrious career as a student, activist-scholar, and distinguished professor.

Path to influence

Taking advantage of the GI Bill, Guzmán obtained an Associate of Arts degree from East Los Angeles Junior College in 1949. He discovered community organizing and advocacy while doing work with the Community Service Organization (CSO). He perfected his writing and investigative skills as a reporter and editor for the *Eastside Sun* and *Los Angeles Free Press* during the 1950s.

In his late twenties, Guzmán enrolled at California State University at Los Angeles and obtained a BA (1958) and an MA (1960) in political science. Guzmán accepted the position of associate director of the Peace Corps, and made tours of Venezuela and Peru.

KEY DATES	
1924	Born in Moroleón, Guanajuato, Mexico.
1958	Attains BA in political science.
1970	Publishes *Mexican American People: The Nation's Second Largest Minority*.
1976	Publishes *The Political Socialization of the Mexican American People*.
1978	Becomes deputy assistant secretary of state for Latin America.
1985	Dies on October 10.

An academic career

On his return to the United States in 1963, Guzmán pursued his doctoral degree at the University of California at Los Angeles (UCLA). He became the first Chicano to receive a PhD in political science from the school. During this time, Guzmán became an outspoken supporter of César Chávez and the United Farm Workers Union. During the heyday of the Chicano movement, Guzmán was a frequent speaker at political events. He opposed U.S. involvement in Vietnam. He protested the Vietnam War on several grounds, including the disproportionately higher casualty rate among Chicanos and other ethnic groups compared to white soldiers (19.4 percent to 10 percent). He remarked: "I am partisan. I speak to you as a Mexican."

In 1969 Guzmán was invited to join the politics faculty at the University of California (UC) and help build programs for minority students at the new UC campus at Santa Cruz. Guzmán cofounded Oakes College, and later became provost of Merrill College. He also helped develop the Latin American studies program and the Third World Teaching Resource Center.

A writer and politician

Guzmán also published several acclaimed articles and books. He worked with Leo Grebler and Joan Moore on their groundbreaking five-year study, *Mexican American People: The Nation's Second Largest Minority*. Guzmán's second book, *The Political Socialization of the Mexican-American People*, published in 1976, met with greater acclaim, however. It was a major contribution to the study of both Mexican Americans and political socialization.

In 1978 President Jimmy Carter appointed Guzmán as deputy assistant secretary of state for Latin America, the first such appointment of a Mexican American in the State Department. Guzmán designed the policy to coexist with the new Sandinista regime in Nicaragua, and advised on developing Chicano–Mexico relations.

See also: Chávez, César

Further reading: Guzmán, Ralph. *The Mexican American People: The Nation's Second Largest Minority*. New York, NY: The Free Press, 1970.
http://texts.cdlib.org/xtf/view?docId=hb967nb5k3&doc.view=frames&chunk.id=div00025&toc.depth=1&toc.id= (obituary).

HAYEK, Salma
Actor, Filmmaker

Sultry Mexican-born actor Salma Hayek rose to prominence as a soap star in her native country. After moving to Hollywood, Hayek was offered a series of stereotypical Latina roles, and was often cast as a mistress or a maid. She fought against being typecast for many years. In 2002 Hayek finally received the acclaim she deserved for her performance in the title role of *Frida*, based on the turbulent life of the revered Mexican artist Frida Kahlo (*see box on page 78*).

Early life
Born on September 2, 1966, in the city of Coatzacoalcos in Veracruz, Mexico, Hayek was the daughter of Sami Hayek Domínguez, a wealthy Lebanese–Mexican businessman, and Diana Hayek, a Spanish-Mexican opera singer. Educated first in elite schools in Mexico, Hayek was sent, aged 12, to a Catholic boarding school in New Orleans, Louisiana. She was expelled for playing practical jokes, however, and returned to Mexico to finish school.

Hayek majored in international relations at the Universidad Iberoamericana in Mexico City. However, she dropped out to pursue a career in acting. After auditioning for television and theater roles, Hayek was cast as Fabiola in the daytime soap opera *Nuevo Amanecer*, which also starred a young Gael García Bernal (star of *The Motorcycle Diaries*, 2004). In 1989 Hayek received her big break in Mexico: She was cast in the title role of the soap opera *Teresa*, which established her as a star in Latin America.

▲ *An A-list Hollywood star, Salma Hayek was the first Mexican, and only the second Latina, to be nominated for an Oscar for best actress.*

Hollywood
After two years in the show, Hayek decided to try to establish a career in North America: In 1991 she moved to Los Angeles, California. Although Hayek's beauty was obvious, she found it difficult to get work, other than in stereotypical Latina roles. Hayek's English was not fluent and this also hindered her progress. Determined to succeed, Hayek enrolled at the Stella Adler Academy in order to improve her acting and English skills.

In 1993, Allison Anders cast Hayek in the popular independent film, *Mi vida loca* (*My Crazy Life*), a role that enabled her to join the Screen Actors Guild. Hayek went on to star in Jorge Fons's acclaimed movie *El callejón de los milagros* (*Midaq Alley*, 1994). She also appeared in a series of small character roles on U.S. television.

In 1994 Hayek's luck changed: The rising Latino director Robert Rodríguez saw her on a talk show. Rodríguez was casting his second movie, *Desperado*, the sequel to his highly successful debut film, *El mariachi* (1992). He gave Hayek a role in the movie, starring alongside Spanish actor Antonio Banderas: The film was

KEY DATES	
1966	Born in Coatzacoalcos, Veracruz, Mexico, on September 2.
1989	Cast in *Teresa*, a soap opera.
1991	Moves to Los Angeles, California.
1993	Appears in Allison Anders's *Mi vida loca*.
1995	Cast in Robert Rodriguez's movie *Desperado*.
2002	Produces and stars in the acclaimed movie *Frida*, for which she receives an Oscar nomination for best actress.
2003	Produces and directs *The Maldonado Miracle*.

INFLUENCES AND INSPIRATION

Salma Hayek's fascination with the Mexican artist Frida Kahlo led her to campaign hard to produce and star in a film about the artist's life. After fending off such established stars as Madonna and Jennifer Lopez, Hayek finally landed the role, although it took a number of years for the project to get off the ground. Hayek said: "There was something about the woman and the times in which she lived that I just found fascinating. She was never conventional … [but] was always herself, which was not easy."

Hayek collaborated with director Julie Taymor to adapt Hayden Herrera's book on Kahlo. She persuaded a cast of well-known actors to work at union rates in order to get the film made: Alfred Molina came on board as the artist Diego Rivera, Ashley Judd played photographer Tina Modotti, Antonio Banderas played muralist David Alfaro Siqueiros, and Geoffrey Rush played Leon Trotsky.

Hayek's determination paid off: On its release *Frida* was critically well reviewed. The movie received six Academy Award nominations, including a best actress nomination for Hayek, who became the first Mexican actress to receive such an honor. *Frida* won two Oscars, for best make-up and best original score.

a commercial success. In the following year Hayek appeared in Rodriguez's vampire movie, *From Dusk till Dawn*, starring George Clooney and Quentin Tarantino. The role involved a scantily clad Hayek dancing with a python draped around her body.

After a number of supporting roles, Hayek got a lead part in the movie *Fools Rush In* (1997), alongside *Friends* star Matthew Perry. Although the film received a lukewarm response from critics, it gave Hayek some well-needed exposure. She went on to appear in such films as Kevin Smith's *Dogma* (1999), Barry Sonnefeld's *Wild Wild West* (1999), and Mike Figgis's *Time Code* (2000). She also took roles in Mexican films, appearing in an adaptation of Gabriel García Marquez's novella *El coronel no tiene quien le escriba* (*No One Writes to the Colonel*, 1999).

A major player

Determined to prove that she was more than just a beautiful face, Hayek set up her own production company, Ventanarosa, which was specifically designed to foster Latin creativity in Hollywood. In 2001 the company produced Julia Alvarez's *In the Time of the Butterflies*. It then produced *Frida* (2002).

It was Hayek's determination to play the artist Frida Kahlo that brought her into Hollywood's big league (*see box*). Hayek originally auditioned to play Kahlo in a 1994 film. The producers needed a big-name actor and Hayek was not well-known enough in the United States to merit the role. The film did not come off, however. After Hayek became better known as an actor in the United States, she was able to convince Miramax, which had acquired the film rights, that she could do the job. Hayek still had to work hard to get the project off the ground. The film was finally shot in 12 weeks, and released in 2002 to critical acclaim. Some Mexican commentators debated whether Hayek was really Mexican enough to play such an important role, however. The film received several awards and six Oscar nominations: It won two Oscars. *Frida* also established Hayek as a major player in Hollywood. In 2003 Hayek's company produced the Emmy-award winning *The Maldonado Miracle* (2003), which Hayek also directed.

Life after Frida

Since *Frida*, Hayek has worked on a range of projects, including, with Robert Rodriguez, *Once Upon a Time in Mexico* (2003). She also starred in Brett Ratner's comedy-heist movie *After the Sunset*, playing the girlfriend of Pierce Brosnan's jewel thief character. In 2006 Hayek starred with her good friend Penelope Cruz in Joachim Roenning and Espen Sandberg's movie *Bandidas*; she also appeared with John Travolta in Todd Robinson's *Lonely Hearts*.

Hayek was a member of the jury of the prestigious Cannes Film Festival. She has endorsed a range of products—from make-up lines to luxury cars. A well-known philanthropist, Hayek has worked with the Avon Foundation as a spokesperson against domestic violence.

See also: Alvarez, Julia; Lopez, Jennifer; Rodríguez, Robert

Further reading: Menard, Valerie. *Salma Hayek*. Hockessin, DE: Mitchell Lane Publishers, 1999.
http://www.imdb.com/name/nm0000161 (biography and filmography).

HAYWORTH, Rita
Actor

Rita Hayworth was the star of more than 50 movies in a career that spanned four decades.

Born Margarita Carmen Dolores Cansino in Brooklyn, New York, in 1918, she was the daughter of a professional dance couple: Eduardo Cansino, a native Spaniard who had immigrated in 1913, and Volga Haworth, an Irish American who had appeared with *The Ziegfeld Follies*. While still a child Margarita became part of her parents' nightclub act, The Dancing Cansinos, which also featured her elder sister, Elisa. In 1926 they appeared together in a short film, *La Fiesta*.

In 1934 Margarita Cansino was spotted in a nightclub by Winfield R. Sheehan, vice president of the Fox Film Corporation, and invited for a screen test. There she overcame her youthful shyness and displayed such accomplishment as a dancer that she was immediately offered a film contract.

Her movie career began with a role as a dancer in *Dante's Inferno* (1935), starring Spencer Tracy. After that she appeared in 10 more "B" features, including *Charlie Chan in Egypt* and *Meet Nero Wolfe*, all under her real name, Rita Cansino. She did not distinguish herself in any of her early roles, but Sheehan remained convinced that she had star quality—he saw her as the next Dolores del Rio—and cast her as the lead in his next intended production, *Ramona*. The project never got off the ground, however, because in 1935 Fox merged with 20th Century Pictures to become 20th Century Fox. New production head Darryl F. Zanuck fired Sheehan and took Cansino off the film.

From bit parts to stardom
Cansino's faltering career was salvaged by her first husband, Edward C. Judson, who in 1937 secured her a seven-year contract with Columbia Pictures. She took the name Rita Hayworth and underwent a cosmetic makeover that some commentators have suggested was intended to downplay her Hispanic appearance and "Americanize" her. Although she now had regular work, the films in which she appeared were still largely nondescript. Her real breakthrough came when she played a married woman who tries to seduce Cary Grant in Howard Hawks's *Only Angels Have Wings* (1939).

After reprising the femme fatale role in *The Lady in Question* (1940), *Blood and Sand*, and *The Strawberry*

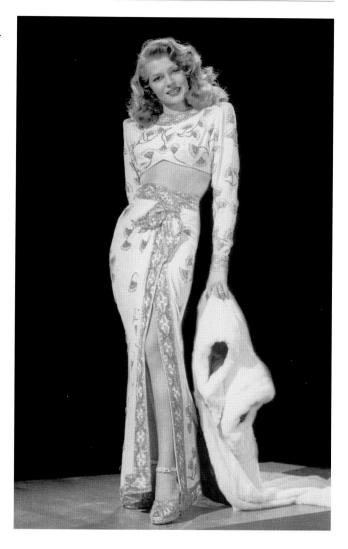

▲ *This still from the movie* **Gilda** *shows Rita Hayworth in the role that established her as a star.*

Blonde (both 1941), Hayworth played opposite Fred Astaire in *You'll Never Get Rich* (1941) and *You Were Never Lovelier* (1942), showcases for the dancing talents of both stars.

During World War II (1939–1945) Rita Hayworth was a favorite pinup with GIs. Columbia capitalized on her widespread popular appeal as a sex symbol in *Cover Girl* (1944), in which she starred with Gene Kelly.

Postwar peak
Two of the films in which Hayworth appeared immediately after the war are widely regarded as her greatest work. In Charles Vidor's *Gilda* (1946) she starred opposite Glenn Ford as a classic temptress, simultaneously

HAYWORTH, Rita

vulnerable and dangerous. In *The Lady from Shanghai* (1948) she gave an acclaimed performance as a manipulative seductress for director Orson Welles, who had become her second husband in 1943 shortly after her divorce from Judson. There was one child of the marriage, Rebecca Welles (1944–2004).

Public legend, private reality

In the late 1940s *Life* magazine began calling Hayworth "The Love Goddess." She disliked the term, but it stuck to her for the rest of her life. Her marriage to Welles ended in 1948, and in the following year she married Prince Aly Khan, the playboy son of the Aga Khan, leader of the world's Ismaili Muslims. On the birth of their daughter, Yasmin, in December 1949, Hayworth took two years away from the limelight to devote her full attention to the child. When she returned to movies in 1951 she struggled to recapture her former glory, although there are hints of it in *Pal Joey* (1957) and *Separate Tables* (1958).

KEY DATES	
1918	Born in Brooklyn, New York, on October 17.
1926	Performs for the first time in The Dancing Cansinos.
1935	Has her first film role in *Dante's Inferno*.
1939	Plays a leading role in *Only Angels Have Wings*.
1946	Stars in *Gilda*, her most acclaimed movie.
1972	Makes final film appearance, in *The Wrath of God*.
1980	Is diagnosed with Alzheimer's disease.
1987	Dies in New York City, New York, on May 14.

In the meantime Hayworth's private life remained turbulent. In 1953 she divorced Khan and married the actor and singer Dick Haymes. They divorced two years later, and in 1958 she took her fifth and final husband, the film producer James Hill. In 1961 that marriage also ended in divorce. Looking back in later life Hayworth reflected: "Every man I have ever known has fallen in love with Gilda and awakened with me."

In the 1960s Hayworth became disillusioned with Hollywood, and she acquired a reputation for erratic behavior and drunkenness. Her final film appearance was in *The Wrath of God* (1972), a Western with Robert Mitchum and Frank Langella.

Chronic illness

In 1980 Rita Hayworth was diagnosed with Alzheimer's disease, although with hindsight it seems that she may have been suffering from the illness for the previous 10 years. It would certainly account for her increasing difficulty in memorizing her lines, which at the time was attributed to alcohol abuse. When her condition deteriorated she moved in with her younger daughter, Yasmin Aga Khan, who nursed her until her death in New York City in 1987. After her funeral Rita Hayworth's remains were interred at the Holy Cross Cemetery in Culver City, California.

A television biopic of Rita Hayworth was produced in 1983, starring Lynda Carter in the title role.

See also: Carter, Lynda; Del Rio, Dolores

Further reading: McLean, Adrienne L. *Being Rita Hayworth: Labor, Identity, and Hollywood Stardom*. New Brunswick, NJ: Rutgers University Press, 2004.
http://www.imdb.com/name/nm0000028/ (filmography).

HERNÁNDEZ, Adán
Artist

Adán Hernández is a Mexican American artist. His work has been described as "post-Chicano": It often deals with the condition of alienation that is still present in the Chicano community after the Chicano civil rights movement. Hernández has described his often highly charged images and work as reflecting "the day-to-day epic struggle of life in the barrio."

Early life
Born in Childress, Texas, on October 15, 1951, Hernández was the son of migrant workers who moved to Robstown, Texas, to find work. When Hernández was nine, he moved with his family to San Antonio, Texas. While studying at local schools Hernández began to experience the alienation and dislocation felt by many Hispanic American children in U.S. schools. He later dropped out of school.

An alienated artist
In 1972 Hernández began studying at the Fine Art Department of San Antonio College, but he was not inspired by its teaching and he eventually quit. Working as a laborer during the day, he continued to paint at night. Urged on by his future wife, Debi Fischer, Hernández finally decided to concentrate on his art. From 1980 he dedicated his time to painting; he also studied artistic techniques and styles in books from the local library. He had his first solo exhibition in 1985.

Hernández often uses black paper (representing the night), and works with brightly colored pastels that lend a surreal atmosphere to his subjects. He uses the image of the "pachuco"—a phrase used in the 1930s to describe young Latinos who wore dandyish clothes such as zoot suits— placing it in different surrealistic contexts to evoke

▲ *In 1999 Adán Hernández produced the painting* **Mi mano (My Hand).**

the alienation of Chicano existence. Many art critics have categorized his work as a merging of neo-expressionism and "Chicano-noir."

In 1991 Hernández's work was exposed to a wider international audience when film director Taylor Hackford used more than 30 of his paintings and murals in *Blood In ... Blood Out* (1993), a film about barrio life. Several Hollywood celebrities subsequently bought his work. In 1992 the Metropolitican Museum of Art also acquired two of his paintings. His work was included in the exhibition "Chicano Visions: American Painters on the Verge," which opened at the San Antonio Museum of Art in 2001.

KEY DATES

1951   Born in Childress, Texas, on October 15.

1985   Has first solo exhibition, "San Antonio, caras y lugares."

1991   Is commissioned to produce paintings and murals for the Hollywood movie *Blood In ... Blood Out.*

2001   Work is included in the "Chicano Visions: American Painters of the Verge" exhibition.

Further reading: Marin, Cheech. *Chicano Visions: American Painters on the Verge.* Boston, MA: Bulfinch, 2002.
http://www.losquemados.com (features biography and work).

HERNÁNDEZ, Antonia
Civil Rights Activist, Lawyer

Civil rights activist and lawyer Antonia Hernández is a recognized leader in the struggle to protect the voting and educational rights of Latinos across the United States. In 2004 Hernández became the president and CEO of the California Community Foundation, a nonprofit organization that assists local community projects with financial support.

Early life

Born in El Cambio, Mexico, in 1948, Hernández is the daughter of Manuel and Nicolasa Hernández. Although Manuel Hernández was born in Texas and was an American citizen, as a child he had to return to Mexico with his family after the U.S. government introduced a policy that forced Americans of Mexican heritage to go back to Mexico during the Great Depression. In 1956 Manuel returned to the United States in order to give his own children better educational opportunities. Settling in Los Angeles, California, Antonia Hernández attended the local public school, where she excelled in her studies. Hernández also helped care for her younger siblings, sold her mother's homemade tamales in the local neighborhood, and spent summers working as a farm laborer with her family in California's Central Valley.

Fighting for change

After graduating from high school, Hernández attended a community college for two years; she eventually graduated from UCLA with a BA in history in 1970. She received a teaching certificate, and in 1974 completed a law degree at UCLA. Hernández chose to specialize in civil rights; she accepted a position as a legal clerk for California Rural

▲ Antonia Hernández disapproved of the "sink-or swim" method by which she had to learn English: She is a fierce advocate of bilingual education in schools.

Legal Assistance, an organization that protected the rights of farmworkers and rural poor people. She went on to work at the Los Angeles Center for Law and Justice and the Legal Aid Foundation. Hernández was the first Latina to serve as a staff counsel to the U.S. Senate Committee on the Judiciary.

From 1981 to 2004, Hernández worked for the Mexican American Legal Defense and Education Fund (MALDEF), first as regional counsel, and from 1985 as its president and general counsel. She campaigned to protect voting and political representation rights in particular: When California voters passed the 1994 Proposition 187, which would have prevented undocumented immigrants in the state from receiving such services as education and health care, MALDEF got it overturned on the grounds that it was unconstitutional. In 2004 Hernández became president and CEO of the California Community Foundation.

See also: Bilingualism; Political Representation

Further reading: http://www.findarticles.com/p/articles/ mi_m0HSP/is_1_3/ai_66678531 (article on Hernández).

KEY DATES

1948 Born in El Cambio in Mexico.

1956 Moves to the United States with her family to live in Los Angeles, California.

1974 Graduates from UCLA Law School.

1985 Becomes president and general counsel of the Mexican American Legal Defense and Education Fund.

2004 Accepts position as president and CEO of the California Community Foundation.

HERNANDEZ, Ester
Artist

Muralist, painter, and printmaker Ester Hernandez is an influential member of the Chicano art movement. Part of the second wave of Mexican American artists that emerged during the 1970s when Chicano studies started to be taught in art schools, Hernandez uses her art to promote Chicano civil rights.

Early life
Born in Dinuba, California, on December 3, 1944, Ester Medina Hernandez came from a family of farmworkers of mixed Mexican and Yaqui origin. Growing up in an agricultural community in the San Joaquin Valley of California, in the early 1960s Hernandez acquired a first-hand knowledge of the labor movement led by César Chávez and Dolores Huerta to gain better rights for migrant farmworkers. She was actively involved in the struggle to improve labor conditions and wages for *campesinos*.

Las Mujeres Muralistes
A talented artist, Hernandez moved to Oakland, California, where she studied at Laney College and Grove Street College. Hernandez went on to gain a BA in visual arts at the University of California at Berkeley.

In 1974 Hernandez joined Las Mujeres Muralistas (The Muralist Women), the San Francisco-based art collective of Latina feminist artists. The group, which was dissolved in the early 1980s, completed several murals that are today considered an important part of California's artistic heritage.

Significance
Hernandez is most renowned as a printmaker, the art form favored by many Chicano and Chicana artists. In her work, Hernandez takes on well-known images and transforms them into what she believes are their real natures—the Statue of Liberty is portrayed as a pre-Columbian idol (1975), and the Virgin of Guadalupe appears as a karate fighter (1976), for example. Hernandez also depicts iconic women figures in her work, such as the Mexican artist Frida Kahlo in *Frida and I* (1998).

The work that first established Hernandez as a serious Chicana artist was *Sun Mad* (1981). Depicting a skeletal version of the woman on the Sun Maid raisin box, it alludes both to the use of pesticides in grape growing and to the Mexican Day of the Dead.

KEY DATES

1944 Born in Dinuba, California, on December 3.

1960s Part of the farm labor movement in California.

1974 Joins Las Mujeres Muralistas (The Muralist Women).

1981 Produces first major work, *Sun Mad*.

1987 Becomes a teacher at Creativity Explored, San Francisco.

2001 Recipient of second California Arts Council grant.

2006 Work exhibited at the Currier Museum of Art, New Hampshire, in an exhibition of Latin American and Caribbean art from New York's El Museo del Barrio permanent collection.

Traveling showcase
Hernandez's work has subsequently been included in several important exhibitions, including "Chicano Art: Resistance and Affirmation 1965–1985," a traveling exhibition that established the historical importance of Chicano art. Hernandez's work is also held at El Museo del Barrio, the New York City-based museum established in 1969 to showcase important Latin American art. It was also part of the 2006 exhibition made up of works from El Museo del Barrio, held at the Currier Museum of Art in New Hampshire.

Honors
A celebrated Chicana artist, Ester Hernandez has won numerous awards for her work, and received various fellowships and grants from a variety of sponsors, including the National Endowment for the Arts (1992), and the California Arts Council (1998, 2001). Hernandez has been an art instructor and visiting artist at several colleges in California. Since 1987, she has been a teacher at Creativity Explored, a visual art center for developmentally disabled adults in San Francisco.

See also: Chávez, César; Huerta, Dolores

Further reading: Keller, Gary, and Amy Philips. *Triumph of Our Communities: Four Decades of Mexican American Art.* Tempe, AZ: Bilingual Review Press, 2005.

http://www.esterhernandez.com/index.htm (biography).

HERNÁNDEZ, Joseph Marion
Politician, Soldier

Joseph Marion Hernández was a soldier and a politician. He was the first Hispanic American to serve in the U.S. Congress as a representative for Florida.

Early life
Born in St. Augustine, Florida, on August 4, 1793, Hernández's original name was José Mariano. At the time of Hernández's birth, St. Augustine was still a Spanish colony. When the Territory of Florida was established in 1822, Hernández officially transferred his allegiance to the United States and changed his name to Joseph Marion Hernández.

A career in politics
Hernández was interested in politics as a young man. He decided that he wanted to have some say in the United States, and stood for election as the first delegate to Congress from the new Territory of Florida. He was successful and served from January 3, 1823, to March 3, 1825. During that time he impressed his peers with his intelligence. Hernández became a member of the territorial House of Representatives, and was eventually chosen to be its presiding officer.

Hernández was made a brigadier general of the Mounted Volunteers in the Florida militia at the start

▼ *Joseph Marion Hernández was a successful soldier, politician, and landowner in the early 19th century.*

of the conflict with the Native Americans in Florida. In 1835 he enlisted in the U.S. Army, serving for three years in the Seminole War (1835–1842) until his discharge in 1838.

A decisive man
In 1837 Hernández commanded an expedition that captured the Native chief Oceola. On September 10, 1837, the militia under his command took part in a decisive battle with Native Americans near what is now Mosquito Inlet. Hernández used his distinguished military record and his years of service to his country to relaunch his own political career. In 1845 he entered the race for a seat in the U.S. Senate. Hernández ran as a Whig, believing a link with the party would help secure him votes. He lost the race by a clear margin, and Hernández felt rejected by those on whom he had counted for support. His political career came to an abrupt but decisive end.

In the last 12 years of his life, Hernández gave up any involvement with politics and turned his back on public service. He left the United States, moving to Cuba. There he sought his fortune in various business ventures. He eventually became a sugar planter and ran a successful plantation. Hernández remained in Cuba for the rest of his life. He died in Matanzas, Cuba, on June 8, 1857, at age 64.

KEY DATES	
1793	Born in St. Augustine, Florida, on August 4.
1823	Takes office as first delegate of the Territory of Florida on January 3.
1835	Enlists in the United States Army.
1845	Loses his bid for a seat in the United States Senate.
1857	Dies in Matanzas, Cuba, on June 8.

Further reading: Enciso, Carmen. *Hispanic Americans in Congress, 1822–1995*. Washington.D.C.: Government Printing Office, 1995.
http://www.infoplease.com/biography/us/congress/hernandez-joseph-marion.html (biography).

HERNÁNDEZ, Juan
Academic, Politician

In December 2000, Juan Hernández, a Mexican American professor at the University of Texas, Dallas, became the first U.S. citizen to serve in the Mexican cabinet, as chair of Vicente Fox's President's Office for Mexicans Abroad. Although the office proved short-lived, Hernández has since continued to work to improve the social and economic conditions of Mexicans living and working in the United States.

Mexican and American
The son of an American mother and a Mexican father, Juan Hernández was born in Fort Worth, Texas, in 1955. He grew up largely in San Miguel de Allende, in the central Mexican state of Guanajuato. Bilingual in Spanish and English, and holding dual Mexican and U.S. citizenship, Hernández learned how to bridge two disparate cultures from an early age. After high school he went to study in the United States, graduating with a BA in literature from Lawrence University, Wisconsin, in 1975. He subsequently received both a master's degree (1978) and a doctorate (1981) from Texas Christian University in Fort Worth.

After completing his studies, Hernández embarked on an academic career, taking positions at Texas Christian University, California State University, Long Beach, and finally the University of Texas at Dallas (UTD). In 1995 he became the founding director of UTD's Center for U.S.–Mexico Studies. In the following year, Hernández met Vicente Fox, the recently elected governor of Guanajuato state, and together they began to develop ideas regarding Mexican immigration to the United States. In 2000 Fox invited Hernández to work as his senior adviser in his campaign for the Mexican presidency.

After his victory in July 2000, Fox appointed Hernández as director of the newly founded President's Office for Mexicans Abroad and made him a member of his cabinet.

▲ *Juan Hernández has been an important voice in the fight for rights for Mexican migrant workers.*

In his new role, Hernández set out an ambitious new program that sought, on the one hand, to gain social justice for Mexican migrants and, on the other, to decrease emigration by stimulating employment within Mexico itself. Hernández also aimed to strengthen relations between the government of Mexico and the 20 million Mexican migrants who had "one foot in Mexico and one foot in the United States."

Hernández's work drew both criticism and praise. Some U.S. critics attacked his policies because they appeared to discourage migrant workers from settling in their new country; others welcomed his policies, including *Latin Trade Magazine*, which named him its Humanitarian Man of 2001. By 2002, the President's Office for Mexicans Abroad had been closed down. Hernández is still a leading commentator on Mexican immigration. He has appeared on ABC, Fox News, and Univision.

Further reading: www.juanhernandez.org (Hernández's Web site).

KEY DATES	
1955	Born in Fort Worth, Texas.
1973	Moves back to the United States.
1995	Founds the Center for U.S.–Mexico Studies at the University of Texas at Dallas.
2000	Is appointed director of the President's Office for Mexicans Abroad; two years later the office closes.

HERNANDEZ, Keith
Baseball Player

The best first baseman of his time, Keith Hernandez won two World Series championships with two different teams, a shared National League Most Valuable Player (MVP) award, 11 straight Gold Gloves, and a batting title.

Keith Hernandez was born in 1953 in San Francisco, California, the grandson of Spanish immigrants. His father, John, played minor league baseball for 10 years but an eye injury derailed his major league ambitions. Keith showed his athletic prowess early when he became the first Capucino High School student to receive all-league honors in basketball, football, and baseball. He also set the interscholastic league record with a .500 batting average.

Shining star

Hernandez rose quickly through the St. Louis farm system after the Missouri team drafted him in June 1971. In 1975 he became the club's regular first baseman. He excelled with his strong, steady hands, quick feet, and nearly infallible instincts. Six feet (1.8m) tall, and weighing 195 pounds (88.5kg), he was not a typical, hulking first baseman, but he was a selective line-drive hitter who won the batting title in 1979 at .344, along with the first shared

KEY DATES	
1953	Born in San Francisco, California, on October 20.
1979	Named cowinner of the National League Most Valuable Player Award.
1983	Traded from the St. Louis Cardinals to the New York Mets.
1985	Testifies in Pittsburgh drug trials and admits frequent cocaine use.
1986	Leads the Mets to World Series victory.
1992	Retires from baseball.

MVP award in history with Willie Stargell. In 1982 Hernandez's eight runs batted in (RBIs) guided the Cardinals to their first World Series title in 14 years.

Despite Hernandez's award-winning play, the Cardinals shocked baseball fans when in 1983 they traded their first baseman to the New York Mets for pitchers Neil Allen and Rick Ownbey. The Cardinals' manager hinted that Hernandez was traded because he was using drugs. The player later admitted drug use, and called cocaine "the devil on this earth."

New life

With the Mets Hernandez transformed himself into the game's most intense player. In 1985 he helped the team to a second-place finish; in the following season they finished in first place. In Game Seven of the 1986 World Series he hit a bases-loaded single in the sixth inning and a sacrifice fly in the seventh to help New York to an 8–5 victory. The following year New York named him team captain. In 1988 Hernandez experienced the first of many injuries that would eventually end his career in 1992 at the age of 39.

In 1999 Keith Hernandez returned to the New York Mets as an assistant in spring training and started broadcasting games. In the same year he won an Emmy award for his television work.

Further reading: Hernandez, Keith, and Mike Bryan. *If at First: A Season with the Mets.* New York, NY: McGraw-Hill, 1996.
http://www.baseballlibrary.com/baseballlibrary/ballplayers/H/Hernandez_Keith.stm (baseball biographical database).

▼ *Keith Hernandez hits a home run for the New York Mets against his former team, the St. Louis Cardinals.*

HERNÁNDEZ, María Latigo
Civil Rights Activist, Community Leader

María Latigo Hernández is frequently included in lists of the 100 most influential Hispanic Americans in history. Hernández was an influential civil rights activist, educator, and community leader.

Early life
Born in Garza García, near Monterrey, Nuevo León, Mexico, in 1896, Hernández was one of six children born to Eduardo Frausto and Francisca Latigo. The family moved to Hebbronville near the U.S.–Mexico border during the Mexican Revolution in 1910. There, Hernández met and fell in love with Pedro Hernández Barrera. They married in 1915 and settled down to have a family: The Hernándezes eventually had 10 children.

Economic move
In 1918 Hernández moved with her family to San Antonio, Texas. She initially remained at home, looking after her young children while Pedro worked. Pedro soon became involved with local civic organizations established by Mexican expatriates residing in the city. While some Mexican exiles longed to return to Mexico, others—including Pedro and María Latigo Hernández—wanted to integrate into the local society and to become U.S. citizens.

Activism and civic participation
Hernández and her husband were critical of both the main Mexican American civil rights organizations, the Orden Hijos de America and the League of United Latin American Citizens (LULAC). Both organizations only allowed male members, and the Orden Hijos de America operated in Spanish while LULAC conducted its business in English.

In 1929 Hernández and her husband founded the Orden Caballeros de America (Order of the Knights of America), an organization open to Mexicans and Mexican Americans of both sexes; it also conducted its meetings in both Spanish and English. The organization, which was dedicated to civic and political activism, worked to help improve the lives of people of Mexican ancestry living in the United States. It focused particularly on the provision of good education for young Latinos.

Hernández also founded the Asociación Protectora de Madres (Association for the Protection of Mothers), which lasted until 1939. The organization gave support to expectant mothers; it developed instructional programs

▲ *María Latigo Hernández worked with her husband, Pedro, to improve the lives of Mexican Americans.*

that stressed prenatal care and provided essential advice to mothers. Hernández recruited local doctors to provide proper medical information and care to members.

An eloquent woman
Hernández was a brilliant and convincing speaker. Both eloquent and passionate, she had the ability to deliver a powerful speech in either English or Spanish at a moment's notice. Using this ability, in 1932 Hernández became the first female radio announcer in San Antonio. She used her program, *Voz de las Americas* (*Voice of the Americas*) to promote the various organizations in which she was involved. She spoke about her many and varied interests, including her ideas regarding the role of women in society. Hernández also wrote critical essays: The San

Maria Latigo Hernández was greatly influenced by her college professor father; he taught her the importance of education. Hernández's husband, Pedro, also provided her with great inspiration. The couple worked together to improve conditions for their community.

Hernández herself became a role model for many young Mexican American women. She managed to balance family and home commitments with her interest and involvement in civic and political affairs.

For nearly eight decades Hernández was active in promoting the interests of women and the Mexican American community. A talented public speaker, Hernández skillfully spurred people to action. Through Hernández's work, Hispanic Americans achieved better and equal access to education.

Antonio publisher Artes Gráficas printed her monograph *Mexico y Los Cuatro Poderes Que Dirigen al Pueblo (Mexico and the Four Powers That Guide the Community)*.

Education

As a mother and a civil rights activist, Hernández was interested in education. Mexican children had to attend segregated schools with poor facilities. They often had no heating or running water and were infested with rats and other vermin. In the 1930s, Hernández, with her children in tow, led several education protest marches in the streets of San Antonio's West Side barrio. The state superintendent of instruction subsequently visited San Antonio to hear the demands of the activists. In 1934 Hernández also helped the activist Eleuterio Escobar to organize La Liga Pro-Defensa Escolar (School Improvement League) in San Antonio, an organization fighting for better education. Hernández spearheaded fundraising initiatives to support legal actions to challenge school segregation on constitutional grounds.

Labor and politics

In 1938 Hernández heard about the miserable conditions in which women pecan shellers worked in San Antonio. After the pecan shellers went on strike and their leader, Emma Tenayuca, was put in jail, Hernández promoted their cause, making numerous speeches on the women's behalf.

Over the next years, Hernández supported many Mexican American causes, traveling across Texas to highlight Latino community issues. In the 1950s Hernández, supported by Pedro, rallied behind several Democratic presidential candidates and emerging barrio leaders such as Albert A. Peña, Jr., and Henry B. González.

In the 1960s Hernández testified before the U.S. Commission on Civil Rights in San Antonio about the discrimination experienced by Mexican Americans and African Americans. In the late 1960s she also supported the actions of the new younger generation of leaders of the Chicano movement. She took part in several of their protests and demonstrations, particularly the school walkouts of 1968. When the Mexican American Youth Organization (MAYO) formed an alternative political party, La Raza Unida (RUP), both Hernández and her husband joined. They traveled across Texas to campaign on RUP's behalf. Hernández retired to Lytle, Texas, where she lived until her death in 1986.

KEY DATES

1896 Born in Garza García, Nuevo León, Mexico.

1915 Marries Pedro Hernández Barrera, with whom she has 10 children.

1918 Moves to San Antonio, Texas.

1933 Helps organize the Asociación Protectora de Madres.

1934 Helps Eleuterio Escobar organize La Liga Pro-Defensa Escolar.

1938 Supports a strike by Mexican female pecan shellers.

1968 Hosts a bimonthly television program in San Antonio, making speeches about education.

1972 Supports the Raza Unida Party in Texas and campaigns across central and west Texas.

1986 Dies on January 8.

See also: González, Henry B.; Peña, Albert A.; Political Movements; Tenayuca, Emma

Further reading: Sánchez Korrol, Virginia. *Latinas in the United States: A Historical Encyclopedia.* Bloomington, IN: Indiana University Press, 2006.
www.tsha.utexas.edu/handbook/online/articles (biography).

HERNÁNDEZ, Orlando
Baseball Player

Orlando Hernández's distinctive pitching style and his four-pitch arsenal have a formidable reputation in baseball. His sports career began in Cuba and continued in the United States after his defection from his home country. Hernández has played for the New York Yankees and the Chicago White Sox, helping both teams to reach the World Series; at the end of the 2005 season he was traded to the Arizona Diamondbacks. He is known as "El Duque" ("the duke"), a nickname from his childhood.

Early life
Hernández gives his birth date as October 11, 1969, although legal records in Havana indicate that he was actually born in 1965. Hernández's father was a pitcher on the Cuban national team and his mother was a therapist.

From an early age, Hernández was obsessed with baseball. Aged 18, he was selected to play for the Cuban national team. He also pitched for the Industriales of Havana in the Cuban National Series, which they won in 1992 and 1996. He represented Havana in the Selective Series, playing for such teams as Ciudad Habana and the Habaneros. Hernández became known for his unique right-handed pitching style: He rapidly kicks his leg up high, while lowering his glove behind that leg, before throwing the ball. His arsenal of pitches includes a change-up, curveball, slider, and a 90-mile-per-hour (145km/h) fastball.

▲ *Orlando Hernández was banned from playing baseball in Cuba following his half-brother's defection to the United States: He defected a year later.*

KEY DATES	
1969	Born in Havana, Cuba, on October 11, according to Hernández; court records give 1965 as his year of birth.
1992	Pitches for Industriales, Havana; wins the Cuban National Series.
1996	Pitches for Industriale; wins the Cuban National Series for the second time.
1997	Defects from Cuba.
1998	Signs with the New York Yankees.
2003	Signs with the Montreal Expos.
2004	Re-signs with the Yankees.
2005	Signs with Chicago White Sox; wins World Series; is traded to the Arizona Diamondbacks and New York Mets.

To the United States
Hernández's career in Cuba hit a low after he was implicated in his half-brother's defection to the United States. The Cuban authorities labeled Hernández a traitor and banned him from playing baseball in 1996. Overnight Hernández went from being a national star to being ridiculed in the streets. He was forced to work in a psychiatric facility for about eight dollars a month. In December 1997, Hernández boarded a boat with seven other people to sail to the United States. They were forced to land on the island of Anguilla Cay, where they waited for the U.S. Coast Guard to pick them up. Hernández became a resident of Costa Rica, rather than accept a visa for the United States. This enabled him to become a free agent in U.S. baseball instead of being subject to the draft.

On March 7, 1998, Hernández signed a four-year deal with the New York Yankees. He made his professional U.S. baseball debut on the Single-A Tampa team on April 16. He soon moved up to pitch for Triple-A Columbus. He ended his first Major League season 12–4. He pitched for the Yankees until 2002; after a stint with the Montreal Expos, he rejoined the Yankees in 2004. He signed with the Chicago White Sox in 2005; at the end of that season, he was traded to the Arizona Diamondbacks, and then to the New York Mets.

Further reading: http://mlb.mlb.com/NASApp/mlb/index.jsp (the official Web site of Major League baseball).

HERNÁNDEZ BROS., Los
Cartoonists

In the early 1980s a cartoon series entitled *Love & Rockets* achieved great popularity with U.S. youth and inspired a new wave of literary comic strips. The comic strip was the work of the four brothers Hernández: Mario, who thought it up; Gilbert (aka Beto) and Jaime (aka Xaime), who produced most of the drawings; and Ismael, who bankrolled the project.

The Hernández family was ethnically mixed but principally Chicano. At home in the strawberry-farming community of Oxnard, California, the boys and their sister acquired a passion for comics from their mother, who was also a fan of rock music. The children's favorite strips included "Dennis the Menace," "Archie," and the "Captain Marvel" series by Jack Kirby and Steve Ditko.

In the late 1970s the brothers were influenced by the southern California punk scene. In this setting, under the tutelage of a community college art instructor, their work evolved from eye-catching poster art for local bands to an entire narrative universe.

Launch and liftoff

When Gilbert and Jaime released the first issue of *Love & Rockets* in 1981, the comic acquired almost immediate cult status among U.S. youth. The saga centers on the story of Palomar, a fictional Central American village, and the life of two punk lesbians, Maggie Chascarrillo and Hopey Glass, which is related in an ongoing serial entitled "Locas." The Palomar strand was written and drawn by Gilbert; "Locas" was the work of Jaime. Between these two main narratives, there are many interspersed subplots, usually populated by strong and complex female characters who are on a par with their male counterparts.

▲ **The success of Love & Rockets *was founded on a combination of bold artistry and a strong storyline.***

After 50 issues in 15 years *Love & Rockets* ceased publication in 1996, but in 2001 Los Bros. Hernández revived it, releasing three new magazines per year. In 2002 they began to publish compilations in book form. They included *Luba in America*, a collection of stories about the enigmatic matriarch of Palomar, and *Palomar: The Complete Heartbreak Soup*. In 2004 the entire Locas storyline was collected into a 700-page graphic novel.

Gilbert Hernández has also been responsible for the miniseries "Girl Crazy" in *Dark Horse*, "Birdland" in EROS Comix, as well as "Grip" and "Yeah!" for DC Comics. He now resides in Las Vegas, Nevada. Jaime and Mario Hernández live in Pasadena and San Francisco, respectively.

Further reading: Reid, Calvin. "Los Bros. Restart Love and Rockets." *Publishers Weekly*; March 12, 2001. Vol. 248, Issue 11, p. 35.
http://www.fantagraphics.com/artist/losbros/losbros.html (official Web page at Fantagraphics Books).

KEY DATES	
1957	Gilbert Hernández is born in Ventura, California, on February 1.
1959	Jaime Hernández is born in Oxnard, California, on October 10.
1981	*Love & Rockets* is released by Fantagraphics Books.
1996	*Love & Rockets* ceases publication.
2001	*Love & Rockets* is relaunched.

HERNÁNDEZ COLÓN, Rafael
Politician

Puerto Rican politician Rafael Hernández Colón was the youngest member of the country's senate. He was also governor of Puerto Rico (1973–1977; 1985–1993).

Early life

Born in the city of Ponce, Puerto Rico, on October 24, 1936, Hernández Colón was the son of a distinguished lawyer, Rafael Hernández Matos, who later served as a justice on the Puerto Rico Supreme Court. As a young man, Hernández Colón was a brilliant student. He eventually went to the United States to study, graduating with a BA from Johns Hopkins University in Baltimore, Maryland, in 1956. He returned to his native country to complete a doctorate in law at the University of Puerto Rico, graduating first in his class in 1959. Hernández Colón's dissertation dealt with the political relationship between the United States and Puerto Rico. He later sent his thesis to Governor Luis Muñoz Marín, who was so impressed that he appointed the 24-year-old Hernández Colón as associate commissioner of public services in Puerto Rico.

Political achievements

Hernández Colón's political talent and sharpness led to his rising quickly through Puerto Rico's political ranks. In 1965 Muñoz Marín's successor, Governor Roberto Sánchez Vilella, made Hernández Colón secretary of justice. He was first elected to the Puerto Rican Senate in 1968: Aged just 32, Hernández Colón was at the time the youngest person ever to be elected to the senate. In the following year, Hernández Colón became president of the senate and leader of the Partido Popular Democrático de Puerto Rico (PPD, or Popular Democratic Party). The PPD believed in Puerto Rico's commonwealth status and that the country should be viewed as an autonomous nation and not as a single state within the United States of America.

▲ *Rafael Hernández Colón believes that democracy and self-determination are Puerto Rico's way forward.*

In 1973 Hernández Colón became governor of Puerto Rico, a position he stayed in until 1977. He was elected again in 1984, serving from 1985 to 1993. During Hernández Colón's first term, President Gerald Ford suggested that Puerto Rico should become the 51st state of the Union. Hernández Colón was strongly opposed to this proposal, advocating self-determination for his country instead. In Hernández Colón's second term, the governor unsuccessfully called for a referendum on Puerto Rico's status in relation to the United States. He also tried to strengthen Puerto Rico's economic ties with various other countries, especially Japan, Canada, Spain, Mexico, and Venezuela. In 1992 he resigned as president of the PPD and announced that he would not run for the governorship again.

Hernández Colón has written several books on law. He also set up the Rafael Hernández Colón Foundation, an organization that promoted the construction of a library to archive material about the Puerto Rican government. Hernández Colón has received several awards for his work.

See also: Muñoz Marín, Luis; Sánchez Vilella, Roberto

Further reading: Morris, Nancy. *Puerto Rico: Culture, Politics, and Identity.* New York, NY: Praeger Publishers, 1995.
http://www.puertorico-herald.org/issues/vol4n10/ProfileRHColon-en.shtml (profile of Rafael Hernández Colón).

KEY DATES	
1936	Born in Ponce, Puerto Rico, on October 24.
1968	Becomes youngest member of the Puerto Rican Senate.
1973	Becomes governor of Puerto Rico, until 1977.
1985	Serves for a second time as governor, until 1993.

HERNÁNDEZ CRUZ, Victor
Poet

Victor Hernández Cruz is one of the most influential Puerto Rican poets of the diaspora (the migration of people from their homeland). His contribution to American poetry underlines both the multicultural and experimental dimensions of literature.

Early life

Born in 1949 in Aguas Buenas, Puerto Rico, Hernández Cruz came from a family of tobacco growers and traditional singers. In 1954 they migrated to New York City. He studied at Benjamin Franklin School, on Manhattan's Lower East Side, where his talent at writing became obvious and was nurtured by his English teachers.

A writer

In the 1960s, Hernández Cruz played a leading role in the poetry that young Puerto Ricans began to create on the Lower East Side and El Barrio. Aged 17, he published his first book of poetry, *Papo Got His Gun*. Before he turned 20, Random House published his collection *Snaps*, making Hernández Cruz the only poet of his generation published by an established mainstream press.

In 1968 Hernández Cruz moved to Berkeley, California, to work on a project that aimed to make art an important experience for minority high-school students. He spent the next two decades on the West Coast, incorporating elements of the Chicano culture into his work. He also cofounded the Before Columbus Foundation, and worked as a visiting professor at various universities in California and Michigan. During this time, he published six books of poetry, including the experimental *By Lingual Wholes*.

▲ **In 1981,** Time *magazine hailed Hernández Cruz as one of America's leading poets.*

Puerto Rican poet

Hernández Cruz established himself as a Puerto Rican poet in the United States, writing primarily in English about Puerto Rican, Nuyorican (New York Puerto Rican), and Latino cultural and artistic issues. In 1989 he resettled in his native Aguas Buenas. *Red Beans*, winner of the *Publishers Weekly* "Ten Best Books of the Year" in 1991, captures some of the experience of that homecoming.

Since 1999 Hernández Cruz has added Morocco as a location for his poetry. It allows him to further explore the African component in Puerto Rican culture. He spends a lot of time there with his wife and children. Hernández Cruz's legacy is the fusion of the traditional with the experimental. In 2001 he won the Griffin prize for poetry for the anthology *Maracas*.

Further reading: Flores, Juan. *Divided Boarders: Essays on Puerto Rican Identity*. Houston, TX: Arte Publico Press, 1993. http://www.writing.upenn.edu/pennsound/x/Cruz.html (voice of Hernández Cruz reading his poems).

KEY DATES

1949	Born in Aguas Buenas, Puerto Rico, on February 6.
1954	Family migrates to New York.
1969	*Snaps* becomes the first Nuyorican book of poetry published by a mainstream press.
1981	*Time* magazine ranks Hernández Cruz among the leading U.S. poets.
1989	Returns to Aguas Buenas, Puerto Rico.
2001	*Maracas: New and Selected Poems, 1966–2000* wins the Griffin Prize for poetry.

HERRERA, Carolina
Fashion Designer

Carolina Herrera is one of the world's leading fashion designers. Known for her elegant and beautiful designs and fragrances, Herrera has dressed some of the world's most beautiful women, including Jackie Kennedy Onassis.

Early life
Born Maria Carolina Josefina Pacanins y Niño in Caracas, Venezuela, in 1939, Herrera was the daughter of Guillermo and Maria Cristina Pacanins. Her family was socially prominent and Herrera was a member of Venezuela's elite. She traveled, mixed with international socialites, and wore made-to-order clothes. Aged 13, Herrera was taken by her grandmother to Cristobal Balenciaga's fashion show in Paris, France. Herrera later said that her father's dashing style and her mother's "cultivated aura" and insistence on fine tailoring and detail influenced her own fashion taste.

From debutante to fashion designer
Until the age of 40, Herrera led the typical life of a socialite. When she was 17, she married Guillermo Behrens Tello, with whom she had two daughters. In 1964 the couple divorced; four years later she married her first love, Reinaldo Herrera, who came from one of Venezuela's most prominent families. The couple had two children, one of whom, Carolina, Jr., also became a designer.

▲ *Carolina Herrera's friend Jackie Kennedy Onassis wore Herrera's designs for the last 12 years of her life.*

In the 1970s Herrera was rarely off the international best-dressed women's lists, but it was not until the late 1970s that she began to consider a career in fashion. With the backing of her family and friends, such as former editor of *Vogue* Diana Vreeland and fashion publicist Count Rudi Crespi, Herrera moved to New York and established Carolina Herrera, Ltd. In 1981 Herrera made her design debut at New York's Metropolitan Club with a collection of 20 dresses. Her beautifully detailed, expertly crafted creations were soon in demand by women all over the world. She launched a fur collection (1984); the CH collection, a more affordable range of her clothing (1986); and a bridal collection (1987). In 1988 Herrera launched her first perfume. Herrera opened a store on Madison Avenue in 2000, and won the Womenswear Designer of the Year Award given by the Council of Fashion Designers of America (2004).

KEY DATES

1939 Born in Caracas, Venezuela.

1968 Marries Reinaldo Herrera.

1980 Moves to New York to pursue a career as a designer.

1981 Establishes Carolina Herrera, Ltd; launches debut collection at New York's Metropolitan Club.

1984 Launches a fur collection.

1986 Launches the more affordable CH collection.

1988 Launches her first perfume.

2000 Opens a flagship store on Madison Avenue in New York City.

2004 Receives the Womenswear Designer of the Year Award from the Council of Fashion Designers of America.

Further reading: Bowles, Hamish. *Carolina Herrera: Portrait of a Fashion Icon.* New York, NY: Assouline, 2004. http://www.newyorkmetro.com/fashion/fashionshows/designers/bios/carolinaherrera (article on Herrera).

HERRERA, John J.
Civil Rights Activist, Attorney

Civil rights activist John J. Herrera was advised to become a lawyer by his speech teacher in high school, future U.S. president Lyndon B. Johnson, who told Herrera that he would make a fine lawyer one day. Herrera took Johnson's words to heart: He went on to become one of the most significant Latino lawyers in civil rights history, winning several landmark cases that helped improve the lives of many Mexican Americans.

The road to activism

Born in Cravens, Louisiana, on April 12, 1910, John James Herrera was the son of Juan José Herrera, a San Antonio policeman whose ancestors came from the Canary Islands, and Antonia Jiménez. Herrera attended Sam Houston High School in Houston, Texas, graduating in 1934. Disgusted by the discriminatory treatment that Mexican Americans experienced in Texas, Herrera became involved in the civil rights movement in the 1930s.

In 1939 Herrera reestablished Council 60 of the League of United Latin American Citizens (LULAC) in Houston, Texas, campaigning for the Mexican American vote. Herrera went on to organize 53 LULAC chapters across Texas and the Southwest. During this time he also worked as a taxi driver and a laborer to support himself through college. In 1940 Herrera became one of the first Mexican Americans to graduate from South Texas Law School. He became a licensed attorney in 1943.

▲ *John J. Herrera dedicated his life to enforcing the constitutional rights of Mexican Americans.*

Herrera specialized in civil rights cases. Believing that political power would help him fight injustice, Herrera became the first Hispanic political candidate for Harris County in 1947. Over the next 11 years, he stood four times in the elections for state representative, although he was unsuccessful.

Herrera had great success as a lawyer, however. Together with Gustavo C. García, he filed suit to end the school segregation of Mexican American children in Bastrop, Texas. The subsequent landmark decision in *Minerva Delgado v. Bastrop Independent School District* (1948) ruled the practice illegal. In *Pete Hernández v. Texas* (1954), Herrera and García challenged the constitutionality of excluding Mexican Americans from jury service: The U.S. Supreme Court ruled in their favor.

Herrera dedicated his life to civil rights. He remained connected to LULAC, and was its president from 1952. A much respected Mexican American, Herrera died in 1986.

See also: García, Gustavo C.

Further reading: http://www.lib.utexas.edu/taro/houpub/00009/hpub-00009.html (Web site of Herrera's papers; includes a biography).

KEY DATES

1910 Born in Cravens, Louisiana, on April 12.

1939 Reestablishes LULAC's Council 60.

1947 Stands unsuccessfully for election as state representative four times from 1947 to 1958.

1948 Wins the landmark civil rights case *Minerva Delgado v. Bastrop Independent School District*, which rules that segregation of Mexican American children is illegal.

1952 Elected national president of LULAC.

1954 Wins the landmark case *Pete Hernández v. Texas* before the U.S. Supreme Court; it ends discrimination against Mexican Americans in jury service selection.

1986 Dies in Houston, Texas, on October 12.

HERRERA, Silvestre
Soldier

Silvestre S. Herrera was a Mexican American who won a Congressional Medal of Honor for bravery under enemy fire during World War II (1939–1945).

Herrera was born in 1909 in Camargo, Chihuahua, Mexico. Both his parents died of influenza when he was 18 months old, and an uncle brought him to El Paso, Texas. On completing the eighth grade at school, he decided that he wanted to join the military. Although he was not at the time a U.S. citizen, he convinced recruitment officers of his allegiance to his adopted country, and he became both a naturalized American and a professional soldier. When the United States entered World War II in 1941 he was a private first class in Company E, 142nd Infantry of the 36th (Texas) Infantry Division.

Heroism

By March 15, 1945, the conflict in Europe had less than two months left to run. On that day Herrera was an acting squad leader/automatic rifleman at the head of a push into German-held territory near Mertzwiller, to the north of Strasbourg, France. He and his platoon were advancing along a tree-lined road when they came under heavy enemy machine-gun fire. As his men took cover, Herrera singlehandedly stormed the German stronghold, killing three soldiers and capturing the remaining eight.

When the U.S. platoon moved forward again it came under more fire. Herrera moved quickly to take cover behind some nearby rocks, but as he ran he stepped on a landmine, which exploded, throwing him into the air. When he landed, he set off another hidden explosive device that blew off both his legs below the knees.

Herrera bandaged his wounds as best he could, then dragged himself to the rocks. Once safely under cover he began firing at the enemy—he had kept hold of his M-1

▲ *Silvestre Herrera (right) receives the Congressional Medal of Honor from President Harry S. Truman.*

rifle throughout the ordeal. He hit at least one Wehrmacht soldier. Meanwhile his comrades moved in from the side and killed the remaining members of the German machine-gun crew. The U.S. platoon members then picked their way through the minefield and rescued the badly injured Herrera. He was taken back to a field hospital, where he remained until the end of the war.

International recognition

Silvestre S. Herrera received his Congressional Medal of Honor from President Harry S. Truman on August 23, 1945. The following year the government of Mexico awarded Herrera its Premier Merito Militar, making him the only person in history to have received both nations' highest award for valor.

Herrera subsequently became a leather worker and a silversmith. He remained philosophical about his terrible injuries: "I wasn't sorry for it. I felt that I didn't want anybody to be sorry for me. I lived a very happy life."

Further reading: http://www.gojafe.com/herrera1.htm (detailed account of Herrera's actions).

KEY DATES	
1909	Born in Camargo, Chihuahua, Mexico.
1922	Joins U.S. Army.
1945	Wounded in action during World War II.
1946	Awarded Congressional Medal of Honor.
1947	Awarded Mexico's highest military honor, the Premier Merito Militar.

HERRERA-SOBEK, María
Academic

María Herrera-Sobek is an eminent Chicana academic and intellectual. The author of such books as *The Bracero Experiment: Elitelore Versus Folklore*, Herrera-Sobek is also associate vice chancellor of the University of California at Santa Barbara.

Born in Texas, Herrera-Sobek was the daughter of poor farmworkers. She attended segregated schools and helped her family pick cotton. Despite these modest beginnings, she wanted to go to college. She achieved her dream when she went to study at Arizona State University, graduating with a degree in chemistry.

From science to Chicano/a studies

Despite an initial interest in science, Herrera-Sobek went on to specialize in Hispanic-related subjects. She began her graduate studies in Los Angeles, an epicenter of the Chicano movement in the 1960s. Her master's degree (1971) focused on Latin America rather than U.S. Latinos, but her PhD from UCLA focused on Hispanic languages and literatures. As Chicano studies developed during the 1960s, language became a central issue given that while most Chicanos speak Spanish, some do not. Much of the early literature in that decade was either written in English, written in Spanish and translated, or written in both languages. Herrera-Sobek's early career thus reflects the role that language played in dividing Chicano scholars between Spanish and English departments.

Academia

During the years that Herrera-Sobek spent working her way up through the tenure-track and tenure ranks in the University of California, Irvine, system, she participated in one of the most vibrant and important centers for Chicano scholarship and creative writing. UC Irvine's annual prize for Chicano fiction helped discover many of the most influential Chicano authors. Working with Juan-Bruce Novoa and Alejandro Morales, Herrera-Sobek helped establish an ongoing biennial international conference on Chicano studies that has met in France, Germany, Holland, and several other European locations, as well as in Mexico and the United States. This conference has been responsible for generating great interest in Chicano studies in Europe, particularly in Germany, and it has provided an avenue for many European scholars to present their work and gain access to the U.S. academic world.

KEY DATES

1965 Graduates with a BA in chemistry from Arizona State University.

1969 Receives a Ford Foundation grant for field work in Mexico.

1971 Receives an MA in Latin American Studies from UCLA.

1972 Becomes acting assistant professor, Chicano Studies Department, California State, Northridge.

1975 Earns a PhD in Hispanic languages and literatures at UCLA.

1990 Becomes a visiting professor at Stanford University.

1997 Appointed professor and Luis Leal Endowed Chair, University of California, Santa Barbara (UCSB).

1999 Wins the Américo Paredes Folklore Prize, Chicano/Latino Section of American Folklore Society.

2003 Becomes associate vice chancellor for diversity, equity, and academic policy, UCSB.

Literature

Herrera-Sobek's scholarly work has concentrated on folklore in her monographs and Chicana studies in her work as an editor. Her books include: *The Bracero Experience: Elitelore Versus Folklore* (1979), *The Mexican Corrido: A Feminist Analysis* (1990), and *Northward Bound: The Mexican Immigrant Experience in Ballad and Song* (1993). She has edited or coedited several books, including *Chicana Creativity and Criticism* (1988), *Culture Across Borders: The Popular Culture of Mexican Immigration* (1998), *Power, Race, and Gender in Academe: Strangers in the Tower?* (2000). In 2003 Herrera-Sobek became associate vice chancellor at the University of California, Santa Barbara, where she also holds the Luis Leal Endowed Chair in Chicano studies.

See also: Morales, Alejandro

Further reading: Maciel, David R., Isidro D. Ortiz, and María Herrera-Sobek (eds.). *Chicano Renaissance: Contemporary Cultural Trends.* Tucson, AZ: University of Arizona Press, 2000.
http://www.chicst.ucsb.edu/faculty/Personal_Pages/Maria_Herrera_Sobek/index.shtml (biography).

HIDALGO, Edward
Secretary of the Navy

Edward Hidalgo was the first Latino to be appointed secretary of the Navy. Hidalgo, who was also a lawyer, worked hard to improve the opportunities available to members of the Hispanic community in the armed forces.

Early life
Born on October 12, 1912, in Mexico City, Mexico, Hidalgo moved with his family to the United States in 1918. They settled in New York City. As a child Hidalgo decided that he wanted to have a life dedicated to study and the service of the others. Hidalgo put his mind to his studies and graduated magna cum laude from Holy Cross College in 1933. Three years later he graduated from Columbia University Law School. He went on to earn another degree in civil law from the University of Mexico Law School. Hidalgo then practiced law in New York.

World War II
Enlisting in the United States Navy in 1942 during World War II (1939–1945), Hidalgo was immediately assigned to the State Department. He worked there between 1942 and

▼ *Edward Hidalgo actively campaigned to recruit people from ethnic minorities for the U.S. Navy.*

KEY DATES

1912	Born in Mexico City on October 12.
1936	Graduates from Columbia University Law School.
1942	Enlists in the U.S. Navy.
1979	Becomes secretary of the Navy.
1995	Dies on February 1.

1943 as a legal adviser. He was also assigned to the Pacific, serving as an air-combat intelligence officer aboard the aircraft carrier *Enterprise*. Hidalgo was awarded a Bronze Star for his bravery in combat.

Commitment and drive
After the war ended, Hidalgo worked with the Eberstadt Committee on a project for the unification of the Armed Services. From 1945 to 1946, he served as special assistant to Secretary of the Navy James Forrestal.

Hidalgo practiced international law, working in Mexico and Paris, France, broadening his view of the world. In 1977, Hidalgo was appointed assistant secretary of the U.S. Navy, with responsibility for manpower, reserve affairs, and logistics. In October 1979, Hidalgo was promoted to the position of the secretary of the Navy; he was the first Latino to be appointed to the post, which until 1947 had been a cabinet post, after which it was integrated into the Defense Department.

Hidalgo actively campaigned to recruit people from ethnic minorities. He implemented advertising campaigns to advise Hispanic Americans about the opportunities available to them in the U.S. Navy. He created new opportunities for minorities. His own success also showed how anyone, irrespective of race, could achieve high rank in the armed forces. Edward Hidalgo died on February 1, 1995, at age 82.

Further reading: Nominations of Robert W. Komer, Edward Hidalgo, and Dennis P. McAuliffe: Hearing Before the Committee on Armed Services, United States Senate, Ninety-Sixth Congress First Session, October 17, 1979. Washington, D.C.: U.S. Government Printing Office, 1979.
http://www.rmpbs.org/americanfamily/heroes.html (biography).

HIJUELOS, Oscar
Writer

Oscar Hijuelos was the first Hispanic American to win the Pulitzer Prize. It was awarded for his novel *The Mambo Kings Play Songs of Love* (1989), which was later made into a movie. In his work Hijuelos chronicles the Cuban experience in 20th-century America.

Early life
Born in New York, on August 24, 1951, Oscar Hijuelos was the son of Cuban immigrants who came to the United States in the 1940s. His father, José Hijuelos, was a hotel worker, and his mother, Magdalena Torrens, stayed at home to look after the family. After studying at public schools in New York, Hijuelos went to the City College of New York, graduating in 1975 with a BA in English and in 1976 with an MA in English and writing. Between 1977 and 1984, Hijuelos worked as an advertising media traffic manager for Transportation Display Inc.

Chronicling Cuban American life
While working in advertising, Hijuelos dreamed of becoming a professional writer. In 1978 some of his short stories were published in the *Best of Pushcart Press, III* (1978). In that year Hijuelos also won an outstanding writer award from Pushcart Press, and received an Oscar Cintas fiction writing grant and a Breadloaf Writers Conference scholarship, both of which enabled him to concentrate on writing. His first novel, *Our House in the Last World*, was published in 1983. Set in the 1940s, the book follows the lives of a Cuban family living in the United States. Hijuelos concentrated on the experiences of life in America, rather than the nostalgia of the Cuban exiles for their homeland. Hijuelos won the Rome prize for literature; he was also given a creative writing fellowship from the National Endowment of the Arts.

In 1989 Hijuelos published his second novel, *The Mambo Kings Play Songs of Love*. The book follows the

▲ *Oscar Hijuelos (right) with actor Antonio Banderas (left), star of the 1992 film* **The Mambo Kings,** *which was based on Hijuelos's Pulitzer-winning novel.*

lives of brothers Nestor and Cesar Castillo, who move to New York from Havana, Cuba, at the beginning of the 1950s. They form an orchestra and appear on the popular TV show *I Love Lucy,* with Desi Arnaz. A critical and commercial success, the book mixed real-life characters with fictional ones. It was nominated for the National Book Critics Circle Award in 1989 and won the Pulitzer Prize for fiction a year later. In 1992 it was made into a successful movie starring Armand Assante and Antonio Banderas.

Not everyone was happy with Hijuelos's book, however. One of the people Hijuelos mentioned, Gloria Parker, leader of the Glorious Gloria Parker and Her All-Girl Rumba Orchestra, brought a $15 million lawsuit against the author. She claimed that his book had ruined her reputation, although the case was subsequently dismissed.

Hijuelos has published several more novels, including *A Simple Habana Melody* (2002), set in Havana in the 1940s. Hijuelos also contributed to the 1998 CD *Stranger than Fiction.*

KEY DATES	
1951	Born in New York City on August 24.
1983	Publishes first novel, *Our House in the Last World.*
1989	Publishes *The Mambo Kings Play Songs of Love.*
1990	Wins the Pulitzer Prize for fiction.

See also: Arnaz, Desi

Further reading: Hijuelos, Oscar. *The Mambo Kings Play Songs of Love*. New York, NY: Farrar, Straus, & Giroux, 1989. www.oscarhijuelos.com (official site).

HINOJOSA, Maria
Journalist

Maria Hinojosa is an award-winning journalist and author. Hinojosa has reported on the struggles and successes of Latinos in the United States, while increasing awareness on key issues such as workers' rights.

The rise to stardom

Born in Mexico City in 1961, Hinojosa grew up on the south side of Chicago. When she was eight years old she had a life-changing experience: Her mother took her to a rally where workers' rights activist César Chávez made a speech to urge people to boycott grapes. Hinojosa witnessed the struggles of her community, particularly the migrant laborers, and knew that she wanted to help highlight and change the situation.

In 1979 Hinojosa moved to New York City, where she attended Barnard College. She majored in Latin American studies, political economy, and women's studies, graduating magna cum laude in 1984. In 1987 Hinojosa landed a job as a producer for CBS Radio in New York. She worked on such shows as *Newsbreak* and *Where We Stand with Walter Cronkite*. In 1988 she was a producer and researcher on the television show *CBS This Morning*. She

▼ *Maria Hinojosa has won several awards for her coverage of Latino issues.*

KEY DATES	
1961	Born in Mexico City, Mexico.
1979	Moves to New York City to attend Barnard College.
1993	Joins *Latino USA* as host.
1995	*Hispanic Business Magazine* names her one of the 100 most influential Latinos in the United States; publishes her first book, *Crews: Gang Members Talk with Maria Hinojosa*.
1997	Joins CNN as first correspondent assigned to report exclusively on urban affairs.
2005	Joins PBS newsmagazine *NOW* as senior correspondent.

began her radio reporting career in 1990 as a general assignment correspondent for WNYC Radio.

In 1991 Hinojosa moved to television, hosting *New York Hotline*, a live prime-time call-in public affairs show on WNYC-TV. Later in 1991, Hinojosa joined National Public Radio (NPR) as a New York-based general assignment correspondent, while also hosting *Visiones*, a public affairs talk show on WNBC-TV. With considerable experience as a producer, news reporter, and host, Hinojosa was a perfect fit to anchor *Latino USA*, a weekly national program reporting on news and culture in the Latino community. The show was launched in 1993 as a joint production of KUT, a local NPR affiliate, and the Center for Mexican American Studies at the University of Texas at Austin.

In 1995 Hinojosa was named one of the 100 most influential Latinos in the United States by *Hispanic Business Magazine*. In 1997 Hinojosa moved to CNN as a correspondent for their New York bureau; she continued to host *Latino USA*. In 2005 Hinojosa joined the Emmy-winning PBS news magazine *NOW* as senior correspondent. Hinojosa has also written two books about her experiences. She lives in New York with her family.

See also: Chávez, César; Media

Further reading: Hinojosa, Maria. *Raising Raul: Adventures Raising Myself and My Son*. New York, NY: Viking Penguin, 1999.
http://www.npr.org/about/people/bios/mhinojosa.html
(National Public Radio Web site on Maria Hinojosa).

HINOJOSA, Tish
Singer

Tish Hinojosa is a popular Mexican American singer-songwriter. The winner of several awards, she has a distinctive, sensual voice that appeals to both mainstream audiences and members of the Hispanic community.

Early life
Born in 1955 in San Antonio, Texas, a city near the U.S.-Mexico border, Leticia Hinojosa was the 13th daughter of Mexican immigrant parents. San Antonio lies within a region that formed part of "La Nueva España" (New Spain) until 1836, when it became part of an independent Texas. Thanks to these historical circumstances, and its proximity to the Mexican border, parts of the area remain largely bilingual and bicultural. Hinojosa grew up listening to Mexican songs on the radio as well as local country and rock-'n'-roll music. Her unique style is rooted in these disparate traditions.

Hinojosa began playing the guitar and singing folk and pop songs as a teenager. She played at local clubs and soon gained a considerable local fan base.

The long road to stardom
In 1979 Hinojosa moved to Taos, New Mexico. She sang at the Kerrville Folk Festival later that year, and was one of the winners of the competition. She became a backup singer for musician Michael Martin Murphey. In 1983 Hinojosa moved to Nashville, Tennessee, to concentrate on a solo career as a singer-songwriter, but she could not establish herself there and moved back to Taos in 1984.

In 1988 Hinojosa moved to Austin, Texas. Known as the "capital of live music," Austin is home to a thriving "roots music" culture, which has its origins in the American folk tradition, but also focuses on voices often marginalized in U.S. society: Cajuns from Louisiana, African American blues

▲ *Tish Hinojosa says that it is irrelevant that she sings in both English and Spanish: "There are things in [my] songs beyond the lyrics; passions that come out in the textures."*

singers of the deep South, and southern "Tejano" (Texas Mexican) artists. Hinojosa thrived in this setting. In 1989 A&M Records released her debut album, *Homeland,* to critical acclaim.

Hinojosa's *Culture Swing* (1992) was named Folk Album of the Year by the National Association of Independent Record Distributors. A rapid succession of albums followed, including *Destiny's Gate* (1994), *Frontejas* (1995; the title combines the words *fronteras*, meaning "borders," and *Tejas*, meaning "Texas"), *Dreaming from the Labyrinth* (1996), *Cada Niño* (*Every Child*, 1996), *Sign of Truth* (2000), and *A Heart Wide Open* (2005). *Frontejas* and *Cada Niño* were particularly popular with the U.S. Latino community.

Hinojosa sings about important topical issues, including women's rights and the Latino situation in the United States.

KEY DATES

1955 Born in San Antonio, Texas.

1979 Moves to Taos, New Mexico.

1983 Moves to Nashville, Tennessee.

1989 Releases the acclaimed debut album, *Homeland*.

1995 Releases *Frontejas*; gains further recognition in the Latino community.

Further reading: Burr, Ramiro. *The Billboard Guide to Tejano and Regional Mexican Music.* New York, NY: Billboard Books, 1999.

http://www.mundotish.com (Hinojosa's official Web site).

HINOJOSA DE BALLÍ, Rosa María
Rancher

Few vacationers and spring break revelers to Padre Island off the Gulf coast of Texas know it is named after the Mexican priest José Nicolas Balli, son of Dona Rosa María Hinojosa de Ballí, also known as the "cattle queen" of Texas. Hinojosa de Ballí was the matriarch of the Hinojosa–Ballí family, which controlled one-third of the Rio Grande Valley.

Early life
Born the sixth of nine children in the state of Tamaulipas in 1752, Hinojosa de Ballí was the daughter of Captain Juan José de Hinojosa and María Antonia Inés Ballí de Benavides. Her family were pioneers in the Rio Grande Valley of Texas; her grandfather, Nicolas Ballí Perez, received a large grant of land from the Spanish king Carlos III in 1765. Hinojosa de Ballí's father was the mayor of Reynosa, across the border from present day McAllen, Texas. Hinojosa de Ballí was schooled in Reynosa and later married the captain of the local militia, José María Ballí.

When Hinojosa de Ballí's grandfather and father died, she inherited large tracts of land in what are now south Texas and Mexico. At the time the estates were heavily in debt but Hinojosa de Ballí managed to pay off the debts and make her holdings profitable. A smart businesswoman, she applied to the Spanish Crown for more land grants in the names of her brothers and sons. Hinojosa de Ballí based her operations on her favorite ranch, La Florida, located in present day La Feria in Cameron County, Texas. On her lands Hinojosa de Ballí had large herds of cattle, horses, sheep, and goats. Hinojosa de Ballí became the most influential woman in south Texas because of her land holdings and livestock.

Being a devout Catholic, Hinojosa de Ballí also built private chapels on her ranches and endowed churches in Reynosa, Camargo, and Matamoros, Mexico. When she died in 1803, her more than 1 million acres (404,678ha) of

▲ *This plaque at the entrance of Padre Ballí Park on Padre Island commemorates the Ballí family.*

land covered several South Texas counties: Starr, Hidalgo, Willacy, Cameron, Kenedy, and Padre Island.

Legacy
Ballí's descendents later fought over land and property rights in Kenedy County and Padre Island. They won partial rights to South Padre Island. In Kenedy County possible illegitimate children and heirs to the Ballí estate were arguing their right to the vast holdings in 2005.

Further reading: Krismann, Carol H. *Encyclopedia of American Women in Business: From Colonial Times to the Present.* Westport, CT: Greenwood Press, 2004.
http://www.tsha.utexas.edu/handbook/online/articles/HH/fhi50.html (biography).

KEY DATES	
1752	Born in Tamaulipas, Mexico.
1800	Applies for land grants in her grandson's name.
1803	Dies in Reynosa.

HINOJOSA-SMITH, Rolando
Writer

Since his first work was published in the early 1970s, Rolando Hinojosa-Smith has become a key figure in Chicano literature.

Early life

Rolando Hinojosa-Smith was born in 1927 and raised in Mercedes, Texas, a small town in the Rio Grande Valley on the border with Mexico. His family had lived in the region since the 1740s, when his ancestors were among the recipients of land grants that were given to Hispanic people who were willing to settle along what was then the northern frontier of New Spain. Hinojosa-Smith's father was Mexican American; his mother was of Anglo-American descent. As a boy he attended schools for Mexican children with Mexican teachers, but grew up fluent in English as well as Spanish and at ease in both cultures.

On graduating from high school Hinojosa-Smith enlisted in the U.S. Army for two years, at the end of which period he attended the University of Texas at Austin. After two years of his course Hinojosa-Smith was recalled to active service when the United States entered the Korean War (1950–1953). At the end of the conflict he returned to Austin to finish his degree in Spanish language and literature. He then worked for a time in a factory before taking a job as a high school teacher. In 1960 he began graduate studies at Highlands University in New Mexico. He took an MA in Spanish literature before deciding to switch schools. Hinojosa-Smith enrolled at the University of Illinois at Urbana, where he completed a doctorate in Spanish literature in 1969. He spent the next few years writing and teaching at Trinity University in San Antonio, Texas, and at Texas A & I University in Kingsville. In 1976 he was appointed chair of Chicano studies at the University of Minnesota. He remained there until 1981, when he became professor of English and creative writing at his alma mater, the University of Texas at Austin.

Writing career

Hinojosa-Smith has written an extensive range of critical works that have firmly established his reputation in the world of literary academe. His broader fame, however, is founded on the "Klail City Death Trip" series, 13 short novels that follow the fortunes of several generations of Americans and Mexican Americans. The fictional setting bears a strong resemblance to the region in which the

▲ *Rolando Hinojosa-Smith has helped bring Chicano literature to a wider audience than ever before.*

author himself grew up. The works are plainly influenced by early 20th-century folklorists, and are in part an attempt to record the historic cultural traditions of the Rio Grande Valley. The main theme, however, is relations between Mexican Americans and European Americans on the border between Texas and Mexico. Hinojosa-Smith's prose is terse and spare, with few adjectives; his style has been likened to that of Ernest Hemingway. He sets the scene and advances the story by means of brief sketches or snapshots rather than a conventional linear narrative. In the Klail City books there is no omniscient authorial voice: Hinojosa-Smith writes from various characters' points of view, and creates nebulous, or vague, plots that may be disorienting at the outset but are cumulatively atmospheric.

The first title in the series, *Estampas del valle y otras obras*, was originally published in 1972. It won that year's Premio Quinto Sol, the premier national award for Chicano

INFLUENCES AND INSPIRATION

The work of Rolando Hinojosa-Smith is influenced by that of numerous earlier novelists, but the most frequently drawn comparisons are with William Faulkner (1897–1962) and Ernest Hemingway (1899–1961).

His contemporaries inspired him, too, especially Tomás Rivera (1935–1984) and Rudolfo Anaya (born 1927). Hinojosa-Smith first came into contact with them through Quinto Sol, the publishing house based in Berkeley, California, that promoted Chicano writers at the height of the civil rights movement in the 1960s. Rivera in particular encouraged Hinojosa-Smith to submit his work for publication. Both authors were from Texas, had academic training, and wrote in similar styles, primarily in Spanish, although Hinojosa-Smith would later rewrite several of his works in English. Rivera won the Premio Quinto Sol in 1970; two years later his slightly older protégé took the same award.

KEY DATES

1927	Born in Mercedes, Texas, on January 29.
1947	Enrolls at University of Texas at Austin.
1950	Serves in Korean War.
1969	Completes doctorate in Spanish at University of Illinois at Urbana.
1972	Publishes first novel in "Klail City Death Trip" series.
1981	Is appointed professor of English and Creative Writing at University of Texas at Austin.
2006	Publishes *We Happy Few*.

literature. An English-language edition of the novel appeared shortly afterward under the title *Sketches of the Valley and Other Works*. Hinojosa-Smith was not satisfied with it, however, feeling that it lacked what he called the "flavor" of the original. Mindful that many Spanish idioms and thought processes cannot be rendered satisfactorily in English, he produced a new rendition, rather than a translation, which was published in 1983 as *The Valley*.

The series continues

Hinojosa-Smith's second novel, *Klail City y sus alrededores*, was first published in Spanish in 1976, and won that year's international Premio Casa de las Américas award. It appeared in English in 1987 under the title *Klail City*. The pivotal volume of the series, it again relies on the technique of sketches, and introduces dozens of new characters. Each story offers alternating, and often apparently contradictory, descriptions of the Klail City community, yet the characters and stories remain consistent throughout. The other volumes of the series that have appeared in English are *Rites and Witnesses*

(1982), *Partners in Crime* (1985), *Fair Gentlemen of Belken County* (1986), *Becky and Her Friends* (1990), and *We Happy Few* (2006).

Trailblazer

Rolando Hinojosa-Smith's writing helped pave the way for subsequent Chicano writers by awakening the U.S. reading public to the American Latino community. His works have contributed significantly to the transformation of Chicano fiction from a provincial curiosity into an influential mainstream force by asserting the Chicano's place within American society. Juan Rodríguez of Texas Lutheran University has described the work of Hinojosa-Smith as "middle-class stories in a working-class tradition," and the author himself as "sandwiched" between Américo Paredes and Tomás Rivera. Another literature professor, Jaime Mejía of Texas State University at San Marcos, holds the Klail City series in high esteem, asserting that "No other works by an American author to date accomplish as significant or as expansive a project." Yet the Klail City novels have a strong appeal to a general audience, not merely to Hinojosa-Smith's fellow academics. The *New York Times* has called him "a writer for all readers."

In 1998 Rolando Hinojosa-Smith was honored with a Lifetime Achievement Award by the Texas Institute of Letters and an Alumni Achievement Award by the University of Illinois at Urbana. He still teaches at the University of Texas at Austin.

See also: Anaya, Rudolfo; Paredes, Américo; Rivera, Tomás

Further reading: Zilles, Klaus. *Rolando Hinojosa: A Reader's Guide*. Albuquerque, NM: University of New Mexico Press, 2001.
http://www.austinchronicle.com/issues/vol16/issue52/books.hinojosa.html (interview with the author about his works).

HISPANIC IDENTITY AND POPULAR CULTURE

In the last 50 years or so, the Hispanic population in the United States has grown significantly. In 2004, there were more than 41 million Hispanics in the country (about 14 percent of the total U.S. population). About 31 million of the total spoke Spanish at home, while about 15 million claimed to speak English well. The U.S. Hispanic population is made up of people from a range of countries and cultures: In 2004, more than 64 percent of them were of Mexican origin, about 10 percent were of Puerto Rican descent, and a further 3 percent were of Cuban, Salvadoran, and Dominican origin, while the remainder claimed other Central American, South American, or mixed Latino heritage. These diverse groups have contributed to the development of a complex Hispanic identity and culture.

In the United States, Hispanic popular culture has been central to the ways in which Latinos and Latinas are perceived by other communities, and also how they perceive themselves. Popular culture is reflected in many aspects of daily life, including advertising, music, film, fashion, radio, and the arts.

Changing perceptions
Popular culture changes over time, but one constant has been the creation of ethnic stereotypes. The most common representations of Hispanics have included the *bandido* or revolutionary; the *campesino* or peasant; the criminal or drug lord; the Latina vamp ("hot tamale"), Latin lover, and spitfire (*see box on page 108*); the lovable buffoon with an almost incomprehensible Hispanic accent; and the delinquent or gang member.

The media often used these images to reinforce the prejudices of white mainstream society, sometimes with fatal consequences. One example occurred in the 1940s, when many young Mexicans began to wear loose-fitting "zoot suits," also popular among African Americans. Some West Coast newspapers reported that these zoot suiters, or *pachucos*, were responsible for many of society's ills, such as juvenile delinquency, prostitution, and drugs. Tensions between white West Coast servicemen and the zoot suiters reached a climax in 1943. In the week-long series of riots that followed in Los Angeles, California, many Mexicans were injured or killed. The riots often featured the ritualistic stripping of the zoot suiters. Luis Valdéz later wrote about the riots in his popular play and movie, *Zoot Suit*.

In the last 40 years of the 20th century, many popular images of Latinos were challenged. Civil rights movements, such as the Chicano and women's rights movements, the introduction of positive discrimination in favor of Latinos, protective legislation, and the introduction of cultural

Actor and playwright Luis Valdéz (center), flanked by his brother Daniel (right) and an actor, stands in front of the Broadway theater where the play Zoot Suit *was staged in 1978.*

awareness programs have helped create more positive images of Hispanics, who as a group have become more prominent in every sector of U.S. society.

Fairer representation

Increasingly, negative racial stereotypes have been replaced by more representative images of Hispanics in the media and society at large. Hispanics have been able to create a much more complex and nuanced vision of their lives in popular culture, focusing on key issues such as family, cultural identity, language, education, work, politics, and different aspects of nationality. Hispanic food, especially Mexican food, has become an accepted part of U.S. culture. Similarly, the lowrider (an automobile or truck that has had its suspension system modified to ride as close to the ground as possible), once seen as unique to Chicano culture, is now an accepted part of West Coast hip-hop culture.

The late 20th century marked a turning point in Hispanic popular culture, as "Latinization" became a trend in mainstream U.S. culture and a lucrative market opportunity that was difficult to ignore. Non-Hispanics went to clubs to dance and listen to Latin music. Artists such as Jennifer Lopez, Enrique Iglesias, and Christina Aguilera became superstars, selling millions of records listened to by Latin and white audiences alike. Actors, such as Cameron Diaz and Salma Hayek, regularly cast in lead roles in Hollywood movies, became box-office draws. International audiences also go to see films that celebrate Latin history and culture, by such directors as Robert

Rodríguez (*El Mariachi*) and Salma Hayek, whose biopic of the Mexican artist Frida Kahlo received several Oscar nominations.

Despite such cultural advances, some critics argue that Latinos are still not fairly represented in the media. In 2004 Angel Rivera, the Screen Actors Guild's national director of affirmative action and diversity, stated that Latino performers had seen their share of roles fall below their representation in the population.

The *mestizo* and identity

The negative representation of Hispanics in popular culture originated in the 16th century, when Spanish settlers moved to Central and Latin America. Most of the settlers were men, and interracial relationships were common, initially between the Spanish and Native Americans, and later between both groups and people of African origin. The offspring of such relationships were known as *mestizos*, from the Spanish meaning products of a

Musician, actor, and cultural icon Jennifer Lopez is one of the most successful Latinas in the United States. A role model for millions, Lopez launched a brand of clothing and fragrances in 2005.

racial mixture. The first mestizos were considered essential to the survival of the Spanish colonies, but over the years, as more Europeans settled in these regions, a hierarchy evolved based on race and skin color. Those born in Spain or to Spanish parents were given the highest status, while those with the most obvious levels of Native American or black blood were designated a lower position in the social order.

In the 19th century, increasing numbers of immigrants from Latin America settled in the United States, particularly after the 1848 Treaty of Guadalupe Hidalgo, which ceded more than 50 percent of Mexican territory to the United States. Many white people viewed Hispanics as racially inferior; their children were sent to separate schools and the speaking of Spanish was discouraged and often punished. Hispanic intellectuals and activists began to organize into groups to fight for better rights and to retain their native language and cultures; some embraced the idea of the *mestizaje* as the foundation of a Latino *fraternidad*, or brotherhood.

As early as the 1890s, the Cuban writer and intellectual José Martí declared that there was no racial hatred in "*mestizo* America because there are no races." José Vasconcelos also used the idea of the *mestizaje* to create common ground between culturally and racially diverse Hispanic groups. The idea was taken up by various civil rights movements in the 20th century, including the Chicano movement in *El Plan Espiritual de Aztlán* (1969), which celebrated the idea of the mestizo and the notion of a "bronze nation." The Chicano movement, and other such movements, promoted the celebration of Latin culture and identity, just as the black civil rights movement had for African Americans.

Broadcasting and music

Historically, Hispanic music has had a great influence on U.S. culture. Immigrants to the United States brought with them a range of musical styles, from *norteño* and salsa to *corridos* and *cumbias*. Hispanic musicians performed their native songs to non-Latino audiences, passing on information about their native history and cultures and keeping the Spanish language alive.

Discouraged from speaking Spanish in schools and in the workplace, many Hispanics began to tune in to the Spanish-language radio stations that emerged in the 1920s and 1930s in the U.S. Southwest. The stations not only featured Spanish-language music, but also news and public-information programming, discussing issues of key interest to their communities, such as segregation and the forced repatriation of Mexicans, some of whom were U.S. citizens.

One of the most influential musicians and broadcasters of the 1930s was Pedro J. González, who performed with Los Madrugadores. The band sang a range of folk and contemporary Mexican *canciones* and *corridos*. González used his radio show to promote social justice issues. He had such a large following among the Los Angeles Spanish-speaking community that local officials claimed he was a threat to mainstream white America. After being accused of rape, González was sent to prison, although the victim later revealed that the broadcaster had been set up.

Other important Spanish-language networks emerged in the postwar period, such as the Hispanic Broadcasting System (1949) and the Spanish Broadcasting System (1960). Some commentators took the stations as evidence that Hispanics are an important part of U.S. popular culture. Yet by the early 21st century, *Latino USA*, distributed by National Public Radio (NPR), was the only English-language radio program for Latinos.

In contrast, however, a large number of Hispanic musicians emerged and became influential in the 20th century. Musicians such as Flaco Jiménez, big-band leaders such as Xavier Cugat and Tito Puente, and singer Desi Arnaz became big stars. Some forged relationships with U.S. musicians, playing and recording with such legends as Charlie Parker, and

KEY DATES

1848	Treaty of Guadalupe Hidalgo signed.
1890s	José Martí and other intellectuals promote pride in Latino heritage.
1933	Good Neighbor Policy introduced to improve relations with Latin America; more Latinos/as cast in movies.
1943	Zoot Suit Riots break out on the West Coast.
1950	Puerto Rican actor José Ferrer wins an Oscar for *Cyrano de Bergerac*.
1951	*I Love Lucy* airs.
1959	Ritchie Valens has hit with "La Bamba"; dies in air crash.
1961	*West Side Story* wins several Oscars; Rita Moreno becomes the first Latina to win an Academy Award (for best supporting actress).
1978	Luis Valdéz's play *Zoot Suit* is produced on Broadway.
1998	Big Pun becomes first Latino solo rapper to achieve a platinum record.
2000	Latin Grammys launched.
2003	*Frida* receives nine Oscar nominations.

In the 1950s Desi Arnaz played opposite his real wife, Lucille Ball, in the hugely successful TV series I Love Lucy. *Arnaz was a successful musician and actor.*

infusing jazz and other music genres with new energy and exciting rhythms.

Crossover stars

Played by local DJs and recorded by independent record labels, some Latino and Latina stars crossed over to become popular with young white Americans. Ritchie Valens, the first Chicano rock 'n' roll star, had a big hit with "La Bamba," a reworking of a traditional Mexican folk song. Valens appeared on *The Dick Clark Show* before his early death in the 1959 plane crash that killed singer Buddy Holly.

By the 1960s, country artists such as Freddie Fender, folk singers such as Joan Baez, pop artists such as Trini López, rock stars such as Carlos Santana, and *salseros* such as Celia Cruz were all popular stars in the United States. Most acquired a fan base among both Spanish- and English-speaking audiences. The trend continued with the next generation of artists,

such as Los Lobos, Gloria Estefan, and the Miami Sound Machine, Ricky Martin, and Jennifer Lopez, all of whom popularized Latin music and made it acceptable for Hispanic stars to sing and record in Spanish. As the musicians' fame increased, so did their ability to move into other media, such as film.

Hispanic artists also began to emerge as stars in music genres not immediately associated with Latinos, such as hip-hop (*see box*). Incorporating their own rhythms, cultural references, and language into their songs, musicians and DJs such as Cypress Hill, Big Pun, and Fat Joe became popular with

Latino and non-Hispanic rap fans, influencing how they spoke, acted, and dressed.

Visual representation

At the same time that music was helping change the way Hispanics were viewed by other cultural groups and the way they viewed themselves, racial stereotypes were being both enforced and challenged in film, TV, and theater.

Since the Hollywood silent era, Hispanic actors have been marginalized, playing stereotypical roles such as the buffoon or bandit, while non-Hispanic actors were often cast as Latin characters. The Hays Code prevented the

LATIN RAP

Hispanics have been involved in the hip-hop scene since the 1970s. Several Puerto Ricans were MCs, breakdancers (Rock Steady Crew), and graffiti artists. In the 1980s, Chicano producers, such as Tony G, and rappers, such as Kid Frost, came to the forefront of the genre. They created a distinctive form of hip-hop that fused Latino street

vernacular with break beats and elements of rhythm and blues and Mexican traditional songs. Cuban rapper Sen Dog formed the leading Los Angeles-based rap group Cypress Hill. Low Profile Records helped San Diego become the second biggest Chicano rap scene, with artists such as Lil' Rob and Aztec Tribe. In the 1990s, Puerto Rican

rappers began to take precedence: New Yorkers Fat Joe and the Terror Squad and Big Pun, whose album *Capital Punishment* went double platinum, dominated Latino rap. Daddy Yankee and Ivy Queen were among the musicians to popularize reggaeton, which fuses hip-hop with elements of many Latin music genres.

LATIN LOVERS AND LATINA VAMPS

Among the most often seen Hispanic stereotypes on the Hollywood screen in the early 20th century were those of the Latin lover, vamp, or spitfire. Seen as suave, passionate, and heroic, Latin lovers were most often Spanish or South American and were frequently played by non-Hispanic actors, including the Italian Rudolph Valentino in *The Four Horsemen of the Apocalypse*, and U.S. screen idol Douglas Fairbanks in *The Mark of Zorro*.

In the 1930s Carmen Miranda, Lupe Velez, and Dolores del Rio emerged as the leading Latina Hollywood vamps. Brazilian-born Miranda was known for her colorful costumes, fruit-laden headwear, and broken English (in reality she spoke English perfectly).

Mexican-born beauty Velez was most often cast in her short career as a Latina vamp or Mexican spitfire. Del Rio fared slightly better, however. Known for her sultry looks and often cast as a Latina temptress, the Mexican-born aristocrat eventually returned to her native country to star in Spanish-language films. Del Rio became a national hero in Mexico.

---

depiction of interracial romance on the screen until the 1950s. Instead, Latinas such as Carmen Miranda or Lupe Velez often played "hot tamales" in movies. Latin lovers were alluring but were not usually played by Hispanics. The stereotypes and restrictions would be picked up by Latinos of later generations and mocked in comedies that they themselves had directed, as for example in the work of Cheech Marín.

In the 1930s, President Franklin D. Roosevelt introduced the Good Neighbor Policy to encourage a more positive and economically beneficial relationship with Latin America. In October 1940, Nelson Rockefeller became head of the new Office of the Coordinator for Inter-American Affairs (CIAA), and John Hay Whitney headed the agency's Motion Picture Division. In addition to improving the representation of Latinos in U.S. films and encouraging U.S. films with Latin American topics, such as Disney's popular *Saludos Amigos* (1942) and Orson Welles's unfinished film *It's All True* (1942), the CIAA fostered the exchange of talent between Mexico and the United States.

Actors with pale skin and Anglo features were able to cross over to appear in mainstream Hollywood movies. Puerto Rican-born José Ferrer was among the actors who benefited from the opening up of more interesting roles for Latino actors: Ferrer won an Oscar for his performance as the French character Cyrano de Bergerac in 1950. Rita Hayworth also regularly appeared opposite A-list Hollywood male stars such as Cary Grant, often cast as an all-American girl such as Judy MacPherson in Howard Hawks's *Only Angels Have Wings* (1939). However, mainstream white actors were still often chosen to play Hispanic roles, darkening their skin, eyes, or hair to appear more authentic. While 1950s' audiences were tuning in to see Desi Arnaz and his American wife, Lucille Ball, in the TV comedy *I Love Lucy,* at the same time in the cinema they

Lupe Velez was a popular Hollywood movie star of the 1930s and 1940s, often typecast in Latin spitfire and vamp roles.

HISPANIC IDENTITY AND POPULAR CULTURE

watched a heavily made-up Charlton Heston play Ramon Miguel "Mike" Vargas in Orson Welles's movie *A Touch of Evil* (1958). Similarly, audiences watched pale-skinned, dark-eyed Anglo-American Natalie Wood play the Puerto Rican Maria in the movie version of *West Side Story.*

West Side Story was important in changing the way Hispanics were represented and perceived in the United States. Based on William Shakespeare's *Romeo and Juliet,* it examined racism among the immigrant communities and gangs in New York. Rita Moreno, who played Anita in the movie version, also showed that Hispanic actors were being taken seriously when she became the first Latina to win an Oscar.

In the 1960s, the Chicano movement led Latinos to take more responsibility for the way in which they were perceived in art and literature. Prominent in the new movement was Luis Valdéz, who made one of the first Chicano documentary films, *Yo Soy Joaquin* (1969), a visual celebration of Corky Gonzáles's epic poem of the same name.

Although Desi Arnaz had been the first Latino to achieve commercial television success through *I Love Lucy* and Desilu, the company he co-owned with Lucille Ball, for the most part Latino TV actors still appeared as bandidos in Westerns such as *Bonanza* or as modern-day gang members or drug lords in *The Rockford Files* and *Hill Street Blues*. In the 1970s, *Chico and the Man*, starring Freddie Prinze, stood out. However, even though it focused on life in the barrio, Prinze's character was still a stereotype, a lovable

buffoon, with a thick accent and a big mustache.

From the 1980s, Latinos and Latinas began appearing as token characters on popular TV shows such as *Miami Vice* and *ER*. They also became more visible on public affairs programs. Latino-themed feature films, such as *Stand and Deliver* and *The Milagro Beanfield War*, were also released during this time, opening the doors for later filmmakers such as Robert Rodríguez and Lourdes Portillo to make Hispanic-themed movies and documentaries in the future.

Spanish-language television also became important. Major networks include the Spanish International Network (SIN), started in 1955, which became Univisión in 1987; Telemundo, founded in 1986; and Azteca America, founded in 2000. In 2001, NBC and its parent company, General Electric (GE), bought Telemundo for $2.7 billion. It became the first English-language network to invest in Spanish-language television, signifying how important Spanish-language audiences are in the United States.

Visual art has been a key feature of U.S. Latino communities. The mural was a popular way to bring art to the people and present important cultural stories. The Mexican mural movement in the early 20th century was an inspiration, not only to Mexicans, but to other Latinos as well. Chicanos adapted the medium in the 1960s, as did Puerto Ricans in Chicago and New York.

Posters and almanac/calendar (*almanaques*) art were another avenue for artistic expression. Loyal customers at Latino businesses were given calendars with Aztec gods or virgin mothers;

they often stayed up on the walls of family homes for years as an affordable form of art. Poster art was also an important medium for artists. Protests, concerts, and meetings provided the opportunity to create art and distribute it widely.

Murals and posters paved the way for the inclusion of Latino art in major galleries. Artists moved beyond oils and inks to create sculpture, mosaics, carvings, and prints. Galleries specifically devoted to Hispanic art opened; examples include the Mexican Fine Art Museum in Chicago, El Museo del Barrio in New York, and Self-Help Graphics in Los Angeles.

Conclusion

As the U.S. Hispanic community has grown, achieving greater rights and status, its influence on popular culture has also increased. This has enabled it to challenge existing negative stereotypes and to create more accurate representations of racial and cultural identity.

See also: Aguilera, Christina; Arnaz, Desi; Baez, Joan; Big Pun; Cruz, Celia; Cypress Hill; Daddy Yankee; Del Rio, Dolores; Diaz, Cameron; Estefan, Gloria; Fat Joe; Ferrer, José; Gonzáles, Corky; González, Pedro J.; Hayworth, Rita; Iglesias, Enrique; Jiménez, Flaco; Lopez, Jennifer; López, Trini; Martí, José; ; Miranda, Carmen; Moreno, Rita; Prinze, Freddie; Puente, Tito; Queen, Ivy; Rodríguez, Robert; Valdéz, Luis; Valens, Ritchie; Velez, Lupe

---

Further reading: Habell-Pallan, Michelle, and Mary Romero (eds.). *Latino/a Popular Culture.* New York, NY: New York University Press, 2002. http://latino.si.edu/ (Smithsonian Latino Center).

HOMAR, Lorenzo
Graphic Artist

Arguably the most influential Hispanic artist known to have worked in the silkscreen medium, Puerto Rican-born Lorenzo Homar created posters and drawings that elevated Puerto Rican graphic arts to a new level of sophistication. He influenced generations of students and graphic designers with his distinctive and exquisite lettering and bold images, illustrating the texts of such writers as Pablo Neruda and Julia de Burgos.

Early life

Born in 1913 to Spanish parents, Homar grew up in Puerta de Tierra, a barrio outside San Juan, Puerto Rico. His father, Lorenzo Homar Zampol, was an art and social events promoter, and his mother, Margarita Gelabert, was an accomplished pianist. They encouraged Homar's artistic interests as he grew up. Seeking greater opportunity in America, Homar's parents moved the family from Puerto Rico to New York City in 1928. However, the family struggled, and Homar was forced to leave Dewit Clinton School to help support them by working in a textile factory.

Resuming his education in 1931, Homar, who was a talented artist, attended the respected Art Students League of New York, where he studied under the famous anatomist George Bridgeman. In 1937 he attended Pratt Institute and apprenticed as a designer with the renowned Cartier jewelers. Following the outbreak of World War II (1939–1945), Homar served in the U.S. Army. After being wounded in combat, he received a Purple Heart. He returned to work at Cartier in 1946. Determined to refine his artistic techniques, Homar attended the Brooklyn School of Art before returning to Puerto Rico in 1950.

Back in Puerto Rico

Shortly after his arrival in Puerto Rico, Homar joined other Puerto Rican artists, including José Antonio Torres Martinó, to establish the Centro de Arte Puertorriqueño (the Puerto Rican Arts Center). Two years later, he became director of the graphic workshop of the Institute of Puerto Rican Culture, the most important school of its kind in Puerto Rico. Over the next 15 years, he produced more than 500 posters and several portfolios of screenprints, such as *Casals Portfolio* (1970), which were admired for their distinctive style and sophisticated technique. Homar became a prolific and versatile craftsman, whose graphic output encompassed everything from screenprinted

KEY DATES

1913 Born in San Juan, Puerto Rico.

1928 Family moves to New York City.

1931 Studies under famous anatomist George Bridgeman at the Art Students League of New York.

1937 Begins apprenticeship as a designer at Cartier; attends Pratt Institute.

1950 Returns to San Juan; cofounds the Centro de Arte Puertorriqueño (the Puerto Rican Arts Center); begins his career as a graphic artist.

1975 Establishes his own studio.

2003 Awarded the National Medal of Honor by the Institute of Puerto Rican culture.

2004 Dies on February 16.

posters, woodcuts, and engravings to political cartoons, book illustrations, logos, and stage designs. He stayed at the center until 1975, when he established his own studio.

A great influence

Credited as the artist most responsible for promoting printmaking in Puerto Rico, Homar organized workshops abroad to share his typographic methods with a new generation of Latin American artists, some of whom became influential in their own right. He exhibited his work at Princeton University in 1983, when he was a visiting printmaker there.

Toward the end of Homar's life, the Metropolitan Museum of Art purchased a number of his works. He was also awarded a doctorate "honoris causa" by the University of Puerto Rico. In 2003 he was given the National Medal of Honor by the Institute of Puerto Rican Culture. In 2004, surrounded by his family, Homar died. As Homar's ashes were scattered off the shores of San Juan, his family tossed roses into the sea.

See also: De Burgos, Julia

Further reading: http://www.atelier-rc.com/Atelier. RC/LHomar.html (Web site featuring biographical information and examples of Lorenzo Homar's work).

HOSTOS, Eugenio María de
Writer, Activist, Educator

Considered by many a key figure in Latin American literature, Eugenio María de Hostos was a philosopher, teacher, writer, sociologist, and journalist. He was an activist in the Puerto Rican independence movement, and lobbied for the rights of women and minorities.

Early life

Hostos was born on January 11, 1839, in the rural village of Río Cañas, Mayagüez, a city on the west coast of Puerto Rico. He began his studies at the Liceo de San Juan, where he received the award for best math student in 1847. In 1852, his parents, Eugenio María de Hostos and María Hilaria Bonilla, sent him to complete his schooling in Spain. After finishing high school at the Institute for Secondary Education in Bilbao, Hostos went to the University of Madrid School of Law in 1858. Dissatisfied with the teaching methods at the university and with the unstable political situation in Spain at the time, Hostos decided not to continue with his law career. He chose to join fellow Puerto Ricans who were agitating for the abolition of slavery and the independence of Cuba and Puerto Rico from Spain.

Influential activist

While in Spain, Hostos collaborated on the publication of various newspaper articles in Madrid and Barcelona. He also wrote his first novel, *La peregrinación de Bayoán* (The Journey of a Puerto Rican, 1863), a sociopolitical work that openly criticized Spanish colonialism in America. He would later publish *Viaje a la América Latina* (Journey to Latin America), in which he described the natural wonders of Argentina, Brazil, Chile, and Panama. Hostos became a member of the Sociedad Abolicionista de la Esclavitud (an abolitionist organization), and a leading member of the Ateneo de Madrid (Madrid Athenaeum).

In 1869, having been disappointed by the election of Spain's new president, Emelio Castelar, Hostos immigrated to New York City, where he spent a year helping immigrant Cubans in their struggle for Cuban and Puerto Rican independence. He became a member of the Cuban Revolutionary Junta, edited its official newsletter, *La Revolución*, and coedited *América Ilustrada* (1874).

From 1870 to 1874, Hostos toured Latin America raising support for the abolition of slavery in Cuba and Puerto Rico. During this period, he worked on various

▲ *Eugenio María de Hostos fought for the independence of Spain's American colonies.*

newspapers, becoming a well-known figure internationally. While in Chile, Hostos became a member of the Academia de Bellas Artes in the capital, Santiago, and the first person to advocate for the rights of women in science education. Hostos later published several works, including *Hamlet* (1873), a critical essay on Shakespeare's play that is widely regarded as the finest work of its kind in Spanish. In Argentina, Hostos initiated a project to build a railroad system that would cross the Andes. Hostos also spoke out against the exploitation of Chinese immigrants in Peru.

Further travels

In 1875, Hostos moved to the Dominican Republic and then settled in Venezuela, where he met and married Belinda de Ayala. He founded and directed the newspapers *Las Tres Antillas* and *Los Antillanos*, and collaborated on *Las Dos Antillas*. In 1878, Hostos published *Cuentos a mi hijo* (Stories for My Son), in which he described the

---

LEGACY

Eugenio María de Hostos's influence as a writer, social activist, and educator continues to this day. His moral strength, passionate idealism, and personal magnetism are well remembered, and his writings—more than 50 titles—are still read throughout the Spanish-speaking world. Commemorating the centennial of his birth, the government of Puerto Rico published *Obras Completas (Edición Crítica, Eugenio María de Hostos)*— Hostos's complete works—in 20 volumes. Hostos even wrote his own epitaph, which reads: "I wish that they will say: In that island [Puerto Rico] a man was born who loved truth, desired justice, and worked for the good of men."

---

experience of becoming a father. That same year, he temporarily interrupted his anticolonial political activism to take a teaching post in the Dominican Republic.

Teaching reformer

For the next nine years, Hostos worked on reforming education, establishing the Dominican Republic's first pedagogy (teaching) school in 1880. Many of his teaching methods were widely adopted, and some of his writings on the subject became university textbooks. In his principal work, *Lecciones de Derecho Constitucional* (Lectures on Constitutional Right, 1887), he discusses his philosophy of law and its applications in American contexts. In *Moral Social* (1888), he sets out his position on ethics. Hostos also collaborated on various newspapers and magazines, such as *Revista Científica, Literaria y de Conocimientos Utiles*; *Eco de la Opinión*; and *Telégrafo*.

Hostos continued his educational career in Chile, where he was chosen by President José Manuel Balmaceda to direct the Miguel Luis Amunátegui high school. He taught courses in geography and constitutional law at the University of Santiago, and collaborated with other institutions as a journalist and a writer. During his stay in Chile, Hostos published *Geografía Evolutiva* (Evolutionary Geography, 1895) and *Cartas públicas acerca de Cuba* (Public Maps of Cuba, 1895).

After Puerto Rico became a territory of the United States in 1898, as a result of that year's Spanish–American War, Hostos felt the need to return to his native island and to raise Puerto Rican support for independence. Hostos traveled to Washington, D.C., as leader of a commission, along with Julio Henna and Manuel Zeno Gandía, to lobby for the rights of Puerto Ricans. Discovering that the U.S. government was not going to relinquish control over the island, Hostos decided to move back to the Dominican Republic, where he spent the rest of his days.

Lasting legacy

Eugenio María de Hostos died on August 11, 1903, in Santo Domingo, Dominican Republic. He had made a remarkable contribution to achieving the political independence of the Spanish colonies in the Caribbean and securing the rights of women. His writings embraced a wide range of subjects, including politics, pedagogy, sociology, philosophy, ethics, biography, law, and history. He further demonstrated his talents through the genres of poetry, critical essays, novel, journalism, short stories, and theater. As part of an agreement at the eighth America International Conference, held in Peru in 1938, Hostos was officially proclaimed a "Citizen of America" for his lifelong fight for liberty and for his dedication to educational leadership in Latin America.

See also: Zeno Gandía, Manuel

Further reading: Hostos, Eugenio Carlos de (ed.) *Eugenio María de Hostos, Promoter of Pan Americanism.* Madrid, Spain: Juan Bravo, 1954.
Palmer, Joy A., Liora Bresler, and David Edward Cooper (eds.). *Fifty Major Thinkers on Education: From Confucius to Dewey.* New York, NY: Routledge, 2003.
http://www.hostos.cuny.edu/library/Hostos%20Page/Index.html (biography and criticism).

KEY DATES

1839 Born in Mayagüez, Puerto Rico, on January 11.

1863 Publishes his first work, *La peregrinación de Bayoán,* which sets his social and political tone.

1868 Delivers a famous anti-Spanish colonialism speech at the Ateneo de Madrid on December 20.

1880 Founds Escuela Normal (a teacher's college) in the Dominican Republic.

1902 Becomes the Dominican Republic's Director General de Enseñanza (Director General of Education).

1903 Dies in Las Marías, Santo Domingo, on August 11.

HUERTA, Dolores
Labor Leader

Dolores Huerta was one of the founders and the first vice president of the United Farm Workers (UFW), which was formed in the early 1960s. Although her contribution to the labor organization is sometimes described as less important than that of its president, César Chávez, their roles were much more equal than their titles suggest. Huerta was a fiery character who represented nontraditional U.S. Latina women, and became the union's chief negotiator. Her presence alongside Chávez influenced, shaped, and guided the organization's development.

Early life
Huerta was born Dolores Fernández in 1930 in the small mining town of Dawson, New Mexico. Her parents, Juan Fernández and Alicia Chávez, were both born in New Mexico, where her mother's family had resided since the area was still part of Mexico. Following her parents' divorce, she moved with her mother to Stockton, California, where Alicia Chávez bought a small hotel (*see box on page 114*) that catered to farmworkers and working-class Mexicans and Mexican Americans. Fernández graduated from Stockton High School in the mid-1940s, after which she enrolled at Stockton Junior College. She qualified as a teacher, a remarkable achievement for a young Mexican American woman in the early 1950s. She was twice married, first to Ralph Head, and then to Ventura Huerta. Both marriages ended in divorce, but she retained her second husband's name.

▲ *In collaboration with César Chávez, Dolores Huerta helped change the lives of millions of workers from ethnic minorities, especially female workers.*

Huerta then taught the children of farmworkers. In her spare time, she became a social activist and labor organizer. In the mid-1950s, she met Fred Ross, who had developed the Community Service Organization (CSO) for Mexican Americans in Stockton. The CSO was an organization that encouraged the political participation of Mexican Americans through voting. Greatly impressed by Ross's commitment to the Mexican community, Huerta soon joined him in his efforts to register Mexican American voters. She also helped him teach citizenship classes to Mexican immigrants.

From CSO to Farm Workers Association
In 1961, Huerta went to Sacramento, California, to work as a lobbyist for the CSO. She campaigned for legislation that provided rights for Spanish-speaking and poor workers and their families. It was during this time that she met César Chávez, head of the local chapter of the CSO in San Jose, California. By 1962, Huerta had become convinced that Chávez's plan to organize field workers into a union could work. They both quit the CSO, and began organizing agricultural workers in California's Central Valley. They founded the Farm Workers Association (FWA), which in 1965 became the National Farm Workers Association (NFWA), and later the United Farm Workers (UFW) union.

KEY DATES

1930   Born in Dawson, New Mexico, on April 10.

1962   Forms the Farm Workers Association (FWA), the predecessor to the National Farm Workers Association (NFWA) and the United Farm Workers union (UFW), alongside César Chávez.

1988   Severely beaten by San Francisco police at a peaceful demonstration against the presidential candidate George H. W. Bush.

1993   Inducted into the National Women's Hall of Fame.

1998   Selected as one of three women of the year by *Ms. Magazine*; receives the Eleanor Roosevelt Award.

INFLUENCES AND INSPIRATION

The most influential figure in the early life of Dolores Huerta was her mother, Alicia Chávez Fernández. After leaving her husband in the mid-1930s, Chávez Fernández moved her family from New Mexico to Stockton, California, where she became the successful owner of a small hotel and restaurant. The money she earned enabled her to provide her children with financial security and the chance of a good education. Huerta later said: "My mother was one of those women who do a lot. She was divorced, so I never really understood what it meant for a woman to take a back seat to a man."

Having experienced racial prejudice as a young woman, and witnessed the poverty of her pupils while she was teaching, Huerta determined to combat both. CSO founder Fred Ross showed her the potential for good in social activism, and César Chávez convinced her that the way forward was through collective action by workers. She recalled: "When César told me, 'I'm going to start my own union,' I was just appalled, the thought was so overwhelming. But when the initial shock wore off, I thought it was exciting."

In 1964, at Chávez's request, Huerta moved to Delano, California. There, in the following year, she became involved in the Delano grape strike, a labor boycott by Mexican workers to protest low pay and bad working conditions. In her role as picket captain, Huerta laid the foundation for the FWA's bookkeeping system, and set up a hiring hall. In 1966, the Schenley Corporation was the first large grape grower to sign with the union. Huerta took charge of negotiating the contract with the company. The grape strike spread to other parts of the United States, and lasted five years. Huerta was a leading activist throughout, directing the actions and raising money for the workers by speaking at lunches and dinners.

Although César Chávez could have turned to other male union leaders for advice, above all he relied on Dolores Huerta. For more than 35 years, Huerta was Chávez's closest associate.

Throughout the 1970s, Huerta coordinated strikes for the UFW on the East Coast. In the 1980s, she organized KUFW, the union's new radio station. She also testified before the U.S. Congress against grower-supported requests to bring temporary "guest-workers" into the United States.

The role of women

Huerta was influential in developing the role of women in the UFW. One of her greatest advantages was her ability to emphasize the difficulties faced by female farmworkers and their children. She believed that, in most Mexican families, it was the women who decided whether to support the union. She also argued that the active involvement of women and children reduced the chances of their strikes degenerating into violence. Nevertheless, some women were attacked during work stoppages.

Huerta's desire for social equality never diminished. During the 1988 presidential campaign, Huerta took part in a protest against Republican candidate George H. W. Bush. She was severely beaten by San Francisco police officers during a peaceful demonstration. Rushed to the hospital, she was treated for a ruptured spleen and broken ribs. She eventually recovered fully from the attack, and received a large financial settlement for the injuries she had suffered. Huerta used the money to form the Dolores Huerta Foundation, an organization that trains potential organizers in low-income communities of color.

Recognition

In the early 1990s, Huerta resumed her role in the UFW, concerning herself with such issues as immigration reform and pesticide poisoning. Huerta's contributions to labor activism, support for women, the poor, and racial minorities led her to be honored by several institutions and bodies. In 1993, Huerta was inducted into the National Women's Hall of Fame, and she received the American Civil Liberties Union Roger Baldwin Medal of Liberty. In 1998, *Ms. Magazine* named her as one of its three women of the year; in the same year, she received the Eleanor Roosevelt Award. Huerta has also served on several boards of directors. She remained active in the Democratic Party, and maintained her support for the UFW.

See also: Chávez, César; National Organizations

Further reading: Griswold del Castillo, Richard, and Richard A. Garcia. *César Chávez: A Triumph of Spirit*. Norman, OK: University of Oklahoma Press, 1995.
http://www.doloreshuerta.org/dolores_huerta_foundation.htm (biography).

HUERTA, Jorge A.
Theater Director

Jorge A. Huerta is the leading authority on contemporary Chicano and U.S. Latino theater. He has worked as a professional director and has written several landmark books on Chicano theater, as well as founding a number of theater groups.

Early life

Jorge Alfonso Huerta was born on November 20, 1942, in East Los Angeles, California, the only boy in a family of six children. His father, Jorge Rodriguez, was a musician, and his mother, Elizabeth, a nurse. Raised in East Los Angeles, Huerta developed a love of the theater at an early age. During the 1950s, he played "that cute little Mexican kid" on several nationally televised programs.

After high school, Huerta attended California State College in Los Angeles. He graduated with a BA in 1965, earning an MA in 1967. He went on to become the first Chicano to earn a PhD in theater from the University of California at Santa Barbara in 1974.

A love of theater

While working on his PhD, Huerta became the founder and artistic director of El Teatro de la Esperanza (The Theater of Hope) in San Francisco. Huerta's belief that Chicanos/Chicanas were not represented in the theater across the country later led him to start several other Chicano theater groups. He was a founding director of El Teatro Nacional de Aztlán and Teatro Mil Caras (now Teatro Nuevo Siglo) in the 1970s. He was also director of the Teatro Meta of the Old Globe theater in San Diego between 1982 and 1986.

While working in professional theaters, Huerta lectured in Chicano studies before teaching drama at the University of California at San Diego. After Huerta's appointment as

▲ *Jorge A. Huerta has traveled around the United States, Western Europe, and Latin America, lecturing on Chicano theater.*

professor of theater in 1988, the following year he launched a new graduate program, the country's first MA program in Hispanic American theater.

Huerta has written widely about Chicano and Hispanic American theater. In addition to writing many articles, he has also published three anthologies of plays and two important books on Chicano theater, *Chicano Theater: Themes and Forms* (1982) and *Chicano Drama* (2000), which explores the diversity and energy of the Chicano theater.

Huerta has dedicated his life to Chicano theater: He believes that the theater is part of the strong contribution Hispanic Americans can make to the United States. His productions examine Chicano identity and explore the way in which Chicanos are caught between Mexico and the United States.

In 2005 Huerta was appointed associate chancellor and chief diversity officer of the University of California at San Diego. He is married to Virginia (Ginger) De-Mirijian; the couple has two grown-up sons.

Further reading: Huerta, Jorge A. *Chicano Theater: Themes and Forms.* Ypsilanti, MI: Bilingual Press, 1982.

KEY DATES	
1942	Born in Los Angeles, California, on November 20.
1974	Becomes the first Chicano to receive a PhD in theater from the University of California at Santa Barbara.
1989	Launches first MA program in Hispanic American theater.
2005	Appointed associate chancellor of the University of California San Diego (UCSD).

IDAR, Jovita
Journalist, Teacher, Activist

A journalist, teacher, and activist along the U.S.-Mexico border and in San Antonio, Texas, Jovita Idar spent a lifetime working for social equality for Mexican Americans and women in Texas at the beginning of the 20th century.

A product of her background

Born in 1885 in Laredo, Texas, Idar was the daughter of Jovita and Nicasio Idar. The publisher of *La Crónica*, a weekly Spanish-language newspaper that served the Mexican American community, Nicasio Idar dedicated his time to promoting better rights for the Hispanic community and writing articles and editorials discussing racial injustices committed in Texas.

After earning a teacher's certificate from the Holding Institute in Laredo in 1903, Idar taught school for a short period. She then became a reporter for *La Crónica*. During Idar's tenure with the newspaper, her parents organized the Primer Congreso Mexicanista (First Mexican Congress) to address the dire educational, social, and economic conditions Mexican Americans faced in South Texas. Along with other women, Idar participated in the week-long congress held in Laredo from September 14 to 22, 1911.

In October 1911, Idar helped found the Liga Femenil Mexicanista (League of Mexican Women); she was the organization's first president. The Liga had as its motto "Por la raza y para la raza" ("By the people and for the people"). Under Idar's leadership, the organization became a social, cultural, political, and charitable group whose members were among the most educated women in the community. The organization was particularly devoted to the education of poor children.

▲ *Jovita Idar was a prominent civil and women's rights activist in the early 20th century.*

During the Mexican Revolution, Jovita Idar joined La Cruz Blanca (The White Cross) in 1913, serving as a nurse for the revolutionaries in northern Mexico. Afterward, she returned to journalism in South Texas, this time working for *El Progreso*. In an editorial for the newspaper, Idar protested President Woodrow Wilson's sending federal troops to the U.S.–Mexico border; she came to the attention of the U.S. Army and the Texas Rangers, a state police force. When the Texas Rangers tried to shut down *El Progreso*, Idar blocked their entry to the office. The Rangers later succeeded, however, and Idar returned to work at *La Crónica*.

After her marriage in 1917 to Bartolo Juárez, Idar moved to San Antonio. She joined the Democratic Party and set up El Club Democrat, an organization facilitating Mexican American political activity in the city. Idar also opened a free bilingual kindergarten for local children.

See also: Idar, Nicasio

Further reading: Acosta, Teresa, and Ruthe Winegarten. *Las Tejanas: 300 Years of History.* Austin, TX: University of Texas Press, 2003.
http://www.tsha.utexas.edu/handbook/online/articles/II/fid3.html (biography).

KEY DATES	
1885	Born in Laredo, Texas.
1911	Helps establish La Liga Femenil Mexicanista and serves as its first president.
1913	Fends off Texas Rangers attempting to shut down publication of *El Progreso*, a newspaper for which she worked.
1917	Moves to San Antonio, where she continues to work for the betterment of the Mexican American people as a community leader, educator, and writer.
1946	Dies in San Antonio, Texas.

IDAR, Nicasio
Publisher, Civil Rights Activist

Nicasio Idar was a journalist, editor, and publisher. Idar dedicated his career to improving the lives of Mexican Americans in Texas. He used the Laredo-based newspaper *La Crónica* to report on racial injustices and to promote Mexican American culture and heritage. From 1910, when he became the proprietor of *La Crónica,* Idar used the newspaper to actively campaign on such subjects as school desegregation and other key civil rights issues. He also tried to promote cultural understanding between the Anglo American and Hispanic communities by organizing community meetings in Laredo.

Early life
Born in Point Isabel, Texas, on December 11 or 14, 1855, Nicasio Idar was the son of Mexican immigrants Manuel and Eluteria Espinoza Idar. Growing up in Texas, Idar became sickened by the prejudice and discrimination that he witnessed against members of the Mexican American community on a daily basis. After graduating from school in Corpus Christi, he decided to become a journalist and write about these issues.

▼ *Nicasio Idar dedicated his life to informing people about social and political injustices in U.S. society.*

KEY DATES

1855 Born in Point Isabel, Texas, on December 11 or 14.

1910 Buys *La Crónica.*

1911 Runs a series of articles highlighting discrimination against Mexican Americans; organizes conference against racial discrimination.

1914 Dies in Laredo, Texas, on April 7.

La Crónica
Aged 25, Idar moved to Laredo, Texas, with his wife Jovita. He worked there for various papers. In the 1890s Idar became editor of the Laredo-based newspaper *La Crónica*, which aimed to inform and educate Texan Mexicans about the political, social, and cultural issues of the day. The paper soon became known for its championship of the civil rights of minority groups, particularly women and Mexican Americans. In about 1910 Idar bought the paper. Over the next few years the Idars published a series of articles highlighting discrimination. Three of Idar's eight children—Jovita, Eduardo, and Clemente—wrote for *La Crónica;* they went on to become prominent journalists.

Working for the good of the community
A popular Laredo citizen, Idar was an active member of several local organizations and was an eager supporter of local business. He was a justice of the peace, and served as the town's assistant marshal. In 1911 Nicasio organized El Primer Congreso Mexicanista, a conference to discuss issues of racial inequality. La Liga Femenil Mexicanista, which campaigned for the education and economic and cultural advancement of Tejana women, arose out of the meeting. Idar also established the Gran Concilio de la Orden Caballeros de Honor, an organization that promoted respect between Anglo Americans and Mexican Americans through intellectual discussion. Idar died in Laredo on April 7, 1914.

See also: Idar, Jovita; Media, Spanish-language

Further reading: http://www.tsha.utexas.edu/handbook/online/articles/II/fid2.html (biography in the Handbook of Texas online Web site).

IGLESIAS, Enrique
Singer

Enrique Miguel Iglesias Preysler, better known to music fans as Enrique Iglesias, has emerged as one of the most popular Hispanic American stars in recent years. Iglesias, the son of Spanish heart throb Julio Iglesias, is the only singer in music history to have had 16 No. 1 *Billboard* Latin hits in the United States as well as in 18 other countries. Iglesias has recorded in Spanish, English, Portuguese, and Italian: He has earned 132 platinum records and more than 250 gold albums.

Early life
Born in Madrid, Spain, on May 8, 1975, Iglesias is one of the three children of Julio José Iglesias de la Cueva and Isabel Preysler Arrastia. When Iglesias was three, his parents divorced. In 1983 Isabel sent him, along with his brother Julio José and sister Chabeli, to live with their father in Miami, Florida. Iglesias grew up hearing and seeing Julio Iglesias sing.

His music career began while he was studying at the prestigious Gulliver private school in Miami, where he debuted in a musical production of *Hello, Dolly!* At age 15 Iglesias started writing songs, but his parents did not realize that he was serious about pursuing a music career.

Music
After studying for a business administration degree at the University of Miami, Iglesias dropped out to pursue his dream of being a singer–songwriter. In 1995 he submitted demos to record companies under the name of Enrique Martinez. He was signed to Fonovisa and recorded his self-titled first album in Toronto, Canada, in five months. The

▲ **Enrique Iglesias has recorded with some of the leading names in U.S. music, such as Whitney Houston and Lionel Richie.**

album went gold in Portugal within a week of its release; it sold more than a million copies in three months. It won Iglesias a Grammy Award for best Latin performer. He released his second album, *Vivir*, in January 1997; it went on to win Billboard's album of the year. A hard-working artist, Iglesias embarked on a world tour and released another album, *Cosas del Amor* (1998).

In 1999 Iglesias's single "Bailemos" ("We Dance"), which appeared on the soundtrack to the movie *Wild, Wild West*, reached No. 1. He released *Enrique*, his first album in English, on Interscope Records. It achieved gold or platinum ranking in more than 30 countries. In 2001 he released the English-language album *Escape*, which spawned the hit No. 1 hit "Hero," after which Iglesias embarked on a worldwide sellout tour. In 2002 he released *Quizas*, for which he won the Latin Grammy for best male pop album. He followed this with the album *Seven* in 2003.

Further reading: Figueroa, Acton. *Famous Families: Julio Iglesias and Enrique Iglesias.* New York, NY: The Rosen Publishing Group, 2005.
http://www.enriqueiglesias.com/bio.asp (Enrique Iglesias's site).

KEY DATES	
1975	Born in Madrid, Spain, on May 8.
1995	Releases his first album, *Enrique Iglesias*.
1996	Wins the Grammy for best Latin performer.
1997	Releases *Vivir*; wins *Billboard*'s album of the year award.
1999	Releases the album *Enrique*.
2001	Releases the album *Escape*.
2003	Wins the Latin Grammy for best male pop album.

IMMIGRATION AND IMMIGRATION LAW

Immigration, either forced or voluntary, has played an important part in the development of North America since the 16th century. Until the middle of the 19th century, the United States had a relatively open immigration policy, and encouraged people to settle in its vast, empty lands. After the end of the Civil War (1861–1865), however, many states introduced laws to limit immigration. From 1875, the regulation of immigration became a federal matter, and in 1891 the United States established the Immigration Service to deal with the increasing numbers of immigrants, most of whom came from Europe. In the 20th century, the United States emerged as the world's leading democracy and superpower, and it became the desired home for many foreign people seeking better lives, particularly those coming from poor or politically unstable nations. In order to deal with the large numbers of immigrants wanting to settle there, the United States, in common with many other nations around the world, introduced legislation to govern and restrict the number of foreign nationals settling on its shores.

Recent developments

In the last quarter of the 20th century, more than 30 million legal and illegal immigrants settled in the United States. In 2005, the U.S. population stood at about 288 million, more than 41 million of whom were of Hispanic origin:

Mexican migrant laborers wait to get their papers to work legally in the United States (1951).

According to the Center for Immigration Studies (CIS), in that year there were about 35 million foreign-born U.S. residents (12.1 percent of the total population), and more than half of that number originated from Latin America. A further 9 percent of the U.S. foreign-born population entered the country illegally. The CIS estimates that by 2055, the U.S. population will stand at more than 400 million, mainly as a result of immigration.

While immigrants have historically contributed a great deal to the United States's development, helping shape its economy, culture, and society, some commentators argue that the nation simply cannot sustain immigration at the current rate. They also claim that, rather than contributing to the economy, many immigrants are draining resources, taking vital services away from U.S. citizens: In 2005, immigrants and their dependant children accounted for almost one in four people living in poverty, and around 29 percent of immigrant-headed households

NATIONAL ORIGINS ACT OF 1924

The Immigration Act of 1924, also known as the National Origins Act, was one of the most important pieces of legislation introduced during the 20th century to help control the numbers of foreign-born people coming to live and work in the United States. The act implemented a permanent quota system and capped total annual immigration to the United States at 164,000. Under quotas, immigration from each country would be limited to just two percent of the total number of people from that country who were living in the United States in 1890. The act banned immigration from East Asia, notwithstanding Chinese and Japanese immigration, which were already restricted under the Chinese Exclusion Act of 1882 and the Gentleman's Agreement of 1907. Revisions to the National Origins Act in 1929 reduced the number of yearly visas to 150,000 immigrants.

used at least one major welfare service. (The national average is 18 percent.) Critics also claim that immigrants are threatening the American way of life, bringing different traditions, foods, and languages with them that are helping destroy U.S. culture. Advocates of immigration counter that the United States has always been a nation of immigrants, and that foreign people work harder than native-born U.S. citizens to succeed in their new country.

The Latin mix
The U.S. government has enacted various bills that have alternately encouraged and discouraged immigration from Latin America.

In the early 21st century, language, bilingual education, and immigration became important topics of debate in the United States. Hispanic immigration has become a particularly contentious issue, especially as Latinos and Latinas make up about 14 percent of the total U.S. population. In 2005, Mexicans made up nearly 64 percent of the total Latino population. In comparison, Puerto Ricans comprised 10 percent, and Cubans accounted for little more than 3 percent of Hispanics. The other Latinos in the United States come from Latin American, South American or Caribbean countries, such as the Dominican Republic, El Salvador, Colombia, and Brazil. Demographers estimate that, by 2050, Hispanic Americans will outnumber African Americans by two to one, and that they will comprise almost one-quarter of the U.S. population (24.5 percent), while the white proportion will constitute just over half (52.8 percent) of the total.

Mexicans
The Mexican presence in the United States began with the annexation of Texas in the 1840s.

KEY DATES

1875	Immigration becomes a federal affair.
1891	U.S. Immigration Service formed.
1917	Jones Act grants U.S. citizenship to Puerto Ricans.
1924	Immigration Act of 1924 establishes quota system; caps annual immigration at 164,000.
1927	Ceiling on overall annual immigration is limited to 150,000.
1929	Immigration capped at 150,000.
1942	Inception of the Bracero Program.
1965	Immigration Act of 1965 rescinds 1924 quota system; institutes family reunification.
1966	Cuban Adjustment Act enacted.
1986	Immigration Reform and Control Act (IRCA) enacted.
1990	Immigration Act of 1990 enacted.
1996	Immigration Reform and Immigrant Responsibility Act makes deportation easier and denies public assistance to non-U.S. citizens.
2005	More than one million immigrants a year settle in the United States.

U.S. border patrol agents process a group of Mexicans at Sunland Park, New Mexico. Sunland Park lies at the junction of Texas, New Mexico, and Mexico.

As a result of the Treaty of Guadalupe Hidalgo (1848), which ended the Mexican–American war, tens of thousands of residents of the Southwest became U.S. citizens. A wave of immigration began with the construction of the U.S. railroads between 1880 and 1920. Although at first most of the building work was carried out by other immigrant groups, by the 1920s they had been replaced by Mexican labor.

In the 1930s, as the United States was plunged into an economic depression, many Anglo-Americans began to denounce Mexicans, accusing them of taking their jobs. The U.S. government began to forcibly repatriate Mexicans, many of whom had legitimate U.S. residency. The move was denounced by civil rights groups around the country, especially since it resulted in the splitting up of families.

In 1941, the United States entered World War II (1939–1945), a move that created an immediate need for labor in U.S. agriculture and industry in order to replace workers drafted into military service. On August 4, 1942, representatives of the U.S. and Mexican governments agreed to the Bracero Program, which allowed the temporary migration of Mexican agricultural workers to the United States. Under the program, more than 4.5 million contracted Mexican laborers migrated to the United States between 1942 and the program's termination in 1964. Denounced by many civil and labor rights groups and the Mexican American community as exploitative and discriminatory, the program did not completely satisfy the labor requirements of U.S. industry. Several employers began to encourage the illegal entry of Mexicans to the United States, resulting in the immigration of many undocumented workers, often known as "wetbacks" or "*mojados*" because they were reputed to have crossed the border by swimming the Rio Grande.

Between 1950 and 1955, the U.S. Immigration and Naturalization Service (INS) launched an aggressive deportation program named "Operation Wetback" to tackle the large number of illegal immigrants. It resulted in the repatriation to Mexico of more than one million undocumented immigrants. Although the theoretical aim of Operation Wetback was to deport illegal aliens, in practice it captured Mexicans, often regardless of whether their presence in the country was legal or undocumented. The operation became the subject of controversy, particularly over the search and seizure tactics employed by the law-enforcement agencies. Police raids and random identification stops in Mexican American neighborhoods rendered almost anyone vulnerable to harassment. Although the United States made efforts to prevent undocumented immigration, the demand for immigrant labor in the United States continued to attract Hispanic people from their home countries even after the Bracero Program ended.

Puerto Ricans
Puerto Ricans began immigrating to the United States shortly after the Spanish–American War. The 1898 Treaty of Paris ceded Puerto Rico, Guam, and the Philippines to the United States. Puerto Ricans did not gain equal status in law

returning to the island from the United States.

Cubans

Cubans have been moving to the United States since before the Spanish–American War in 1898. However, most of today's Cuban American population arrived after 1959, the year of Fidel Castro's revolution. Previously, significant Cuban American communities had existed in a range of locations, notably Tampa and Ybor City, Florida; New Orleans, Louisiana; and New York City.

When Castro seized power, relations between the Caribbean island and the United States soured. In 1961, the U.S. government unsuccessfully attempted to topple Castro in an episode known as the Bay of Pigs invasion. A year later, the Soviet Union, Cuba's ally, deployed nuclear missiles on the island, creating fears of a third world war. The United States later promised never to invade Cuba again, but imposed economic sanctions against it that remained largely in effect into the 21st century.

Cubans were not free to leave the country, although many tried to do so. The United States permitted Cubans who reached its shores to remain in the country. There were several reasons for that policy, including the fear that people forced to return to Cuba would be persecuted, and the hope that encouraging an exodus of talented and able-bodied Cubans to the United States might weaken Castro's regime.

until 1917, when President Woodrow Wilson signed the Jones Act, which gave statutory citizenship to all Puerto Ricans.

During World War I (1914–1918) and World War II (1939–1945), there was a great need for agricultural and industrial laborers. With immigration significantly curtailed by such acts as the 1924 National Origins Act (*see box on page 120*), the United States looked to Puerto Ricans to fill the demand for low-cost labor. By the 1930s, immigrants from the Caribbean island had established major communities in New York, Chicago, Boston, and Philadelphia. In addition to filling jobs vacated by draftees, Puerto Ricans—and numerous other Latinos—fought in the U.S. armed forces.

The mass exodus of Puerto Ricans to jobs in the United States during World War II had a detrimental knock-on effect on the economy of the land they left behind. As the farms were

neglected through understaffing, the Puerto Rican economy faltered, and after the war there was a new wave of immigrants who came to the United States in search of a better life.

In 1947, the government of Puerto Rico responded to the crisis by introducing an industrialization plan, named Operation Bootstrap, which encouraged foreign investment through tax breaks and the availability of low-cost labor. Also in that year, the Puerto Rican Bureau of Employment and Migration was established; it opened offices in Puerto Rico and on the U.S. mainland, in New York City and Chicago.

While Puerto Ricans continue to have a significant presence in the cities in which they originally settled, particularly Chicago, New York, and Philadelphia, they have since spread out to settle across the Northeast and in South Florida. During the 1990s, however, there developed a significant trend of Puerto Ricans

THE ELIÁN GONZÁLEZ CASE

On November 25, 1999, six-year-old Elián González was found floating in a car inner-tube off the coast of Florida. His parents were divorced and Elián's mother, Elizabeth, had taken him, without his father's knowledge, and boarded a boat leaving Cuba for the United States. The boat capsized about 35 miles (56km) off the U.S. coast, and Elián's mother was drowned. In the months that followed, Elián became the focus of a bitter battle between Juan Miguel González, his father, who wanted his son returned to Cuba, and Elián's Miami-based relatives, who wanted him to stay in the United States.

The Immigration and Naturalization Service (INS) allowed Elián to reside temporarily with his Miami relatives. Elián's grandmothers and his father flew to the United States to campaign for his return to Cuba. On January 5, 2000, the INS declared that it was Juan Miguel González's right to decide where his son should live, a position supported by President Bill Clinton and about two-thirds of Americans. The U.S. attorney general set April 13 as the deadline for Elián's return to Cuba; his Miami relatives refused to give Elián up, however. Federal agents forcibly retrieved Elián on April

22, 2000, much to the anger of the Cuban American community. Elián subsequently returned with his father to Cuba.

In Miami, Elián's repatriation alienated many Cuban Americans. Commentators also believe that it damaged the Democrats in the 2000 presidential election, the outcome of which hinged on the vote in Florida. Fidel Castro also used the affair to challenge U.S. perceptions of Cuba, showing that loving, happy families also existed in his regime. Soon after Elián's return, the U.S. government ruled that food and medicine could be sold to Cuba for the first time in 40 years.

Since the revolution, Cubans have immigrated to the United States in five distinct waves. The first, between 1959 and 1962, was composed mostly of Cuba's former political and economic elites, including thousands of professionals and skilled workers. They started to leave the island when the Castro regime began nationalizing foreign and domestic industry, and started to persecute supporters of the previous regime. Most Cuban immigrants in this wave expected their time in the United States to be brief, and looked forward to returning to Cuba as triumphant exiles after Castro's regime was overthrown with the help of the United States.

The second wave of post-revolutionary immigration began in October 1965, when Castro opened Camarioca Harbor to allow Cubans to flee the country via

foreign watercraft. Within two months, President Lyndon B. Johnson had established the Freedom Flight program as part of the Memorandum of Understanding between the United States and Cuba: Two flights a day left Cuba carrying refugees to the United States, and priority was given to Cubans with relatives in the United States. More than 250,000 Cubans immigrated between 1965 and 1973, when the program was halted.

Accepting the new reality
Realizing that the revolution had been consolidated, and that Cuban exiles would not be returning soon, the U.S. Congress enacted the Cuban Adjustment Act in 1966. Under the act, Cubans were able to adjust their legal immigration status to that of permanent residents.

Since Castro did not allow Cubans to emigrate from Cuba after 1973, there was almost no further immigration from the island until 1980. In that year, amid growing unrest, economic decline, and high unemployment, immigration again became a key issue. After many Cubans stormed Latin American embassies, Castro opened the port of Mariel between May and September 1980, encouraging the departure of Cubans who wanted to emigrate to the United States. More than 125,000 undocumented Cubans arrived in the United States, mostly in U.S. vessels and in violation of U.S. law. The U.S. Coast Guard helped deal with the influx of Cuban refugees. Most Cubans were initially detained in refugee camps and federal prisons.

In response to the Mariel boatlift, as the incident became

known, the United States and Cuba entered a bilateral agreement that introduced a quota system for Cuban immigration. The United States agreed to allow Cubans up to 20,000 visas per year, with unlimited visas for family reunification. Commentators claim that, in the 1980s, very few of the 20,000 annual visas were granted. Increasing numbers of Cubans began to take risks to reach Florida, some leaving their country on badly constructed rafts.

On August 19, 1994, Castro declared an open migration policy, and thousands of Cubans left Cuba for U.S. shores. Castro's action led President Clinton to reverse U.S. policy toward Cuban arrivals. He stipulated that any Cubans stopped at sea en route to the United States could be detained indefinitely. More than 32,000 Cubans were taken to detention centers at the U.S. naval base at Guantanamo Bay, Cuba. In May 1995 Clinton announced that those still detained would gradually be allowed into the States. He also stated that in the future, Cubans caught trying to enter the United States illegally by sea would be intercepted and repatriated if they could not show conclusive proof of persecution in Cuba. In 1999, the case of the six-year-old Elián González brought the issue of Cuban immigration to international attention (*see box on page 123*).

Hispanic immigration and law
In the United States in the postwar period, several laws were introduced to limit immigration. The Immigration Act of 1965 allowed foreign migration from all countries, and abolished all previous quotas established by prior immigration acts. It introduced annual visa limitations of 170,000 from Eastern Hemisphere countries, and 120,000 from the Americas. A key element in this legislation was family reunification, which ensured that most visas were issued to immigrants who already had family in the United States.

The Immigration Reform and Control Act of 1986 (IRCA) raised the official limit on immigration to 540,000 people annually, authorized amnesty legislation, introduced penalties for individuals who hired undocumented immigrant workers, increased border enforcement, and created an immigration category of seasonal agricultural workers (SAW). The amnesty program resulted in the legalization of three million undocumented workers (2.3 million of them Mexican). Ironically, one of the long-term consequences of IRCA was to allow an unprecedented level of both legal and undocumented immigration in the 1990s.

The Immigration Act of 1990 increased to 700,000 the annual number of permitted immigrants to the United States. It also included a provision that rescinded the Cuban Adjustment Act on the establishment of democracy in Cuba.

The Immigration Reform and Immigrant Responsibility Act was enacted in tandem with the Welfare Reform Act of 1996, and denied many kinds of public assistance to legal immigrants who had not yet become U.S. citizens. The act also introduced new bars to the reentry of illegal immigrants. However, many critics argued that these laws still did not go far enough, and that the United States was too soft on illegal immigration.

Response to 9/11
The terrorist action against the United States in September 2001 made immigration a contentious issue. Prior to 9/11, President George W. Bush had intended to promote legislation that advocated a guest-worker program aimed at providing U.S. businesses with access to foreign laborers. After 9/11 nothing much happened regarding these measures until Bush again began to push immigration reform in late 2005.

In 2006, the Republican Party remained divided between those who wanted to ensure that the United States continued to benefit from access to cheap labor, and those who demanded that any new legislation strictly enforce existing laws and make undocumented immigration, as well as the aiding or hiring of undocumented immigrants, felony crimes. The provisions were included in H.R. 4437, a House bill passed in 2005. Some politicians advocated other measures: Senator Ted Kennedy, for example, endorsed earned citizenship for undocumented immigrants, after the payment of fines and back taxes. He also advocated that the United States allow up to 400,000 guest workers into the country each year.

See also: Assimilation; Civil Rights

Further reading: Foner, Nancy. *From Ellis Island to JFK: New York's Two Great Waves of Immigration.* New Haven, CT: Yale University Press, 2000.
http://www.census.gov/ (official U.S. government site of the Census Bureau.)
http://www.cis.org/index.cgi (Center for Immigration Studies site).

ISLAS, Arturo
Writer, Academic

Arturo Islas published two novels during his lifetime, *The Rain God* and *Migrant Souls*, both of which helped establish him as one of the premier voices in 20th-century Chicano literature. Islas's books examine such issues as racial identity, gender roles, family relations, homosexuality, and the cultural mapping of the U.S.–Mexico border. Islas's third novel, *La Mollie and the King of Tears*, was published posthumously.

The emergence of a Chicano writer

Islas was born on May 25, 1938, in the border city of El Paso, Texas. Islas and his two younger brothers, Mario and Luis, were raised in a bilingual home. Islas later drew on his early experiences growing up in a border town in a family rife with conflict.

Despite contracting polio as a child, which led to lifelong health problems, Islas managed to graduate as valedictorian from El Paso High School in 1956, the same year in which he entered Stanford University on a pre-med scholarship. He planned to become a neurosurgeon but

▼ *Arturo Islas grew up in a town on the Mexican–U.S. border. He believed that the area had a cultural identity that was unique.*

KEY DATES

1938 Born on May 25 in the Segundo Barrio area of El Paso, Texas.

1946 Diagnosed with polio.

1960 Graduates with a BA in English from Stanford University.

1984 *The Rain God*, his debut novel, is published by Alexandrian Press.

1985 *The Rain God* receives the Border Regional Library Conference fiction prize.

1988 Tests positive for HIV on January 14.

1990 Publishes *Migrant Souls*.

1991 While working on *La Mollie and the King of Tears*, he dies of pneumonia at his home in Palo Alto.

switched instead to study for a BA in English, which he received in 1960. Three years later he finished an MA degree in English, before going on to study for a PhD at Stanford, which he finished in 1971. In that same year, Islas joined the Stanford faculty. Islas helped develop the Chicano Fellows Program to address issues concerning Chicana/o students and faculty. As a result of the program, Stanford set up the first Chicano studies course.

By the early 1980s, Islas had finished his first novel, *The Rain God*, a literary work that fused the social, magical, and psychological to present the Angel family through the eyes of the gay Chicano protagonist, Miguel Chico. The book examines Chico's struggles to reconcile his traditional family heritage with his life as a gay man in San Francisco. Islas won critical acclaim and several awards for this work. He published his second novel, *Migrant Souls*, in 1990. Islas died while writing a sequel to the book, *La Mollie and the King of Tears*. He was inducted into the Writers Hall of Fame by the University of Texas El Paso shortly before his death in 1991.

Further reading: Aldama, Frederick Luis. *Dancing with Ghosts: A Critical Biography of Arturo Islas.* Berkeley: University of California Press, 2005.
http://www.stanford.edu/dept/news/pr/91/910418Arc1431.html (Stanford University article about Islas's death).

ITHIER, Rafael
Pianist, Bandleader

Rafael Ithier has played an important part in the history of Latin music, particularly that of his native country, Puerto Rico. As the founder, bandleader, and arranger of the renowned group El Gran Combo, Ithier has played with some of the world's leading Latin musicians.

Early life
Ithier was born on August 29, 1926, in Rio Piedras, Puerto Rico, into a very musical family; his father was a member of local music groups. Ithier showed early talent as a musician. Although mostly self-taught, he learned to play the guitar. Later, helped by his sister, he took up the piano, which became his main instrument.

A professional musician
In 1944 Ithier began his professional career as a guitarist in Tito Henríquez's group, Conjunto Taone. He formed a band while in the U.S. Army (1952–1954); the group toured

▼ *Rafael Ithier is El Gran Combo's bandleader, pianist, and arranger.*

KEY DATES

1926 Born in Rio Piedras, Puerto Rico, on August 29.

1955 Begins playing with Rafael Cortijo and his band.

1962 Forms El Gran Combo; releases debut album.

1992 Honored at the Festival de la Salsa at Madison Square Garden in New York; Celia Cruz and Cheo Feliciano are among the artists featured.

the United States briefly in 1955. After returning to Puerto Rico, Ithier joined Rafael Cortijo and Ismael Rivera's band. Although very successful in Puerto Rico, the United States, and Latin America, the group's disagreements led Ithier and some other band members to leave. In 1962 he formed El Gran Combo, a 13-piece band, which featured Roberto Roena (percussion), Martín Quiñones (congo), Eddy Pérez and Hector Santos (saxophone), and Kito Velez (trumpet). El Gran Combo went on to have several successful hits, including "Un Verano en Nueva York," "Jala Jala," and "Acangana."

Remaining in Puerto Rico and maintaining a stable lineup allowed the orchestra to remain true to its roots and resist the more fashionable trends of Latin music. In 1972 Ithier added a trombone to the group's lineup, to produce a sound that Ithier liked in the music of Mons Rivera and Willie Colón. By the late 1970s and early 1980s, El Gran Combo was considered to be far too conservative for some music commentators' tastes. By the 1990s El Gran Combo's popularity had increased again, however. In 1992 the band was honored at the Festival de la Salsa in Madison Square Garden, at which musicians such as Celia Cruz and Cheo Feliciano performed.

El Gran Combo celebrated its 40th anniversary with a tour and a live two-CD album that won the group its first Grammy award. This was followed with the release of *Aqui Estamos Y … Verdad!* (2004) on the Sony label.

See also: Colón, Willie; Cruz, Celia; Feliciano, Cheo

Further reading: http://www.musicofpuertorico.com/en/rafael_ithier.html (biography of Ithier, featuring information on El Gran Combo).

ITURBI, José
Pianist, Conductor

José Iturbi was one of the most recognized concert pianists of the 1940s, mainly because of his appearances in Hollywood movies. Iturbi was instrumental in bringing classical music to a wider audience. He performed with brilliance in a varied repertoire, but was most praised for his interpretations of Spanish music.

From Spain to Hollywood

Born in Valencia, Spain, on November 28, 1895, Iturbi was a child prodigy. He began playing the piano in a silent movie theater in Valencia at the age of seven. Iturbi studied at the Conservatorio de Valencia (now the Conservatorio Superior de Valencia), after which he went to Barcelona. He later enroled at the Conservatoire de Musique in Paris, France, where he received the first prize in piano in 1913.

Leaving the Conservatoire during World War I (1914–1918), Iturbi went to Switzerland. He played the piano in cafes before getting a teaching post at the Geneva Conservatoire in 1918. Five years later Iturbi left the Conservatoire to concentrate on a performing career.

Iturbi made his debut in the United States in 1929, playing with the Philadelphia Philharmonic and New York Philharmonic orchestras. He was an instant success in the United States and he decided to settle there. He was joined by his sister, Amparo Iturbi (1898-1969), who was also a pianist and with whom he played four-hand piano pieces. Iturbi was appointed conductor of the Rochester Philharmonic in 1936.

As part of the Good Neighbor Policy, Franklin D. Roosevelt campaigned for the end of racial stereotyping in the media, government, and entertainment industries. As a result, Hollywood started to use Latin American artists in films during World War II (1939–1945). Iturbi starred in several films in the 1940s. He first appeared in *Thousands Cheer* (1943), followed by *Music for Millions* (1944),

▲ *José Iturbi benefited from Franklin D. Roosevelt's Good Neighbor Policy, which encouraged Hollywood to cast more Latinos in movies.*

Holiday in Mexico (1946), and *Three Daring Daughters* (1948), where he mainly played himself. In the highly romanticized film biopic of composer Frederic Chopin's life, *A Song to Remember* (1945), Iturbi provided the piano music for actor Cornel Wilde (Chopin). His recording of the Polonaise in A Flat broke record sales and Iturbi became the first classical musician to achieve sales of more than one million copies for a record. Iturbi's work in Hollywood led to disapproval from music critics, however.

Later work

Iturbi also composed several piano pieces, the most famous of which was "Pequeña Danza Española." Aged 83, he gave a farewell concert at the Ambassador Auditorium in Pasadena, California. He died in 1980. Iturbi received a number of honors, including the Order of St. George (Greece) and the Order of the Légion d'Honneur (France). In California the José Iturbi Gold Medal Series of concerts is held annually at Cerritos to help aspiring musicians. Since the 1990s Iturbi's recordings have been reissued.

Further reading: http://users.adelphia.net/~fvila/Spain/ Conductors.htm (biography).

KEY DATES	
1895	Born in Valencia, Spain, on November 28.
1929	First performs in the United States.
1943	Debuts in Hollywood movies.
1980	Dies in Hollywood, California, on June 28.

JARAMILLO, Cleofas M.
Writer

Cleofas M. Jaramillo was a factual writer whose autobiographical reminiscences are a valuable source of information about life and customs in New Mexico in the last years before it became the 47th U.S. state in 1912.

She was born Cleofas Martínez in 1878 in Arroyo Hondo in northern New Mexico, and raised in a small town outside Taos. Her family had hereditary wealth, having been been granted extensive lands in the region in the 17th century by the viceroy of New Spain (modern Mexico).

Education and marriage
Cleofas Martínez attended the Loretto Convent School in Taos and later the Loretto Academy in Santa Fe. She recalls her experiences in both establishments with affection in her memoirs, *Romance of a Little Village Girl*. On completing her education in 1898 she married Colonel Venceslao Jaramillo, an aide to territorial governor Miguel A. Otero. The couple moved to the colonel's home of El

▼ **The work of Cleofas Jaramillo is an important source of information about life in early 20th-century New Mexico.**

KEY DATES	
1878	Born in Arroyo Hondo, New Mexico, on December 6.
1898	Marries Colonel Venceslao Jaramillo.
1931	Becomes a writer after the murder of her daughter.
1939	Completes her first work, *Cuentos del hogar*.
1956	Dies in El Paso, Texas, on November 30.

Rito, where they settled down and started a family. During the next two decades, Colonel Jaramillo served as a state senator; he was a delegate to the Constitutional Convention that was held when New Mexico joined the United States. When he died in 1920, Cleofas Jaramillo returned with her four-year-old daughter, Angélica, to Santa Fe, where she initiated legal proceedings to gain control of her husband's legacy. A shrewd negotiator, she eventually overcame opposition, took control of all the assets, and finally rescued the estate from the debts it had incurred during the dispute.

In 1931 Angélica was murdered. Jaramillo started writing to assuage her grief. She had long felt resentful about the way New Mexican culture was depicted in the newspapers and literature of the period. In 1939 she responded by writing a history of Hispanic culture in general and of her own family in particular. Her principal aim was to set the record straight, but she also wanted to record details of a way of life that was rapidly disappearing with the advance of European American culture. Her first work, *Cuentos del hogar*, was a compilation of 25 fairytales that her mother had told her as a child. Jaramillo also published *Potajes Sabrosos*, a cookbook of traditional New Mexican recipes. *Romance of a Little Village Girl* depicts episodes from her own life, blending personal, family, and New Mexican history. The book is often considered her most important because it documents Hispanic life and attempts to preserve Hispanic culture as a unique and significant force.

See also: Otero Family

Further reading: Reed, Maureen. *A Woman's Place: Women Writing in New Mexico*. Albuquerque, NM: University of New Mexico Press, 2005.

JARAMILLO, Mari-Luci
Ambassador, Educator

Mari-Luci Jaramillo believes that education is critical in helping defeat poverty and discrimination. Throughout her distinguished career in both elementary and university education, and during her ambassadorship to Honduras, Jaramillo has advocated equality for all.

Early life
Jaramillo was born into a poverty-stricken bicultural family in Las Vegas, New Mexico, in 1928. Her mother, Elvira Ruiz, was a native New Mexican; her family dated back to Spanish colonial settlers. Jaramillo's father, Maurilio Antuna, was a native of Durango, Mexico; he moved to New Mexico, where he opened a shoemaker's shop to support his family.

Education conquers poverty
Jaramillo registered at New Mexico Highlands University dressed in clothing made from flour sacks. After interrupting her studies to marry and start a family, she completed a BA in 1955 and an MA in 1959, both with honors. She went on to earn a PhD from the University of New Mexico (UNM) in 1970.

Jaramillo taught elementary school for several years; she then lectured and taught at UNM, eventually chairing its department of elementary education.

"Madame Ambassador"
In conjunction with the university's Latin American program and the U.S. Agency for International Development, Jaramillo spoke nationally and internationally on civil rights issues. Jaramillo's diplomatic treatment of sensitive issues attracted much attention.

▲ *Mari-Luci Jaramillo was the first Latina U.S. ambassador to Honduras.*

In 1977 Jimmy Carter, the Democratic U.S. president, appointed Jaramillo the U.S. ambassador to Honduras, a Central American country bordering the Caribbean Sea, with a military government. Jaramillo was the first Hispanic woman to serve in the position. She tirelessly campaigned for democracy in Honduras.

After three years' service in Honduras, Jaramillo was replaced after the election of Republican president Ronald Reagan. Jaramillo returned to her chairmanship at UNM. She was promoted to associate dean (1982–1985), and vice president for student affairs (1985–1987).

Jaramillo left UNM for a position as assistant vice president of the Educational Testing Service, one of the largest nonprofit testing firms. She published a memoir, *Madame Ambassador: The Shoemaker's Daughter*, in 2002.

KEY DATES	
1928	Born in Las Vegas, New Mexico, on June 19.
1970	Receives PhD from the University of New Mexico (UNM).
1977	Appointed the U.S. ambassador to Honduras.
1985	Becomes vice president for student affairs at UNM.
2002	Publishes *Madame Ambassador: The Shoemaker's Daughter.*

Further reading: Jaramillo, Mari-Luci. *Madame Ambassador: The Shoemaker's Daughter*. Tempe, AZ: Bilingual Press, 2002.
http://www.hrtnm.org/2001.html (Hispano Round Table on distinguished New Mexico Hispanas).

JIMENEZ, Flaco
Musician

Flaco Jimenez is an accordionist who specializes in conjunto music, a Mexican American musical form that has been influenced by the music of German immigrants to Texas, and features the accordion as well as Mexican elements. His father, Santiago Jimenez, considered by many to be the father of conjunto, was the first accordionist from San Antonio to make recordings in the 1930s. As a teenager, Jimenez was given his father's nickname "Flaco," which means "skinny" or "thin." Known for his technique and entertaining performances, Jimenez has won several awards, including five Grammys.

Early life
Born in San Antonio, Texas, on March 11, 1939, Leonardo Jimenez grew up in a musical household, listening to his father, Santiago, play conjunto-style music. Aged seven, Jimenez began appearing on stage with his father. In 1954 he made his first record, as a member of Los Caporales.

After playing in clubs for several years, Jimenez went to New York with the musician Douglas Sahm, founder of The Sir Douglas Quintet, where he played with many of the leading musicians of the 1960s, including Bob Dylan.

▼ **Flaco Jimenez inherited his love of music from his father, Santiago Jimenez, the "Father of Conjunto."**

KEY DATES	
1939	Born in San Antonio, Texas, on March 11.
1946	Begins performing live.
1974	Featured in an award-winning documentary, *Chulas Fronteras*.
1986	Wins first Grammy for rerecording of his father's song "Ay Te Dejo En San Antonio."
1999	Wins a Grammy for the best Tejano performance and for the best Mexican American performance.
2003	Inducted into the International Latin Music Hall of Fame in New York.

Getting public attention
In 1974 Jimenez was featured in Les Blank's award-winning documentary, *Chulas Fronteras*, which also starred his father, Santiago. The film aired on PBS in the United States, and on national TV in England, Germany, and Sweden; it brought Jimenez's music to international audiences. During this time Jimenez also met the singer-songwriter Ry Cooder, who invited him to tour with him. Cooder later featured Jimenez on his album *Chicken Skin Music*. In 1977 Flaco appeared with Cooder on *Saturday Night Live*. The following year saw Jimenez team up with the country-bluegrass singer Peter Rowan. They became friends and have often toured and recorded together.

The next decades saw Jimenez continue to record and tour with his conjunto band, especially in Europe and Japan. In 1983 Jimenez appeared on Carlos Santana's *Havana Moon* album. In the early 1990s, he worked with the Texas Tornados, comprised of his friends Doug Sahm, Freddy Fender, and Augie Meyers. The band toured and recorded three CDs. He also recorded with Dwight Yoakam, Buck Owens, Linda Ronstadt, Emmy Lou Harris, Los Lobos, The Mavericks, John Hiatt, Bryan Ferry, The Clash, Stephen Stills, The Rolling Stones, and The Chieftains. Jimenez was inducted into the National Hispanic Hall of Fame and the International Latin Music Hall of Fame.

See also: Los Lobos; Ronstadt, Linda; Santana, Carlos

Further reading: http://www.Flacojimenez.com (an informative Web site on Jimenez's career).

JIMÉNEZ, Luis
Artist

Best known for bold, vibrant sculptures and bright, ironic paintings that comment on the American West and the stereotypes associated with it, Chicano artist Luis Jiménez is perhaps one of the finest Hispanic artists to have emerged from the 1970s art scene.

Early life
Born in El Paso, Texas, on July 30, 1940, to Mexican immigrant parents, Jiménez showed an interest in art from an early age. At his father's business, a sign-making shop specializing in neon and large-scale materials, Jiménez learned that bright colors and symbols attract attention and create powerful visual associations in the minds of the viewers.

Education
Choosing to attend college rather than take over his father's shop, Jiménez attended the University of Texas from 1959 to 1964, majoring in art and architecture. He then studied at the Ciudad Universitaria in Mexico for two years, where he worked with the muralist Francisco Zuninga. Jiménez explored his cultural heritage by painting Mexican murals.

Developing his own style
In 1966 Jiménez moved to New York City. Arriving at a fertile moment in the history of contemporary art, Jiménez was impressed by the powerful yet playfully irreverent attitude of pop art. As he began to display his own work—he held his first solo exhibition in 1969—Jiménez experimented with fusing the techniques he had learned in Mexico with the early influences of neon and the sensibilities of pop art. By the time he returned to live in the Southwest five years later, Jiménez had developed a signature style that blended vibrant colors and satirical commentary with the imagery of his cultural heritage.

Experimenting with art
Creating sculpture in addition to painting, Jiménez began employing materials such as fiberglass and plastic to create ironic artwork about U.S. life, which often featured stereotypes of the American West and Mexican iconography. He remarked: "My main concern is creating an American art using symbols and icons.

KEY DATES	
1940	Born in El Paso, Texas, on July 30.
1966	Moves to New York.
1969	First solo show at the Graham Gallery in New York City.
1995	First major retrospective entitled "Man on Fire."

I'm making high art out of low art material. I feel I am a traditional artist working with images and materials that are of my time."

Reinterpreting the American Dream
For more than 25 years, Jiménez has displayed his work in important galleries and museums throughout the United States. His bold, large-scale sculptures can also be found in numerous private collections and in public spaces for which they were specially commissioned. Simultaneously celebrating the American character and parodying American mythology, Jiménez's work sometimes generates controversy owing to what have been described as his "attempts to rethink the 'American Dream' into Hispanic terms."

The driving force behind Jiménez's art is a desire to exalt ordinary men and women, particularly Hispanics, and recast them as dignified and heroic figures. He says: "We must create our own heroes to make us feel good about ourselves. Artists can provide these images."

Honors
Luis Jiménez has received numerous awards and grants, including the 1998 Texas Artist of the Year Award, the New Mexico Governor's Award, and a National Endowment of the Arts Award. In the 1990s "Man on Fire," a comprehensive retrospective, was organized in celebration of Jiménez's rich body of work. Jiménez's work can be found in the collections of the Metropolitan Museum of Art, the Chicago Art Institute, and the Hirshhorn Museum and Sculpture Garden in Washington, D.C.

Further reading: http://newssearch.looksmart.com/p/ articles/mi_m1248/is_n11_v82/ai_15918997 (an article about Luis Jiménez's work and first major retrospective).

JUANES
Musician

Born Juan Esteban Arizabal in Colombia, Juanes (a reduction of Juan Esteban) began his musical career with the rock group Ehkymosis. In the late 1990s, Juanes became a solo artist, releasing *Fíjate Bien* (2000), and *Un Dia Normal* (2002), which stayed in the *Billboard* Latin charts for two years and in the Top 10 for 92 weeks.

Early life
Born in Medellín, Colombia, in 1972, Juanes grew up in a musical family. He began playing the guitar, influenced by the tangos, boleros, and cumbia music that his father played. At an early age he suffered tragedy when his cousin was kidnapped and executed. His father also later died of cancer.

As a teenager, Juanes was influenced by heavy metal. He eventually formed the band Ehkymosis. The group enjoyed success in Colombia, and released seven albums over 11 years. Many of his songs stressed the importance of peace and tolerance. Ehkymosis's song "Mi Tierra," for example, includes the lyrics "Love the land where you were born." Juanes also became known for his sometimes controversial views, including his argument

▼ *Juanes is one of the most successful Latin cross-over artists in modern music.*

KEY DATES	
1972	Born in Medellín, Colombia.
1987	Is a member of the band Ehkymosis, until 1999.
2000	Begins a solo career, releasing *Fíjate Bien*.
2002	Releases *Un Día Normal*.
2004	Birth of his daughter is the inspiration for the song "Tu Guardián."
2004	Releases *Mi Sangre*.
2005	Plays himself in *Bordertown*, alongside Jennifer Lopez and Antonio Banderas.
2006	Contributes to the soundtrack for *Rosario Tijeras*.

that, if drugs were legalized in Colombia, many of the problems between the warring factions in the country would become a thing of the past.

Going solo
In the late 1990s Juanes decided to go solo. He moved to Los Angeles, California, where he met the producer Gustavo Santaolalladía and signed with his label Surco. Fernan Martinez became his manager; he had helped the musician Enrique Iglesias achieve fame.

In 2000 Juanes released *Fíjate Bien*. Although the album reached No. 1 in Colombia, it did only moderately well elsewhere. Despite this, Juanes was nominated for seven Latin Grammys in 2001, winning three. His second album, *Un Día Normal,* debuted at No. 1 on the *Billboard* Latin charts, thanks in part to Juanes's songwriting and sense of rhythm. The album also featured the popular song "Fotografía," sung with Nelly Furtado.

In addition to singing, Juanes costarred with Jennifer Lopez, Antonio Banderas, Martin Sheen, and Sonia Braga in *Bordertown* (2006), a film that deals with the murders of women in Ciudad Juarez, Mexico. Juanes has contributed songs to the film scores of several movies. He continues to tour and record music.

See also: Iglesias, Enrique; Lopez, Jennifer; Sheen, Martin

Further reading: http://www.juanes.net (official Web site).

JULIA, Raul
Actor

The iconic Puerto Rican-born actor Raul Julia was one of the most respected Latino stars of the theater and cinema. A highly skilled performer, Julia had a great stage and film presence. Audiences admired and respected Julia's sense of conviction as an actor and the credibility of his performances. Julia's untimely death in 1994 cut short a pioneering career that had helped improve the type of roles offered to Latino actors.

Early life

Born in San Juan, Puerto Rico, on March 9, 1940, Raul Rafael Carlos Julia y Arcelay grew up with his younger sisters and brother in a prosperous household. His father ran La Cueva del Chicken (The Chicken's Cave), a popular restaurant in the city. Julia received an excellent education; he went first to a school run by Roman Catholic nuns, where he learned English, and then on to the Jesuit-run San Ignacio de Loyala High School.

Although Julia's parents thought that he might like to take over the family restaurant when he left high school, Julia had other ideas. He told *Photoplay* (1986) that: "Having spent my school days in every play I could find and getting my hands on plays and settling down to learn them in their entirety, it seemed that trying for a life in acting made sense."

Julia went on to study at the University of Puerto Rico by day, at night performing with theater groups, such as a cabaret outfit called The Lamplighters. He was also a regular performer at the city's Tapia Theater.

Making it in New York

In 1964 Julia decided to move to New York to pursue a career as an actor. Although actors such as Rita Moreno and José Ferrer had broken through many barriers for Latino and Latina actors, Julia was determined that he would not be typecast in stereotypical roles. He was lucky enough to meet and become friends with Joseph Papp, founder of New York's Shakespeare Festival, which put on free performances of William Shakespeare's plays (*see box on page 134*). Papp cast Julia in several of the plays, including *Macbeth* and *Titus Andronicus*.

▼ **Raul Julia starred as Gomez Addams in the hit movie The Addams Family (1991).**

In 1972 Julia portrayed Valentine in a contemporary musical version of *The Two Gentlemen of Verona*, costarring Stockard Channing and Jeff Goldblum. Julia's performance earned him his first nomination for a Tony award. He was nominated a further four times during his career.

Julia soon established a reputation as a fine stage actor; he appeared in plays by George Bernard Shaw (*Arms and the Man*) and Harold Pinter (*Betrayal*). He also received enthusiastic reviews for his performance in a costly 1982 production of the musical *Nine*.

Getting into movies and television

Julia made his film debut in the crime melodrama *Stiletto* (1969), an adaptation of a Harold Robbins novel. Julia often chose small, provocative projects with a certain social awareness. Off the screen, he was a representative for the Hunger Project and other important charities. He also appeared on television; he was a frequent face among Jim Henson's Muppets in *Sesame Street*.

Julia's other early films included a 1971 adaptation of Richard Farina's book *Been Down So Long It Looks Like Up to Me*, and *The Panic in Needle Park* (1971), a film about heroin addiction starring Al Pacino. Critics took note when

Julia starred in the striking Brazilian feature *Kiss of the Spider Woman* (1985). He played a political prisoner who shares a jail cell with a homosexual played by William Hurt. Critic Roger Ebert wrote that his performance revealed "a poetry that makes the whole movie work."

Displaying astonishing versatility, Julia gave a blazing performance in *Romero* (1989) as Salvadorean Archbishop Oscar Romero, then reprised an earlier stage role on screen, playing MacHeath in *Mack the Knife* (1990). He took the title part in Roger Corman's *Frankenstein Unbound* (1990). Julia then showed off one of his more unusual movie accents as a sadistic German car thief in the Clint Eastwood vehicle *The Rookie* (1990).

Acclaim

It was Julia's performance as the dapper patriarch Gomez Addams in *The Addams Family* (1991) that brought him to the notice of a wider audience. Based on the popular TV series and *New Yorker* cartoons by Charles Addams, the movie showcased Julia's gift for comedy; the chemistry that Julia shared with Anjelica Huston (who played his wife, Morticia) made for a successful movie that spawned a 1993 sequel. The projects were among Julia's last.

John Frankenheimer's TV production *The Burning Season* (1994) was perhaps Julia's greatest work. He played the Brazilian rubber tapper and environmentalist Chico Mendes. The performance earned him an Emmy, a Golden Globe, and a Screenwriters Guild Award in 1995. The accolades were bestowed on the actor posthumously, however. He died, aged 54, on October 24, 1994, several days after suffering a stroke.

KEY DATES

1940	Born in San Juan, Puerto Rico, on March 9.
1964	Moves to New York to become a professional actor.
1968	Appears on Broadway in *The Cuban Thing*.
1972	Wins a Tony nomination for *Two Gentlemen of Verona*.
1985	Appears in *Kiss of the Spider Woman*.
1991	Enjoys box-office success with *The Addams Family*.
1994	Dies on October 24 in New York.

See also: Ferrer, José; Moreno, Rita; Smits, Jimmy

Further reading: Cruz, Barbara. *Raul Julia: Actor and Humanitarian*. Berkeley Heights, NJ: Enslow Publishers, 1998. http://www.cigaraficionado.com/Cigar/CA_Archives/CA_Show_Article/0,2322,813,00.html (interview with Julia).

SET INDEX

Volume numbers are in **bold** type. Page numbers in *italics* refer to captions.

A

9/11 attacks *see* September 11th terrorist attacks
10 Years' War, Fernández Cavada and **3**:*112*
20/20 (news program) **8**:*89*
21 Grams (film) **3**:*46*
500 Years of Chicano History in Pictures (book) **5**:*69*
"Abaniquito" (song) **6**:*39*
Abbott, William **8**:*123*
Abraxas (album) **7**:*120*
Abu Ghraib Prison torture scandal **4**:*42*, **7**:*113*
acculturation **1**:*79–82*
Acevedo-Vilá, Aníbal **1**:*4*
Acosta, José Julián **1**:*5*
Acosta, Juan **1**:*6*
Acosta, Oscar Zeta **1**:*7–8*
activism **1**:*9–14*
actos **1**:*10*
Acuña, Rodolfo **1**:*15*, **6**:*48*
Ada, Alma Flor **1**:*16*
Adolfo **1**:*17*
advocacy groups **8**:*46*
Advocates, The **6**:*107*
affirmative action **8**:*34*
Affleck, Ben **5**:*39*
Agreda, María de Jesús de **3**:*25*; **7**:*34*
AFL-CIO, Linda Chavez-Thompson and **2**:*96–97*
Afro-Cuban Jazz Moods (album) **6**:*77*
Afro-Cuban Jazz Suite, The (album) **6**:*77*
Afro-Cubans, The **5**:*50*, 51
Agosín, Marjorie **1**:*18*
Agricultural Labor Relations Act (ALRA; 1975) **5**:*13*
Agricultural Workers Organizing Committee (AWOC) **5**:*13*
agriculture and migrant labor **1**:*19–24*
see also labor organizations
Aguilera, Christina **1**:*25*, *129–130*, **4**:*105*, **6**:*35*
Airto **1**:*26*
Alamo, the **3**:*24*, **7**:*133*, 134, **8**:*42–43*, 48, 80
Alamo, The (film) **3**:*11*
Alarcón, Francisco X. **1**:*27*
Alarcón, Martín de **3**:*23–24*
Alba, Jessica **1**:*28*
Albino, Johnny **1**:*29*
Albita (Albita Rodríguez) **7**:*51*
Albizu, Olga **1**:*30*
Albizu Campos, Pedro **1**:*31–32*, **2**:*109*, **5**:*23*, 24, **8**:*16*
Alcalá, Kathleen **1**:*33*
Alcaraz, Lalo **1**:*34–35*
Alegría, Fernando **1**:*36*
Alers, Rafael **1**:*6*
Alfaro, Luis **1**:*37*
Algarín, Miguel **1**:*38–39*
Alianza Americana **6**:*42*
Alianza Federal de Mercédes (Federal Land Grant Alliance) **1**:*12*, **2**:*108*, **6**:*125–126*, **8**:*59*

Alianza Federal de Pueblos Libres (Federal Alliance of Free Towns) **8**:*60*
Alien Registration Act (Smith Act; 1940) **5**:*98–99*
Allende, Isabel **1**:*40–41*
Allende, Salvador **3**:*77*
almanaques **4**:*109*
Almaraz, Carlos **1**:*42*
Almeida, Santiago **5**:*78*, **6**:*37*, **8**:*49*
Alomar, Roberto **1**:*43*
Alonso, Alicia **1**:*44–45*
Alou, Felipe **1**:*46*
altarcitos **7**:*37*
Alurista **1**:*47–48*, **4**:*49*
Alvarado, Juan Bautista **1**:*49–50*, 100, **2**:*69–70*
Alvarado, Linda **1**:*51*
Alvarado, Pablo **1**:*52*
Alvarez, Julia **1**:*53*
Alvarez, Luis Walter **1**:*54–55*
Alvarez, Paulina **3**:*13*
Álvarez de Piñeda, Alonso **1**:*56*
Alvariño de Leira, Angeles **1**:*57*
American Civil Liberties Union (ACLU), Anthony D. Romero and **7**:*78–79*
American Communist Party (ACP), leaders on trial (1949) **5**:*98–99*
American Educator (magazine) **2**:*95*
American Family (TV series) **6**:*46–47*
American Federation of Labor (AFL) **5**:*9–10*
see also AFL-CIO
American GI Forum (AGIF) **1**:*11*, *12*, **4**:*10*, 11, **5**:*113*, **6**:*42*, 43, **8**:*32*
Raúl Yzaguirre and **8**:*127*
American Revolution
Bernardo de Gálvez and **3**:*134*
Esteban Rodríguez Miró and **5**:*119*
Amor Prohibido (album) **8**:*5*
Anaya, Rudolfo Alfonso **1**:*58–59*, **2**:*91*, **4**:*103*
Anaya, Toney **1**:*60*
Angelico, Fray *see* Chávez, Angélico
Anguiano, Lupe **1**:*61*
Anthony, Marc *see* Marc Anthony
Antonio Maceo Brigade **2**:*56*
Anzaldúa, Gloria Evangelina **1**:*14*, *62*, **6**:*10*
Aparicio, Luis **1**:*63*
Apodaca, Jerry **1**:*64*
Aponte-Martínez, Luis **1**:*65*
Arana, Marie **1**:*66*
Archuleta, Diego **1**:*67*
"Ardillitas, Las" **4**:*71*
Arenas, Reinaldo **1**:*68*
Areu, José **6**:*59*
Arias, Ron **1**:*69*
Arista, Mariano **8**:*44*
Arizona, and bilingual education **5**:*92*
Armes, Jay J. **1**:*70*
Armstrong, Louis **1**:*113*
Arnaz, Desi **1**:*71–72*, **4**:*98*, 106, *107*, 108–109, **6**:*38*

Arnaz, Desi, Jr. **1**:*73*
Arpa School of Painting **4**:*64*
Arrau, Claudio **1**:*74–75*
Arreguín, Alfredo **1**:*76*
Arrillaga, Mariano Paredes y **8**:*43*
Arriola, Gus **1**:*35*
Arroyo, Martina **1**:*77*
Arvizu, Steven **1**:*78*
Asco (art group) **4**:*4*
Asociación Nacional Mexico-Americana (ANMA) **2**:*108*, 127
Asociación Protectora de Madres **4**:*87*
Aspira **6**:*101*
assimilation **1**:*79–82*
José T. Canales and **2**:*32*
Astaire, Fred **4**:*80*
At War with Diversity (book) **1**:*129*
atomic particles **4**:*12*
Atracciones Noloesca **6**:*59*
Austin, Moses **7**:*132*
Austin, Stephen Fuller **8**:*24*, 42
Autobiography of a Brown Buffalo (book) **1**:*8*
Avila, Carlos **1**:*83*
Avila, Marcus **7**:*127*
Ayala, Francisco J. **1**:*84*
Azpiazu, Don **1**:*85*
Azteca (group) **3**:*88*
Aztecs, music **6**:*35*
Aztec people **4**:*107*
Aztlán **1**:*13*, 47
Aztlán: Chicano Journal of the Social Sciences and Arts **4**:*40*

B

Baca, Elfego **1**:*86*
Baca, Jimmy Santiago **1**:*87–88*
Baca, Judith Francisca **1**:*89–90*, **4**:*38*
Baca, Polly **1**:*91*
Badillo, Herman **1**:*92*
Baez, Joan **1**:*93–94*, **4**:*107*
baianas **5**:*118*
Baird, Lourdes G. **1**:*95*
Bakhunin, Mikhail **3**:*125*
Bakke case **8**:*34*
Balboa, Marcelo **1**:*96*
"Ballad of Gregorio Cortez" (song) **2**:*9*
Ballad of Gregorio Cortez, The (film) **2**:*9*
Ball, Lucille **1**:*71*, 72, 73, **4**:*107*, 108–109
Balmaseda, Liz **1**:*97*
Bamba, La (album) **5**:*46*
Bamba, La (film) **8**:*82*, 84
"Bamba, La" (song) **6**:*38*, **8**:*83*, 84
Banderos, Antonio **4**:*98*
Bandini, José **1**:*99*, 100
Bandini, Juan **1**:*99–100*
Bañuelos, Ramona Acosta **1**:*101*, **6**:*87*
Barceló, Antonio R. **6**:*30*
Barceló, Maria Gertrudes **1**:*102*
Barela, Casimiro **1**:*103–104*
Barela, Patrocino **1**:*105*
Barenboim, Enrique **7**:*129*

Barkley, David Bennes **1**:*106*, **5**:*112*
Barraza, Santa **1**:*107*
Barrera, Aida **1**:*108*
Barretto, Ray **1**:*109*, 132, **6**:*38*, 39
barrios **3**:*74*
Barrymore, Drew **3**:*60*
Batista, Tomás **1**:*110*
Batiz, Xavier **7**:*121*
Bautista de Anza, Juan **1**:*111*
Bauzá, Mario **1**:*112–113*, **5**:*50*, **6**:*38*
Bay of Pigs crisis **4**:*122*, **5**:*88*
Bazar, Philip **5**:*112*
Bazooka: the Battles of Wilfredo Gomez (documentary) **4**:*37*
Bear Flag Republic **2**:*70*
Beaubien, Carlos **1**:*114*
Beltran, Carlos **5**:*115*
Benavides, Alonso de **3**:*25*
Benavides, Cristóbal **1**:*115*
Benavides, Placido **1**:*116*
Benavides, Refugio **1**:*115*, *117*
Benavidez, Roy P. **1**:*118*
Benes, Bernardo **1**:*119*
Benitez, John "Jellybean" **1**:*120*
Benítez, José Gautier **1**:*121*
Benítez, Sandra **1**:*122*
Benítez, Wilfred **1**:*123*, **6**:*100*
Bennett, William **5**:*71*
Berrios, Steve **1**:*124*
Bert, Guillermo **1**:*125*
big bands **6**:*38*
Big Pun **1**:*126*, **3**:*102*, **4**:*107*, **6**:*40*
bilingualism **1**:*127–130*, **3**:*72–73*
Bilingual Education Act (1968) **1**:*128*
Carrascolendas (TV series) and **1**:*108*
code switching **3**:*28*
Biltmore Six **1**:*7–8*
Birth of a City (mural) **7**:*74*
Bithorn, Hiram **1**:*131*
Blades, Rubén **1**:*132–133*, **2**:*120*
Bless Me, Ultima (book) **1**:*58*, 59, **4**:*50*
blowouts, in Los Angeles (1968) **3**:*90*, **4**:*4*
Bobo, Eric **3**:*20*
Bocanegra, Carlos **1**:*134*
Bohemia (magazine) **7**:*127*
boleros **5**:*130*
Daniel Santos and **7**:*125*
Bonilla, Tony **2**:*4*
boogaloo **3**:*16*
border, Mexico-United States **2**:*5–10*, **8**:*46*
Catarino E. Garza and **4**:*22*
cross-border trade **2**:*9*
culture **2**:*9–10*
illegal immigration across **2**:*8–9*, **8**:*27*
maquiladoras **2**:*9*, *10*
suspicious deaths of women along **4**:*25*, **5**:*39*
twin cities **2**:*8*
Border Arts Workshop/Taller de Arte Fronterizo (BAW/TAF) **6**:*75*
Border Incident (film) **5**:*131*
Border Industrialization Program (BIP) **1**:*23*

Set Index

Border Protection, Antiterrorism, and Illegal Immigration Control Act, amendment (2005) **8**:105
Border Realities (mural) **6**:75
Bordertown (film) **4**:132, **5**:39
Bori, Lucrezia **2**:11
"Borinqueña, La" (song) **5**:4, **7**:73
Borinqueneers **5**:114
Botero, Fernando **2**:12
Botiller v. Dominguez (1899) **8**:32
boveda catalan **4**:68
Boy Without a Flag, The (book) **7**:50
Bracero Experience: Elitelore Versus Folklore, The (book) **4**:96
Bracero Program **1**:21–23, **2**:8, 107, **3**:72, 130, **4**:121, **5**:13, **6**:44, **8**:27, 46
Brando, Marlon **8**:12
Brandon, Jorge **6**:119
Briseno, Rolando **2**:13
Bronx Remembered, El (book) **5**:121
Brooks, Gwendolyn **2**:104
Brown, Lee **5**:71
"browning of the Midwest" **1**:24
Brown v. Board of Education (1954) **2**:106, 107, **6**:126–127
"Bruca Manigua" (song) **7**:54
Buffalo Nickel (book) **7**:98
bugalu **3**:16
Bujones, Fernando **2**:14–15
Bulge, Battle of the **5**:40
Bullock, Sandra **5**:36
Burciaga, José Antonio **2**:16
Bush, George H.W.
  and drug czars **5**:70, 71
  and Lauro F. Cavazos **2**:73–74
Bush, George W.
  Alberto Gonzales and **4**:41–42
  Rosario Marin and **5**:60
Bustamante, Cruz **2**:17

C

Caballero (book) **4**:56
Cabana, Robert Donald **2**:18
Cabeza de Baca, Ezekiel **2**:19
Cabeza de Baca, Fabiola **2**:20
Cabrera, Lydia **2**:21
Caesar, Sid **2**:114, 115
Cahuenga, Treaty of (1847) **6**:116
Cahuenga Pass, Second Battle of **2**:70
Calderón, Alberto **2**:22
Calderón, Gilberto Miguel (Joe Cuba) **3**:16
Calderón, Sila María **1**:4, **2**:23–24
Calendar of Dust (book) **7**:95
calendars **4**:109
California
  affirmative action in **8**:34
  bandits (1800s) **3**:120
  Gold Rush **8**:26
  language **1**:129, **5**:92
  Mariano Guadalupe Vallejo and **8**:88
  Proposition 187 (1994) **4**:82, **6**:58
  Proposition 227 (1998) **8**:33
  state prison **5**:123
  transfer from Mexico to the United States **6**:116, 117

Treaty of Guadalupe Hidalgo and **4**:66
Calleros, Cleofas **2**:25
caló **4**:70
Calvillo, María Del Carmen **2**:26
Camacho, Héctor **2**:27–28
Camillo, Marvin **6**:122
Campaign 3 P.M. **7**:53
Campeche y Jordán, José **2**:29, **7**:49, 74
Campos, Juan Morel **2**:30
Canales, José T. **2**:31–32
Canales, Laura **2**:33, **8**:5
Canales, Nemesio **2**:34
"Canción de invierno" (elegy) **6**:9
"Canción Mexicana" (song) **4**:70, 71
cancións (songs) **6**:36
"Candida" (song) **6**:85
Canícula (book) **2**:37
Cannery and Agricultural Workers Industrial Union (CAWIU) **5**:11
Canseco, Jose **2**:35
Cansino, Rita *see* Hayworth, Rita
Cantor, Andrés **2**:36
Canto y Grito Mi Liberacíon (book) **7**:111
Cantú, Norma Elia **2**:37
Capetillo, Luisa **2**:38
Capirotada (book) **7**:43
Capital Punishment (album) **4**:107
Capobianco, Tito **2**:40
Capó, Bobby **2**:39
Cara, Irene **2**:41
CARA–Chicano Art: Resistance and Affirmation (exhibition) **6**:6, 75
Caramelo (book) **2**:104
Caras Viejas y Vino Nuevo (book) **6**:12
"Caravan" (song) **8**:61
Carbajal, José María Jesús **1**:116, **2**:42, **3**:6
Carbajal, Michael **2**:43
Carew, Rod **2**:44
Carey, Mariah **2**:45–46
Carlito's Way (book and film) **8**:63
Carmona, Richard H. **2**:47–48
Carollo, Joe **8**:30
Carpenter, John **7**:72
Carranza, Venustiano **7**:26
Carrasco, Barbara **2**:50
Carrascolendas (TV series) **1**:108
Carrera, Barbara **2**:51
Carreta, La (play) **5**:62
Carreta Made a U-Turn, La (poetry) **5**:19
Carrillo, Elpidia **2**:52
Carrillo, Leo **2**:53
Carrillo, Leopoldo **2**:54
Carr, Vikki **2**:49
Cartéles (magazine) **7**:127
Carter, Lynda **2**:55, **4**:80
Caruso, Enrico **3**:18
CASA (Centro de Acción Social Autónoma) **6**:9
Casal, Lourdes **2**:56
Casals, Jordi **2**:57
Casals, Pablo **2**:58
Casals, Rosemary **2**:59
Casares, Oscar **2**:60
Casas, Juan Bautista de las **2**:61
Casas Revolt **2**:61, **7**:132
Casino de la Playa band **7**:54
Castaneda, Carlos **2**:62–63

Castañeda, Carlos Eduardo **2**:64–65
Castillo, Ana **2**:66
Castillo, Leonel **2**:67
Castro, Fidel **1**:119, **2**:110, **4**:122, **7**:37
  Daniel Santos and **7**:125
  and the Elián González case **4**:123
  and Jorge Mas Canosa **5**:88
  and José Martí **5**:64
Castro, George **2**:68
Castro, José **2**:69–70
Castro, Raúl **2**:71
Catholicism **7**:33–38
  mariachi masses **6**:36
  María Elena Durazo and **3**:82
  Virgilio Elizondo and **3**:84
Caucasian Race Resolution, of Texas **8**:47
Cavazos, Bobby **2**:72
Cavazos, Lauro F. **2**:73–74, 75
Cavazos, Richard E. **2**:75–76, **5**:113
Center for Latino Educational Excellence (CLEE) **7**:47
Centro de Arte Puertorriqueño **7**:85
Cepeda, Orlando **2**:77
Cerro Maravilla incident **7**:83
Cervantes, Lorna Dee **2**:78
Cesar Pelli Associates **6**:106
Chacón, Eusebio **2**:79
Chacón, Felipe Maximiliano **2**:80
Chacón, Iris **2**:81
Chagoya, Enrique **2**:82
Chang-Díaz, Franklin R. **2**:83
Chapa, Francisco A. **2**:84, **3**:14
Chaplin, Charlie **3**:17
Charanga Duboney **6**:98
Charca, La (book) **8**:133
Charlie Brown TV animations **5**:101
Chata, La (La Chata Noloesca) **6**:59
Chaves, J. Francisco **2**:85
Chaves, Manuel Antonio **5**:112
Chávez, Angélico **2**:86–87
Chávez, César **1**:12, 81, **2**:88–89, 108, 121, **6**:44, 124, **8**:81
  and the Delano grape strike **5**:12
  Dolores Huerta and **4**:113, 114
  holiday devoted to **5**:14
  Maria Hinojosa and **4**:99
Chávez, Denise **2**:90–91
Chavez, Dennis **1**:60, **2**:92–93, **6**:7
Chavez, Julio Cesar **3**:32
Chavez, Julz **2**:94
Chavez, Linda **2**:95
Chávez, Thomas E. **2**:87
Chávez Fernández, Alicia **4**:113, 114
Chavez Ravine (play) **4**:71
Chavez-Thompson, Linda **2**:96–97
Cheech and Chong **5**:57–58
Chicanismo (film) **1**:37
Chicano (book) **8**:93
Chicano Art: Resistance and Affirmation *see* CARA
Chicano moratorium **7**:100
Chicano movement **1**:81, **2**:108–109, **4**:104–105, 106, 109, **6**:125–126
  Bert Corona and **2**:127
  bilingual newsletters **5**:93

Corky Gonzales and **4**:49
Gloria Molina and **5**:122
Luis Omar Salinas and **7**:101
Mario Compeán and **2**:121
Martha P. Cotera and **3**:10
Oscar Zeta Acosta and **1**:7–8
Réies López Tijerina and **8**:59, 60
Rodolfo Acuña and **1**:15
Chicanos
  meaning of the term **1**:15
  muralists **1**:89–90, **4**:65, 83, 109
  theater **4**:115
Chicano studies **1**:9–10, 13, 59, **6**:48
  international conference on **4**:96
Chico and the Man (TV series) **7**:13
Chicxulub crater **6**:70
"Child of the Americas" (poem) **5**:27
Chinese Exclusion Act (1882) **4**:120
CHiPs (TV series) **3**:98
Chong, Tommy **5**:57–58
Christian, Linda **2**:98
Chulas Fronteras (documentary) **4**:130
Cibola, Seven Cities of **2**:129–130, **3**:49–50
"Cierra los Ojos" (song) **5**:129
Cinco de Mayo holiday **8**:131, 132
Cintrón, Nitza Margarita **2**:99
Cisneros, Evelyn **2**:100
Cisneros, Henry G. **2**:101–102
Cisneros, Sandra **2**:103–104
Ciudad Juarez murders **5**:39
civil rights **2**:105–110, **6**:42–43
  see also Chicano movement
Civil Rights Act (1964) **2**:107
Civil War **5**:111–112
  Cristóbal Benavides and **1**:115
  Fernández Cavada and **3**:112
  Francisco J. Chaves and **2**:85
  Loreta Janeta Velazquez and **8**:103
  Refugio Benavides and **1**:117
  Texas in **8**:45
Clark, Ellen Riojas **2**:111
Clark, Georgia Neece **6**:87
Clemente, Roberto **2**:112–113, **8**:19
Clinton, Bill **6**:45
  and Bill Richardson **7**:42
  and Federico Peña **6**:110
Clooney, Rosemary **3**:116, 117
Coca, Imogene **2**:114–115
Codex Delilah: a Journey from México to Chicana (artwork) **6**:5
Coca-Cola Company, Roberta Goizueta and **4**:30–31
Colmenares, Margarita **2**:116
colonias **8**:26
Colón, Jesús **2**:117, **8**:98
Colón, Miriam **2**:118
Colón, Willie **1**:132–133, **2**:119–120, 50, 51
Colquitt, Oscar B. **2**:84
comancheros **8**:35
Combs, Sean "Puff Daddy" **5**:38, 39
Coming Home Alive (book) **5**:27
Coming of the Night, The (book) **7**:32

Comisión Femenil Nacional (CFMN) **5**:122
Comité, El **6**:128
communism, trial of American Communist Party leaders **5**:98–99
Community Service Organization (CSO)
  César Chávez and **2**:89
  Dolores Huerta and **4**:113
Comonfort, Ignacio **8**:131
Compeán, Mario **2**:*121*
Confederación de Uniones Oberos Mexicanos (CUOM) **1**:21, **2**:106
conga, the **1**:72
Congreso de Pueblos que Hablan Español, El **6**:21
Congress of Industrial Organizations (CIO) **5**:12
  Luisa Moreno and **6**:21
Congressional Hispanic Caucus (CHC) **6**:132–133
Conjunto La Perfecta **6**:99
conjunto music (*musica norteña*; *norteño*) **5**:46, **6**:35, 37, **8**:49, 50
  Arsenio Rodríguez and **7**:54, 55
  Narciso Martínez and **5**:77, 78
Cooder, Ry **4**:130
Coordinator of Inter-American Affairs (CIIA) **4**:108, **8**:46
Cordero, Angel, Jr. **2**:*122*–123
Cordero, Rafael **1**:5, **8**:38
Córdova, France Anne **2**:*124*
Corea, Chick **1**:26, **2**:*125*–126
Corona, Bert **2**:*127*, **7**:89
Corona, Juan **2**:*128*
Coronado, Francisco Vásquez de **2**:*129*–130, **3**:49, 50, 51, **8**:23, 35
Coronel, Antonio F. **2**:*131*–132
Corpi, Lucha **2**:*133*
Corretjer, Juan Antonio **2**:134, **7**:125
"Corrido de Delano, El" (song) **4**:71
corridos (songs) **2**:9, **6**:36–37, **8**:48, 49
Cortés, Carlos E. **3**:4
Cortés, Hernán **3**:53, 54, **7**:33
Cortez, Gregorio **2**:84, **3**:5, 14
  film about **6**:81
Cortijo, Rafael **4**:126
Cortina, Juan Nepomuceno **3**:6–7
Cortines, Ramón C. **3**:8
Corzine, Jon **5**:106
Coser y Cantar (play) **7**:11
Cota-Cárdenas, Margarita **3**:9
Cotera, Martha P. **3**:10
Crawford, James **1**:129
Cristal, Linda **3**:11
Crónica, La (newspaper) **2**:105, **4**:116, 117, **5**:92, **6**:42
Cruz, Carlos **6**:89
Cruz, Celia **3**:*12*–13, 75, 83, **4**:107
Cruz, Pablo **3**:*14*
Cruzada para la Justicia (Crusade for Justice) **2**:108, **4**:49
Cruz González, José **3**:*15*
Cuba
  constitution (1940) **7**:55
  diaspora **4**:53
  mass emigration of children from **5**:75, 76, 102

U.S. trade embargo **5**:89
  see also Cubans
Cuba, Joe **3**:*16*
Cuban Adjustment Act (1966) **4**:123
Cuban American National Council (CNC) **3**:61–62, **6**:129
Cuban American National Foundation (CANF) **5**:89, **6**:129
Cuban Americans, activism **1**:13–14
Cuban Liberty and Democratic Solidarity Act (Helms-Burton Act; 1996) **5**:106, **7**:86
Cuban Representation in Exile (RECE) **5**:88
Cubans **2**:110
  Elián González case **4**:123
  Freedom Flight and **4**:123
  as immigrants **1**:82, **2**:110, **3**:35–36, **4**:*122*–124, **8**:25
  Mariel Boatlift **3**:35, **4**:123–124
  music **6**:37–38, 40
  and newspapers **5**:93
  political movements **6**:129
  political representation **6**:131–132
Cucaracha, La (cartoon strip) **1**:34, 35
"*cuentó puertorriqueno, el*" **5**:121
Cuentos del hogar (book) **4**:128
Cugat, Xavier **1**:72, **3**:*17*–18, **4**:106, **6**:38
Culture Swing (album) **4**:100
Cunningham, Glenn **5**:106
Cursillo movement **3**:121
Cybrids: La Raza Techno-Crítica, Los **5**:130
Cypress Hill **3**:*19*–20, **4**:107, **6**:40

D

Daddy Yankee **3**:*21*, **4**:107, **6**:40
Dallas (TV series) **7**:12
Dallmeier, Francisco **3**:*22*
Dancing with Cuba (book) **4**:72
danzas **2**:30
Danzas Mexicanas **5**:30
danzas puertorriqueñas **1**:6
danzón music **7**:55
Dawn (backing duo) **6**:85
Day of the Dead **7**:34, 38
De Alarcón, Martín **3**:*23*–24
Dean, James **8**:12
Death of an Anglo (book) **6**:12
Death and the Maiden (play) **3**:76–77
De Benavides, Alonso **3**:*25*
De Burgos, Julia **3**:*26*–27
Decastro, Joseph H. **5**:112
De Hoyos, Angela **3**:*28*
de la Garza, Carlos **3**:29
de la Garza, Eligio "Kika" **3**:*30*
De La Hoya, Oscar **2**:28, **3**:*31*–32, **5**:124, **8**:90
Delano grape strike **4**:114, **5**:12, 13
Delano-Sacramento march (1994) **2**:89, **7**:56
de la Renta, Oscar **3**:*33*
de la Rocha, Zack **3**:*34*
del Castillo, Adelaida R. **6**:9
del Castillo, Siro **3**:35–36
de León, Alonso **3**:37

de León de Vega, Sonia Marie **3**:*38*
De León family **2**:42, **3**:39–40
  Fernando De León **1**:116, **3**:39
  Martin De León **3**:39
  Patricia De La Garza De León **3**:39, 40
  Silvestre De León **3**:39–40
Delgado, Abelardo **3**:*41*
del Olmo, Frank **3**:*42*
del Río, Dolores **3**:43–44, **4**:108
Del Toro, Benicio **3**:*45*–46
Del Valle, Ygnacio **3**:*47*
Del Villard, Sylvia **3**:*48*
Democracia, La (newspaper) **6**:32
de Niza, Marcos **3**:49–50, **8**:22
de Oñate, Cristóbal **3**:51, 52
de Oñate, Juan **3**:*51*–52
"Deportado, El" (song) **6**:36
Deporting the Divas (play) **7**:39
"descargas" **5**:37
Desert Blood (book) **4**:25
De Soto, Hernando **3**:*53*–54
Desperado (film) **4**:77–78
de Vargas, Diego **3**:*55*, **8**:23
de Varona, Donna **3**:*56*
de Zavala, Lorenzo **3**:*57*–58
de Zavala, Lorenzo, Jr. **3**:58
Día de los Muertos (Day of the Dead) **7**:34, 38
Día Normal, Un (album) **4**:132
Diaz, Cameron **3**:*59*–60, **4**:105
Díaz, Guarioné M. **3**:*61*–62
Díaz, Junot **3**:*63*
Díaz, Justino **3**:*64*
Diaz Dennis, Patricia **3**:*68*
Diddy (Sean Combs) **5**:39
"Diepalismo" **6**:96
Dihigo, Martin **3**:*69*
Dimas, Trent **3**:*70*
Dinos, Los **8**:5
Diputación, Pío Pico and **6**:117, 118
"Discriminación a un Mártir" (song) **6**:37
discrimination **3**:71–74
D'León, Oscar **3**:*75*
Dolores Huerta Foundation **4**:114
"Donna" (song) **8**:83, 84
Don Pedro *see* Albizu Campos, Pedro
Dorfman, Ariel **3**:76–77
Dreaming in Cuba (book) **4**:9
D'Rivera, Paquito **3**:*78*–79
drug czars **5**:70, 71
Duran, Alfredo **3**:*80*
Durazo, María Elena **3**:*81*–82
Dying to Cross (book) **7**:27

E

Eastern Airlines **5**:44
East L.A. 13, the **1**:7
East L.A. Blowouts **3**:90, **4**:4
Echo Amphitheater Park **8**:60
Edición Critica, Eugenio María de Hostos (book) **4**:112
education **3**:72–73, **5**:127
  language in **1**:127–128, 129, 130, **3**:73, **5**:92
  Lauro F. Cavazos and **2**:73–74
  multicultural **6**:54

Sara Martinez Tucker and **5**:87
segregation in *see* segregation in education
Ehkymosis (band) **4**:132
Elektric Band **2**:126
Elephant Butte Dam **2**:7
El General **3**:*83*
Elizondo, Virgilio **3**:*84*
El Mozote massacre **4**:72
El Paso, Texas **2**:6
El Salvador, El Mozote massacre **4**:72
Elvira, Rafael **5**:130
employment **3**:72
  see also Bracero Program; labor organizations
enganchistas **1**:20
En Mi Imperio (album) **7**:17
Environmental Protection Agency (EPA) **6**:53
Escalante, Jaime **3**:*85*
Escandón, José de **3**:*86*, **4**:24
Escobar, Eleuterio **4**:88
Escobar, Sixto **3**:*87*
Escovedo, Pete **3**:*88*
Escuela Tlatelolco, La **4**:49
Espada, Martín **3**:*89*
Esparza, Moctesuma **3**:*90*
Espejo, El (book) **7**:77
Espíritu Santo land grant **4**:24
Estampas del valle y otras obras (book) **4**:102–103
Estefan, Emilio **3**:*91*, 92, 93, **6**:40
Estefan, Gloria **3**:91, *92*–93, **4**:107, **7**:131
Estés, Clarissa Pinkola **3**:*94*–95
Estevanico (Esteban) **3**:49–50
Esteves, Sandra María **3**:*96*
Estevez, Emilio **3**:*97*
Estrada, Erik **3**:*98*
Estrada, Miguel **3**:*99*, **8**:31
Estrella de Mora, La (newspaper) **8**:74
evolutionary theory, teaching **1**:84
Executive Order 9981 **5**:113
"Eyes of Father Margil, The" (miracle) **5**:55

F

"Fade Into You" (single) **7**:118
Fairbanks, Douglas **4**:108
Fania All-Stars **3**:*100*–101, **6**:39, 94, **7**:20
Fania Records **6**:94
Farm Labor Organizing Committee (FLOC) **1**:23, **5**:14, **6**:44, **8**:101
Farm Workers Association (FWA) **4**:113
"Father of California" *see* Serra, Junípero
"Father of Modern Puerto Rico" *see* Muñoz Marín, Luis
"Father of Texas" *see* Austin, Stephen Fuller
Fat Joe **3**:*102*, **4**:107, **6**:40
Federal Art Project **1**:105
Federal Land Grant Alliance *see* Alianza Federal de Mercedes
Feliciano, Cheo **3**:*103*
Feliciano, José **3**:*104*–105
Felita (book) **5**:121
feminists, Latina **1**:14
Fender, Freddy **3**:*106*, **4**:107

Set Index

Fernández, Emilio **3**:44
Fernandez, Evelina **3**:*107*, **8**:87
Fernández, Gigi **3**:*108*
Fernández, Manny **3**:*109*
Fernández, Mary Joe **3**:108, *110*
Fernández, Ricardo R. **3**:*111*
Fernández Cavada, Federico **3**:*112*
Ferré, Luis A. **3**:*113*–114
Ferré, Maria Luisa **3**:114
Ferré, Rosario **3**:114, 115
Ferrer, José **3**:*116*–117, **4**:108
Ferrer, Mel **3**:118
Ferrer, Miguel **3**:*119*
Flipper (TV series) **1**:28
Flores, Hector **4**:10, **6**:44
Flores, Juan **3**:120, **6**:116
Flores, Patrick F. **3**:*121*, **4**:34
Flores, Pedro **3**:*122*, **7**:125
Flores, Tom **3**:*123*
Flores Magón, Ricardo **3**:*124*–125
Floricanto en Aztlán (poetry) **1**:48
Florida
   Ponce de León and **7**:4, 5
   population (2000) **8**:25
food, Tex-Mex **8**:50–*51*
Foraker Act (Organic Act; 1900) **6**:33
Fornes, Maria Irene **3**:*126*, **6**:11
Foto-Novelas (TV series) **1**:83
Four, Los **7**:81
Fox, Vicente **4**:85
Franklin, Aretha **2**:46
Freak (show) **5**:25
Fredonia, Republic of **2**:5
Freedom Flight **4**:123
Freese, Louis **3**:19
Fremont, John Charles **2**:70
Frida (film) **4**:77, 78, **6**:46
Frisco War **1**:86
Fuente, Ivon **8**:30
Fuentes, Daisy **3**:*127*
FUERZA Inc. **5**:60

G

Gabaldon, Diana **3**:128
Gadsden Purchase **2**:6, **7**:104, **8**:25–26
Galán, Héctor **3**:*129*
Galarza, Ernesto **3**:130
Galindo, Rudy **3**:*131*
Gallegos, Herman **3**:*132*
Gallegos, José Manuel **3**:*133*
galleries **4**:109
Gallo: La Vaz de la Justicia, El (newspaper) **4**:49
Gálvez, Bernardo de **3**:*134*, **5**:119
Gamboa, Harry, Jr. **4**:4, 38
Gamio, Manuel **4**:5
Gandhi, Mohandas K. **2**:89
Garcia, Andy **1**:129–130, **4**:6–7, **5**:37, **7**:116
García, Clotilde **4**:8
Garcia, Cristina **4**:9
García, Gustavo C. **4**:10, 17, 94, **7**:29, **8**:33, 34
García, Héctor P. **1**:11, *12*, **4**:8, *11*, **5**:113
   and the funeral of Felix Longoria **5**:34
   and José Angel Gutiérrez **4**:73
García, J.D. **4**:12
Garcia, Jeff **4**:13
Garcia, Jerry **4**:*14*–15
García, Lionel **4**:16
García, Macario **4**:17
García, Rupert **4**:18

García Lorca, Federico **2**:91
García Márquez, Gabriel **1**:41, **8**:21
Garciaparra, Nomar **4**:*19*, **7**:52
Garza, Ben F. **4**:*20*–21
Garza, Catarino E. **4**:*22*
Garza, Reynaldo G. **4**:*23*
Garza Falcón, María de la **4**:24
Garza War **4**:22
Gaspar de Alba, Alicia **4**:*25*
Gauss, Christian **5**:99
Gavin, Christina **4**:27
Gavin, John **4**:*26*–27
gay community, Ileana Ros-Lehtinen and **7**:87
Gell-Mann, Murray **1**:55
Geneva Convention, war against terrorism and **4**:42
Gentleman's Agreement (1907) **4**:120
Geographies of Home (book) **6**:112
Geronimo **8**:26
Geronimo (mural) **6**:75
Get Real Girls **2**:94
GI Forum *see* American GI Forum
Gil, Federico **4**:28
Gillespie, Dizzy **6**:40, 77
   Arturo Sandoval and **7**:116, 117
   Chano Pozo and **7**:9
   Lalo Schifrin and **7**:128
Gioia, Dana **4**:29
Giuliani, Rudolf W. **3**:8
Giumarra, John **6**:*124*
Global Change Research Program (GCRP) **6**:53
Going Home (folk duo) **7**:118
Going to the Olympics (mural) **7**:81
Goizueta, Roberto **4**:*30*–31
Goizueta Family Foundation **4**:31
Goldemberg, Isaac **4**:32
Gold Rush, Californian **8**:26
Gómez, Edward **4**:33
Gómez, José H. **4**:34
Gomez, Scott **4**:35
Gomez, Vernon "Lefty" **4**:36
Gomez, Wilfredo **4**:37
Gómez-Peña, Guillermo **4**:*38*–39
Gómez-Quiñones, Juan **4**:40
Gonzales, Alberto **4**:*41*–42, 63
Gonzales, Boyer **4**:43
Gonzales, Manuel **4**:44
Gonzales, Manuel C. **4**:*45*
Gonzales, Ricardo **4**:*46*–47
Gonzales, Rodolfo "Corky" **1**:12, 14, 47, **2**:108, 109, **4**:*48*–49, **6**:*126*
Gonzales-Berry, Erlinda **4**:*50*
Gonzalez, Alfredo Cantu **4**:51, **6**:132
Gonzalez, Antonio **4**:*52*
González, Celedonio **4**:53
González, Elián **1**:14, **4**:123, 124, **5**:96
González, Henry B. **4**:*54*–55
González, Jovita **4**:56
Gonzalez, Juan **4**:*57*, **5**:96
Gonzalez, Juan D. **4**:*58*
Gonzalez, Kenny "Dope" **4**:*59*, **8**:99
González, Odilio **4**:*60*
González, Pedro J. **2**:106, **4**:*61*–62, 106, **5**:94, 95
González, Raúl **4**:*63*
González, Sila Mari **2**:23

González, Xavier **4**:64
Good Neighbor Commission **8**:46
Good Neighbor Policy **4**:108, 127
Gordo (cartoon strip) **1**:35
Gordon, Milton M. **1**:80
Gráfico (journal) **8**:98
Gran Combo, El (band) **4**:126, **7**:69
Gran Concilio de la Orden Caballeros de Honor **4**:117
Grateful Dead, The (rock band) **4**:14, 15
Great Depression
   anti-Hispanic feelings **8**:15
   Felix H. Morales and **6**:15
   and Mexican workers **1**:21, **2**:7, **4**:62, **5**:11, 94, **6**:48, **8**:27, 46
   and Spanish-language radio **5**:94
Great Wall of Los Angeles, The (mural) **1**:90
Green, Jerome **2**:106–107
Gregorio T. v. Wilson (1997) **1**:658
Grisman, David **4**:15
Grito, El (magazine) **7**:77
Grito de Dolores **2**:61
Grito de Lares, El (play) **8**:66
Grito del Norte, El (newspaper) **5**:69
Gronk **4**:4, *65*
Guadalupe, the Virgin of **7**:34, *36*
Guadalupe Hidalgo, Treaty of (1848) **1**:9, 10, 12, 47, **2**:6, **3**:71, 120, **4**:*66*–67, 105, **7**:34, **8**:25, 44
   and Mexicans **4**:67, 121, **5**:9, **6**:36, **7**:26, **8**:31, 32, 45, 48–49
   religion after **7**:34–35
   and Texas **8**:44
   and settlement in the Southwest **8**:22, 32
   violations **4**:67, **8**:59
Guadalupe Victoria, Texas **3**:39, 40
"Guantanamera" (song) **5**:63
Guantanamo Bay, Cuba, prison camp **4**:42, **5**:76
Guastavino, Rafael **4**:68
Guerra, Manuel **4**:69
Guerrero, Eduardo and Concepción **4**:71
Guerrero, Lalo **4**:*70*–71, **6**:38
Guerrero, Vicente **8**:24
Guillermoprieto, Alma **4**:72
"Guns for Toys" program **5**:91
Gutiérrez, José Angel **1**:13, **2**:109, **4**:*73*, 74
Gutiérrez, Luz Bazán **4**:74
Gutierrez, Theresa **4**:75
Guttierez, José Antonio **5**:114
Guzmán, Ralph **4**:76

H

habanera (musical style) **6**:37
Hamlet (essay) **4**:111
Hardscrub (book) **4**:16
Hayek, Salma **4**:*77*–78, 105
Haymarket Massacre **3**:125
Hays Code **4**:107–108
Hayworth, Rita **3**:18, **4**:*79*–80, 108
Heart That Bleeds, The (book) **4**:72

Helms-Burton Act *see* Cuban Liberty and Democratic Solidarity Act
Henna, Julio J. **8**:133
Hepburn, Audrey **3**:118
Hermanos al Rescate **6**:125
Hernández, Adán **4**:81
Hernández, Antonia **4**:*82*
Hernandez, Ester **4**:83
Hernández, Gilbert and Jaime **1**:35; **4**:*90*
Hernández, Joseph Marion **4**:84
Hernández, Juan **4**:85
Hernandez, Keith **4**:*86*–87
Hernández, María Latigo **4**:*87*–88
Hernández, Orlando **4**:89
Hernández, Pedro **4**:88
Hernández, Pete **8**:33, 34
Hernandez, Rene **5**:51
Hernández Bros., Los **1**:35; **4**:*90*
Hernández Colón, Rafael **4**:*91*
Hernández Cruz, Victor **4**:92
Hernández Mayoral, José **1**:4
Hernandez v. Texas (1954) **4**:10, **6**:43, **8**:33
Herrera, Carolina **4**:*93*
Herrera, John J. **4**:*94*, **8**:33
Herrera, Silvestre **4**:95
Herrera-Sobek, María **4**:96
Herrera y Tordesillas, Antonio de **7**:4, 5
Herrón, Willie **4**:4
Hidalgo, Edward **4**:*97*
High Chapparal, The (TV series) **3**:11
Hijuelos, Oscar **4**:98
Hinojosa, Maria **4**:*99*
Hinojosa, Tish **4**:*100*
Hinojosa de Ballí, Rosa María **4**:*101*
Hinojosa-Smith, Rolando **4**:*102*–103
hip-hop **4**:107
Hispanic (magazine) **5**:94
Hispanic Causing Panic (album) **6**:40
Hispanic identity and popular culture **4**:*104*–109
Hispanic National Bar Association **6**:45
Hispanic Scholarship Fund (HSF) **5**:87
Historic Cookery (book) **2**:20
H.O.L.A. (record label) **1**:120
Homar, Lorenzo **4**:110, **7**:85
Hombre Que Le Gustan Las Mujeres (picture) **5**:72
Homeland (album) **4**:100
Home Owner Loan Corporation **2**:93
Hostos, Eugenio María de **4**:*111*–112, **8**:133
Hotel Employees and Restaurant Employees (HERE) **3**:81, 82
House on Mango Street, The (book) **2**:103, 104
House of the Spirits, The (book and film) **1**:41
housing, social zoning and **3**:73–74
Houston, Sam **8**:42, 43
How the Garcia Girls Lost Their Accents (book) **1**:53
How to Read Donald Duck (book) **3**:76
Huerta, Dolores **1**:81, **4**:*113*–114, **5**:14
   and César Chávez **4**:114

Huerta, Jorge A. **4**:*115*
Huerta, Victoriano **7**:26
human rights, Ileana Ros-
Lehtinen and **7**:86
Hunter, Robert **4**:14
Huston, Walter **7**:19

I

Idar, Jovita **4**:*116*, 117
Idar, Nicasio **2**:105, **4**:116, *117*,
5:*92*, **6**:42
identity and popular culture
4:*104–109*
"If I Had a Hammer" (song) **5**:42
Iglesias, Enrique **4**:105, *118*, **6**:35
I Love Lucy (TV series) **1**:*71*, 72,
73, **4**:98, *107*, 108–109,
6:47
Imagine (magazine) **8**:112
immigration and immigration
law **1**:82, **2**:8–9, 105,
107–108, **4**:*119–124*,
6:44–45, **8**:27, 45–46
Immigration Act (1924;
National Origins Act)
4:120, 122
Immigration Act (1965) **4**:124
Immigration Act (1990) **4**:124
Immigration Reform and
Control Act (IRCA; 1986)
1:23, 24, **4**:124
Immigration Reform and
Immigrant Responsibility
Act (1996) **4**:124
poverty and immigrants
4:119–120
see also assimilation;
bilingualism; civil rights;
Cubans; Mexicans; Puerto
Ricans
"Imparcial, El" (poem) **6**:96
Imperial Valley Workers Union
5:11
*Importancia de Llamarse Daniel
Santos, La* (book) **7**:109
ImpreMedia **5**:94
Incas, de Soto and **3**:*53*
In the Dark (album) **4**:15
Infante, Pedro **5**:95
Infinito Botánica **5**:128
Initiative on Race **2**:97
Insular Labor Relations Act
(ILRA; 1945) **5**:12
International Ladies Garment
Workers Union (ILGWU)
2:106
Irakere **3**:79, **6**:40
Arturo Sandoval and **7**:116
Iraq, war in *see* Persian Gulf
War, Second
Irvin, Monte **2**:113
Islas, Arturo **4**:*125*
Ithier, Rafael **4**:*126*
Iturbi, José **4**:*127*
Iturbide, Agustin de **8**:24

J

Jackson, Helen Hunt **2**:132
Jaramillo, Cleofas M. **4**:*128*
Jaramillo, Mari-Luci **4**:*129*
Jarvel, Dagmar **6**:*98*
Jayuya Uprising **1**:32
jazz
bebop **6**:38
Cubop **6**:77
Latin (Afro-Cuban) **1**:113,
5:50, 51, **7**:16
Jazz Meets the Symphony
(music) **7**:129

Jet Capital Corporation **5**:44
Jeter, Derek **7**:52
Jimenez, Flaco **3**:106, **4**:106,
130, **8**:49, 50
Jiménez, Jose "Cha Cha" **2**:109
Jiménez, Luis **4**:131
Johnson, Bert "Bobo" **6**:68
Johnson, Lyndon B.
and the Civil Rights Act
2:107, 108
and the funeral of Dennis
Chavez **2**:93
and the funeral of Felix
Longoria **5**:34
and Porfirio Salinas **7**:103
Jones-Shafroth Act (Jones Act;
1917) **2**:109, **4**:122, **6**:33
Juanes **4**:*132*
Juárez, Benito **4**:49, **8**:131
Julia, Raul **4**:*133–134*
Juncos, Manuel Fernández **5**:4
Jurado, Katy **5**:*5*

K

Kahlo, Frida **4**:78, **5**:120
Kanellos, Nicolás **5**:*6*
Kapp, Joe **5**:*7*
Karatz, Bruce **6**:58
Katenback v. Morgan (1966) **3**:73
Keane, Bob **8**:83, 84
Kennedy, John F. **2**:108, **6**:132
Henry B. González and **8**:55
Kennedy, Ted **4**:124
Kesey, Ken **4**:14
Kid Frost **4**:107, **6**:40
Kid Gavilan **5**:*8*
King, Martin Luther, Jr. **2**:89,
3:77, **8**:60
"King of Latin Music" *see*
Puente, Tito
Kino, Eusebio Francisco **8**:*24*
"Klail City Death Trip" (books)
4:102–103
Klail City y sus alrededores
(book) **1**:3
KLVL (radio station) **6**:15
KMEX-TV **5**:96
"Knock Three Times" (song)
6:85
Koch, Frederick H. **6**:55, 56
Korean War **5**:113
the Borinqueneers **5**:114
Edward Gómez and **4**:33
Richard E. Cavazos and **2**:75
Kornberg, Arthur **6**:74
Krause, Martin **1**:75
Kreiten, Karlrobert **1**:75
Kreutzberg, Harald **5**:29, 30

L

"La Bamba" (song) **4**:107
labor, migrant *see* agriculture
and migrant labor
labor organizations **2**:106,
5:*9–14*, **6**:43–44
Ladies LULAC **5**:52
Lagos, Ricardo **4**:28
Laguerre, Enrique **5**:15–16
La India **4**:59, **5**:*17*
Lair, Clara *see* Negrón Muñoz,
Mercedes
Lalo y Sus Cinco Lobos **4**:70
laminas **1**:107
Lamy, Jean Baptiste **5**:68
Lane, Abbe **6**:*38*
Langoria, Felix **5**:113
language **1**:79–80, *81*, **5**:92
and education **1**:127–128,
129, *130*, **3**:73, **5**:92

Spanglish **8**:48
Spanish-language radio
stations **4**:106
of Tejanos **8**:51
and voting **3**:73
see also bilingualism
LaPorte, Juan **4**:37
La Providencia, Battle of **2**:70
La Raza Unida Party *see* Raza
Unida Party
Laredo **3**:86
Larrazolo, Octaviano **5**:*18*
Lasater, Edward C. **4**:69
las Casas, Juan Bautista de **2**:*61*
Lassa fever **2**:57
Latina (magazine) **5**:94
Latina Feminist Group **5**:27
Latin American Studies
Association (LASA) **4**:28
Latin Business Association (LBA)
6:45
Latino National Political Survey
(LNPS) **6**:131
Latinos and Latinas
feminist Latinas **1**:14
Latinas in World War II **5**:112
population **1**:80
the term 'Latinos' **1**:14
Latino Theater Company (LTC)
8:87
Latino USA (radio program)
4:106
Lau v. Nichols (1974) **1**:128, **8**:33
Laviera, Jesús **5**:*19*, **6**:119
Lavoe, Hector **5**:*20*
Layne, Alfredo **4**:37
League of Mexican Culture
5:93–94
League of United Latin American
Citizens (LULAC) **2**:106,
3:14, **4**:10, 17, **6**:42–43,
45, 125, **8**:26, 32, 46
Belén Robles and **7**:48
Ben F. Garza and **4**:*20*, 21
conference (2005) **6**:83
Esther N. Machuca and **5**:52
Felix Tijerina and **8**:57
first conference **4**:20
George Isidore Sanchez and
7:107
John J. Herrera and **4**:94
Ladies LULAC **5**:52
Manuel C. Gonzales and **4**:45
María Latigo Hernández and
4:87
Pete Tijerina and **8**:58
Vilma Martínez and **5**:85
Leal, Luis **5**:*21*
Leaños, John Jota **5**:*22*
Leaving Home (book) **4**:16
Lebrón, Lolita **1**:11, **5**:*23–24*
LeClerc, Juan Marco **6**:36
Lee, Wen Ho **7**:42
Leguizamo, John **5**:*25*
Lemon Grove case **1**:127–128,
2:107, **3**:72, 73, **8**:33
León, Alonso de **3**:37
León, Tania **5**:*26*
Letter From Santa Fe Jail, A **8**:60
Levins Morales, Aurora **5**:27
Lewis and Clark Expedition,
Manuel Lisa and **5**:31
libraries **5**:93–94
Lifshitz, Aliza **5**:*28*
Liga Femenil Mexicanista **2**:105,
4:116, **6**:42
Liga Pro-Defensa Escolar, La
4:88
"Light My Fire" (song) **3**:104

Lil' Rob **4**:107
Limón, José **5**:*29–30*, **6**:103
Lisa, Manuel **5**:*31*
Little Joe y La Familia **5**:104
"Livin La Vida Loca" (song) **5**:65
Llamarada, La (book) **5**:15
Lockridge, Rocky **4**:37
Lomas Garza, Carmen **5**:*32*, 72
Longoria, Felix **1**:11, **2**:107,
4:11, **5**:*33–34*
song about **6**:37
Lopez, Al **5**:*35*
Lopez, George **1**:129, **5**:*36*
Lopez, Israel "Cachao" **3**:93,
4:6, 7, **5**:*37*, **7**:55
Lopez, Jennifer **1**:129–130,
4:*105*, 107, **5**:*38–39*, 54,
6:113, **8**:4
López, José M. **5**:*40*
Lopez, Nancy **5**:*41*
Lopez, Trini **4**:107, **5**:*42*, **6**:39
López, Yolanda **5**:*43*
Lopez Portillo, José **6**:*48*
Lorenzo, Frank **5**:*44*
Los Angeles
Edward Roybal and **6**:132
plans for a prison at Boyle
Heights **5**:123
school walkouts (blowouts;
1968) **3**:90, **4**:4
Villaraigosa as mayor **6**:*133*,
8:*113*, 114
Zoot Suit Riots **4**:104
"Los Angeles 13" **3**:90
Los Angeles Star (newspaper)
5:92
Los Lobos **4**:107, **5**:*45–46*,
6:39–40, **8**:50, 84
Love & Rockets (cartoon series)
1:35, **4**:*90*
Loving Pedro Infante (book) **2**:91
lowriders **4**:105
Lozano, Ignacio **5**:93
Lujan, Manuel Luis **5**:*47*
Luján, Tony **5**:*48*
LULAC *see* League of United
Latin American Citizens
Luminarias (film) **8**:87
Luna, Solomon **5**:49, **6**:92, 93
"Luv Dancin" (song) **7**:114
Luz de Luna (album) **5**:129
Lymon, Frankie **7**:124

M

MacArthur, Douglas **5**:112
Machito **1**:113, **5**:*50–51*, **6**:39,
7:9
Macho Camacho's Beat (book)
7:109
Machuca, Esther N. **5**:52
MAD (magazine) **1**:35
Madrugadores, Los **2**:106, **4**:*61*,
62, 106, **5**:94
magazines, bilingual **5**:94
Malcolm in the Middle (TV
series) **6**:25
MALDEF *see* Mexican American
Legal Defense and
Education Fund
"Mal Hombre" (song) **5**:104
Malinche, La **1**:107, **3**:28
mambo **5**:51
Arsenio Rodríguez and **7**:54
Pérez Prado and **7**:10
Tito Puente and **7**:15–16
Manhattan Project **1**:54
Manifest Destiny **2**:5–6, **8**:24–25
in Texan history **8**:45
"Manteca" (song) **6**:77

Set Index

Manzano, Sonia **5**:*53*
maquiladoras **2**:*9, 10*
maquilas **1**:23
Maravilla, La (book) **8**:*97*
Marc Anthony **5**:39, *54*
Marcantonio, Vito **8**:*54*
Margil de Jésus, Antonio **5**:*55*
Mariachi, El (film) **7**:*71*
mariachi music **6**:36
Marichal, Juan **5**:*56*
Mariel Boatlift **3**:35, **4**:*123–124*
Marin, Cheech **1**:129, **4**:108, **5**:*57–58*, **8**:*87*
Marin, Rosario **1**:101, **5**:*59–60*
Marisol **5**:*61*
Marqués, René **5**:*62–63*
Márquez, Gabriel García **4**:72
Martí, José **1**:10, **4**:106, **5**:*63–64*
Martin, Ricky **1**:129, **5**:*65–66*, 109
Martinez, A. **5**:*67*
Martínez, Antonio José **5**:*68*
Martinez, Betita **5**:*69*
Martinez, Bob **5**:*70–71*
Martinez, Cesar A. **5**:*72*
Martinez, Felix **5**:*73*
Martínez, Manuel Luis **5**:74
Martinez, Mel (Melquiades) **3**:67, **5**:*75–76*
Martínez, Narciso **5**:*77–78*, **6**:37, **8**:*49*
Martínez, Oscar **5**:*79*
Martinez, Pedro **5**:*80*, 115
Martinez, Tomas Eloy **5**:*81–82*
Martinez, Victor **5**:*83*
Martínez, Vilma **5**:*84–85*
Martinez, Xavier **5**:*86*
Martinez Tucker, Sara **5**:*87*
Mas Canosa, Jorge **5**:*88–89*
Masters at Work **4**:*59*; **8**:*99*
Mata, Eduardo **5**:*90*
Mateo, Fernando **5**:*91*
Maxwell Land Grant **1**:114
Mazzy Star **7**:*118*
McCaffrey, Barry **5**:*71*
McDonnell, Donald **2**:*88–89*
McKernan, Ron "Pigpen" **4**:*14*
McLaughlin, John **7**:*121*
MEChA (Movimiento Estudiantil Chicano de Aztlán) **1**:*47*, 48, **6**:*126–127*
Medal of Honor, Congressional **1**:*106*, 118
media, Spanish-language **5**:*92–97*
see also radio; television
Medina, Battle of **8**:*80*
Medina, Harold R. **5**:*98–99*
Medina, Pablo **5**:*100*
Medrano v. Allee (1972) **4**:*23*
Melendez, Bill **5**:*101*, **7**:*76*
"Memorias de Melgarejo" **7**:*6*
Mendez v. Westminster (1943) **6**:*126–127*, **8**:*33*
Mendieta, Ana **5**:*102*
Mendoza, Antonio de **2**:*130*
Mendoza, Leonor Zamarripa **5**:*104*
Mendoza, Lydia **5**:*103–104*
Menéndez, Robert **3**:67, **5**:*105–106*
Menendez de Avilés, Pedro **5**:*107–108*
Menudo **5**:*66, 109*
Men on the Verge of a His-Panic Breakdown (book) **7**:*39*
Merchant, Jimmy **7**:*124*
Messiaen, Olivier **7**:*129*

mestizaje **3**:*84*
mestizajes **4**:*105, 106*
META Inc. **8**:*62*
Mexican American Cultural Center (MACC) **3**:*84*
Mexican American Education Council (MAEC) **2**:*67*
Mexican American Legal Defense and Education Fund (MALDEF) **3**:73, 132, **6**:44, 58, 107, **8**:32, 47
Antonia Hernández and **4**:*82*
Luis G. Nogales and **6**:*57*, 58
Mario Obledo and **6**:*67*
Pete Tijerina and **8**:*58*
Vilma Martínez and **5**:*84–85*
Mexican American Political Association (MAPA) **7**:*89*
Mexican Americans
as activists *see* Chicano Movement
assimilation **1**:*79*
deported to Mexico (1930s) **5**:11, 94, **6**:*48*
and discrimination **3**:71, 72
feminism **7**:*25*
labor organizations and **5**:*9–14*
in the military **5**:111, 112, *113*
Treaty of Guadalupe Hidalgo and **4**:67, 121, **5**:9
see also Mexicans
Mexican American Unity Council **8**:*102*
Mexican-American War *see* Mexican War
Mexican American Youth Organization (MAYO) **3**:*10*, **4**:73, 74, **8**:*47*
Mexican Constitution (1824), abolished **8**:*42*
Mexican Federal Union **5**:*10*
Mexican Immigrant, His Life Story, The (book) **4**:*5*
Mexican Immigration to the United States (book) **4**:*5*
"Mexican Madonna" *see* Selena
Mexican Revolution, and the Plan de San Diego **6**:103, **7**:26
Mexican Robin Hood (Joaquín Murrieta) **6**:*34*
Mexicans **4**:*120–121*
as agricultural or migrant workers **1**:*19–24*, **2**:*7–8*, **4**:*119*
repatriation (1930s) **4**:*121*
see also Mexican Americans
Mexican Side of the Texas Revolution, The (book) **2**:*65*
Mexican Village (book) **6**:*55, 56*
Mexican War (U.S.-Mexico War) **2**:5–6, **4**:66, **5**:92, **7**:94, **8**:25, 43–44, 48
Los San Patricios **8**:*44*
see also Guadalupe Hidalgo, Treaty of
Mexico
area ceded to the United States **1**:19, 80, **4**:66, **5**:9, 92
the Gadsden Purchase and **8**:*25–26*
independence from Spain **7**:34, **8**:24
see also border, Mexico-United States

Mexterminator **4**:*38*
Meyerhof, Otto **6**:*74*
Miami Sound Machine **1**:78, **3**:91, 92–93, **6**:40
Jon Secada and **7**:*131*
Mickey Mouse comic strips **4**:*44*
migrant labor *see* agriculture and migrant labor
Miguel, Luis **1**:29, **5**:*110*
Milian, Emilio **5**:*96*
military **5**:*111–114*
the Borinqueneers **5**:*114*
see also American GI Forum; Civil War; Korean War; Persian Gulf War; Vietnam War; World War I; World War II
Million to Juan, A (film) **7**:*68*
Mi mano (painting) **4**:*81*
Minaya, Omar **5**:*115*
miners, labor organizations **5**:*10–11*
Minerva Delgado v. Bastrop Independent School District (1948) **4**:*94*
"Minga y Petraca al Nuevo Senado" (essay) **7**:*109*
Minoso, Minnie **5**:*116*
Mi Otro Yo (book) **4**:*38*
Miranda, Carmen **4**:108, **5**:*117–118*, 134
Miranda, Guadalupe **1**:*114*
Miranda v. Arizona (1966) **8**:*34*
Mireles, Edmundo E. **4**:*56*
Miró, Esteban Rodriguez **5**:*119*
Mislán, Angel **1**:*6*
missionaries, Spanish **8**:*23–24*
Mitchell, Arthur **5**:*26*
Mi Tierra (album) **3**:*93*
Mohr, Nicholasa **5**:*120–121*
mojados (wetbacks) **2**:107, **4**:121
"Mojado sin Licensia, Un" (song) **8**:*49*
Mojados, Los (book) **7**:*105*
Molina, Gloria **5**:*122–123*
Molina, John John **5**:*124*
Molina, Mario **5**:*125–126*
Moll, Luis **5**:*127*
Mondini-Ruiz, Franco **5**:*128*
Monge, Yolandita **5**:*129*
Monroe Doctrine **8**:*44*
Monroig, Gilberto **5**:*130*
Montalban, Ricardo **5**:*131–132*
Monte, El (book) **2**:*21*
Montero, Mayra **5**:*133*
Montez, Maria **5**:*134*
Montoya, Carlos Garcia **6**:*4*
Montoya, Delilah **6**:*5*
Montoya, José **4**:38, **6**:*6*
Montoya, Joseph **1**:60, **6**:*7*
Montoya, Nestor **6**:*8*
Monument Valley **8**:*22*
Moor's Pavane, The (dance) **5**:*30*
Mora, Magdalena **6**:*9*
Moraga, Cherríe **1**:14, 62, **6**:*10–11*
Moraga, Elvira **6**:*11*
Morales, Alejandro **6**:*12*
Morales, David **6**:*13*
Morales, Esai **6**:*14*
Morales, Felix H. **6**:*15*
Morales, Noro **5**:*51*
Morales, Pablo **6**:*16*
Morales Carrión, Arturo **6**:*17*
Moratorium March **3**:*90*
Morel Campos, Juan **1**:*6*
Moreno, Antonio **6**:*18–19*
Moreno, Arturo **5**:93, **6**:*20*

Moreno, Luisa **6**:21, **8**:*15*
Moreno, Rita **4**:109, **6**:*22–23*
Morin, Raul **6**:*24*
Mothers of East Los Angeles **5**:*123*
Mrs. Vargas and the Dead Naturalist (book) **1**:*33*
Muggerud, Lawrence **3**:*19*
Mujeres Muralistas, Las **4**:*83*
Muniz, Frankie **6**:*25*
Muñiz, Ramsey **6**:*26*
Muñoz, Anthony **6**:*27*
Muñoz, Elías Miguel **6**:*28*
Muñoz, Luis **6**:*29*
Muñoz Marín, Luis **1**:32, **3**:*64*, **4**:91, **5**:24, **6**:*30–31*, **7**:*115*
Jesus T. Piñero and **6**:120, 121
Muñoz Rivera, Luis **6**:*32–33*
murals **1**:*89–90*, **2**:16, 50, **4**:64, 65, 83, 109, **6**:*75*, **7**:*81*, **8**:36
Murrieta, Joaquín **6**:*34*
music **4**:106, **6**:*35–40*
Aztec **6**:35
Cuban **6**:*37–38*, 40
habanera **6**:*37*
mariachi **6**:36
orquestas **6**:*37*
Spanish-language musicians on the radio **5**:*95*
tejano **8**:5
Tex-Mex **5**:46, **6**:39, **8**:*49–50*
see also conjunto music; rap; salsa
musica norteña see conjunto music
Musto, William Vincent **5**:*106*
mutualistas (mutual aid societies) **2**:105, **5**:10, **6**:42, **8**:26
My Family (Mi Familia) (film) **6**:46, *47*

N

Nacogdoches, Texas **2**:5, **8**:*125*
Najera, Eduardo **6**:*41*
Narvaez, Panfilo de **6**:64, 65
National Affordable Housing Act (1990) **4**:*55*
National Association for the Advancement of Colored People (NAACP), Vilma Martínez and **5**:*84*
National Association of Latino Elected Officials (NALEO) **6**:*132*
National Chicano Moratorium **6**:*127*
National Chicano Youth Liberation Conference (1969) **2**:*108–109*, **6**:*126*
National Council of La Raza (NCLR) **6**:43, 107, **8**:*128*
National Day Laborer Organizing Network (NDLON) **1**:*52*
National Farm Workers Association (NFWA) **2**:89, **4**:113, **5**:13, **6**:84
National Hispanic Leadership Conference (NHLC) **2**:*4*
National Hispanic Media Coalition **6**:*45*
National Industrial Recovery Act (NIRA) **5**:*12*
National Labor Relations Act (NLRA; Wagner Act; 1933) **5**:12, 13

National Labor Relations Board (NLRB) **5**:12, 13
National Organization for Mexican American Services (NOMAS) **8**:128
national organizations **6**:42–45
National Origins Act (Immigration Act; 1924) **4**:120, 122
Nation of Yahweh **8**:29
Native Americans
the Pueblo Revolt **8**:23
and religion **7**:35, 36, 37
in the Southwest **8**:22, 23, 26
Nava, Gregory **6**:46–47
Nava, Julián **6**:48
Navarro, José Antonio **6**:49
Navarro, Max **6**:50
Navas, William A., Jr. **6**:51
needle exchanges **5**:71
Negrete, Jorge **5**:95
Negrón Muñoz, Mercedes **6**:52
Neighborhood Youth Corps (NYC), Corky Gonzales and **4**:48–49
Nelson, Eugene **6**:84
Neruda, Pablo **8**:21
New Deal **1**:21, 105
New Faces of 1934 (revue) **2**:114
New Formalism movement **4**:29
New Mexico **2**:80
explored and colonized by de Oñate **3**:51–52
Ezekiel Cabeza de Baca and **2**:19
Nestor Montoya and **6**:8
reconquered by de Vargas **3**:55
newspapers, Spanish-language **1**:127, **5**:92–93
New World Border, The (book) **4**:38, 39
New York City, the Bronx **7**:50
Nicondra, Glugio *see* Gronk
Niebla, Elvia **6**:53
Nieto, Sonia **6**:54
Niggli, Josefina **6**:55–56
Nilda (book) **5**:121
Nineteenth Amendment **6**:93
Nixon, Richard M., Charles Rebozo and **7**:30
Niza, Marcos de **3**:49–50, **8**:22
Nogales, Luis G. **6**:57–58
Noloesca, Beatriz **6**:59
nonviolence **1**:94
Noriega, Carlos **6**:60
Norte, El (film) **6**:46, 83
norteño music *see* conjunto music
North American Free Trade Agreement (NAFTA) **1**:23–24, **5**:9, 14
Nosotros **5**:132
Noticieros (TV program) **7**:27
Noticiero Univision (TV program) **7**:102
Novarro, Ramon **6**:61
Novello, Antonia **6**:62–63
Nueva Ola, La **5**:129
Nueva York (book) **5**:121
Nuevo Herald, El (newspaper) **5**:94
Nuevo Teatro Pobre de América **7**:119
Núñez Cabeza de Vaca, Álvar **3**:49, **6**:64–65
Nureyev, Rudolf **2**:15
Nuyorican movement **5**:17

Nuyorican Poets Café **3**:96, **6**:119, 122
Nuyorican renaissance **1**:38–39
NYPD Blue (TV series) **8**:14

O

Obejas, Achy **6**:66
Obledo, Mario **6**:67
Obregón, Eugene Arnold **6**:68
O'Brien, Soledad **6**:69
Ocampo, Adriana **6**:70
Occupied America (book) **1**:15
Ochoa, Ellen **6**:71
Ochoa, Estevan **6**:72
Ochoa, Severo **6**:73–74
Ochoa, Victor **6**:75
Ochoa, Victor L. **6**:76
O'Farrill, Arturo "Chico" **6**:77
Ofrenda para Antonio Lomas (artwork) **5**:32
Old Spain in Our Southwest (book) **6**:93
Olivas, John **6**:78
Oller, Francisco **6**:79, **7**:49
Olmos, Edward James **6**:80–81
Once Upon a Time in Mexico (film) **7**:72
Ontiveros, Lupe **6**:82–83
Operational Technologies Corporation (Optech) **6**:50
Operation Bootstrap **4**:122, **6**:31
Operation Jobs **2**:8, **3**:72
Operation Peter Pan **5**:75, 102
Operation Serenidad (Serenity) **6**:31
Operation Wetback **1**:23, **2**:8, 107–108, **3**:72, **4**:121, **8**:27
Opinión, La (newspaper) **5**:93
Optech (Operational Technologies Corporation) **6**:50
Orden Caballeros de America **4**:87
Orden Hijos de America **2**:106, **4**:87
Order of Sons of America **7**:96
Orendain, Antonio **6**:84
Organic Act (Foraker Act; 1900) **6**:33
Orlando, Tony **6**:85
Orozco, Jose Clemente **5**:120
orquesta (orquesta tejana) music **6**:37
Orquesta Tropicana **7**:69
Orquesta Cubana de Música Moderna (OCMM) **7**:116
Orquesta Juvenil de Música Moderna **7**:116
Ortega, John **5**:112
Ortega, Katherine **1**:101, **6**:86–87
Ortega y Gasca, Felipe de **6**:88
Ortiz, Carlos **3**:87, **6**:89
Ortiz Cofer, Judith **6**:90
Otero Family **6**:91–92
Adelina Otero Warren **6**:92, 93
Antonio Jose Otero **1**:67
Mariano S. Otero **6**:92
Miguel A. Otero I **3**:133, **6**:91, 92
Miguel A. Otero II **6**:91–92
Miguel A. Otero IV **6**:92
Solomon Luna and **5**:49, **6**:92, 93
Otero Warren, Adelina **6**:92, 93
Our Catholic Heritage in Texas (book) **2**:65
Outlander (book) **3**:128
Oviedo, Lope de **6**:65

P

P. Diddy *see* Combs, Sean "Puff Daddy"
Pacheco, Johnny **5**:51, **6**:94
Pacheco, Romualdo, Jr. **6**:95
Pacheco y su Charanga **6**:94
pachucos **4**:70, 104
Palés Matos, Luis **6**:96
Palmeiro, Rafael **6**:97
Palmieri, Charlie **5**:37, **6**:98
Palmieri, Eddie **5**:17, **6**:38, 39, 99
Palomino, Carlos **6**:100
Palooka (film) **8**:107
Pan-American Union **5**:12–13
"Pancho López" (song) **4**:70
Pantín, Leslie **8**:62
Pantoja, Antonia **6**:101
Paoli, Antonio **6**:102
Papp, Joseph **4**:134
Paredes, Américo **6**:103, **8**:67
Paredes y Arrillaga, Mariano **8**:43
Paris, Treaty of (1898) **4**:121
Paris Philharmonic **7**:129
Parker, Gloria **4**:98
Parra, Derek **6**:104
Parrot in the Oven: Mi Vida (book) **5**:83
Partido del Pueblo (PPD) **7**:115
Partido Liberal **6**:120
Partido Liberal Mexicano (PLM) **3**:124, **6**:125
Sara Estela Ramírez and **7**:25
Partido Nuevo Progresista (PNP) **7**:88
Partido Popular Democrático de Puerto Rico (PPD; Popular Democratic Party) **4**:91, **6**:30, 120–121
Paterson (book) **8**:123
Pau-Llosa, Ricardo **6**:105
Paz, Juan-Carlos **7**:129
pecan shellers' strike (1938), in San Antonio **5**:11, **8**:15, 41
Pedro J. González and his Madrugadores (radio show) **2**:106, **5**:95
Pelli, Cesar **6**:106
Peña, Albert A., Jr. **6**:107
Peña, Amado **5**:72, **6**:108
Peña, Elizabeth **6**:109, **8**:68
Peña, Federico **6**:110
Penn, Sean **3**:45, 46
Perales, Alonso S. **5**:84, 85
"Perdido" (song) **8**:61
Pérez, Jorge **6**:111
Pérez, Loida Maritza **6**:112
Perez, Rosie **5**:38, **6**:113
Pérez, Tony **6**:114
Pérez Firmat, Gustavo **6**:115
Perfecta, La (band) **7**:20
Perón, Eva **5**:82
Perón, Juan **5**:82
Perón Novel, The **5**:82
Persian Gulf War
First **5**:113, **7**:112
Second **5**:111, 114
Pete Henández v. Texas (1954) **4**:94
Petronas Towers **6**:106
Phoenix, Arizona **8**:27
Pico, Andrés **6**:116
Pico, Pío **1**:100, **2**:70, **6**:116, 117–118
"Piel Canela" (song) **2**:39
Pierce, Franklin **8**:25
Pietri, Pedro **6**:119
Pimentel, George C. **5**:126
Piñero, Jesus T. **1**:32, **6**:120–121

Piñero, Miguel **1**:38, **3**:106, **6**:119, *122*
Plan de Ayutla **8**:131
Plan de San Diego **6**:103, **7**:26
Plan de Santa Barbara, El **1**:13, 48, **6**:126, 127
Plan Espiritual de Aztlán, El **1**:47, 48, **2**:109, **4**:48, 49, **6**:126
Plan of San Diego **3**:125
Plessy v. Ferguson (1897) **8**:32
Plunkett, Jim **6**:123
Plyler v. Doe (1982) **5**:84, 85, **8**:34
Pocho (book) **8**:116
Pocho (magazine) **1**:34–35
Political Association of Spanish-speaking Organizations (PASO: *later* PASSO) **6**:132
political movements **6**:124–129
see also Chicano movement; MEChA
political representation **6**:130–133
Polk, James Knox **2**:6, **4**:67, **8**:25, 43–44, 45
Ponce, Mary Helen **6**:134
Ponce de León, Juan **1**:56, **5**:108, **7**:4–5
Ponce de León Troche, Juan **7**:6
Ponce Massacre **1**:32
Poor People's March on Washington (1968) **8**:60
Popé **8**:23
popular culture *see* Hispanic identity and popular culture
Popular Democratic Party (PPD), Sila María Calderón and **2**:23–24
population, Hispanic American **1**:80, **4**:104, 119
Latin mix **4**:120
see also Cubans; Mexicans; Puerto Ricans
Portes, Alejandro **7**:7
Portillo, Lourdes **4**:109
Portillo Trambley, Estela **7**:8
Portrait of the Artist as the Virgin of Guadalupe (painting) **5**:43
posters **4**:109
poverty, immigrants and **4**:119–120
Power, Tyrone **2**:98
Poyesis Genetica **4**:38
Pozo, Chano **1**:99, **6**:38, **7**:9
Prado, Pérez **7**:10
Prensa, La (newspaper) **5**:93
Price of Glory (film) **1**:83
Prida, Dolores **7**:11
Prince, Sheila E. and **8**:13
Principal, Victoria **7**:12
Prinze, Freddie **4**:109, **7**:13, 14
Prinze, Freddie, Jr. **7**:14
Professional Air Traffic Controllers Organization (PATCO) **5**:14
Protagonist of an Endless Story, The (portrait) **7**:74
Proudhon, Pierre-Joseph **3**:125
Public Health Service Commissioned Corps **6**:62–63
Puebla, Battle of **8**:132
Pueblo Revolt **8**:23
Puente, Tito **3**:13, *16*, 93, **4**:106, **5**:48, 51, 130, **6**:38, 39, **7**:15–16

Set Index

Puente in Percussion (album) **6**:39
"Puerto Rican Bombshell" *see* Chacón, Iris
Puerto Rican Embassy, El (play) **6**:119
Puerto Rican Herald (newspaper) **6**:33
Puerto Rican Legal Defense and Education Fund (PRLDF) **3**:73, **6**:44
Puerto Ricans **2**:109–110, **4**:121–122
  as immigrants **1**:82, **4**:121–122
  in the military **5**:111
  nationalism **6**:127–128
  political representation **6**:131
  Young Lords **2**:109, 110, **6**:128, **7**:45
  see also Puerto Rico
Puerto Rican Socialist Party **6**:128
Puerto Rico
  agricultural workers from **1**:24
  and conservation **5**:16
  Father of Modern Puerto Rico *see* Muñoz Marín, Luis
  labor relations **5**:12
  language **5**:92
  oral story telling **5**:121
  Ponce de León and **7**:4–5
  Ponce de León Troche and **7**:6
  rule by the United States **6**:32–33
  slavery abolished **1**:5
  U.S. commonwealth status **2**:110, **4**:91, **6**:30, 31, 121
  see also Puerto Ricans
Puff Daddy **5**:39

Q

Queen, Ivy **4**:107, **7**:17
"Queen of Reggaetón" *see* Queen, Ivy
"Queen of Technicolor" *see* Montez, Maria
"Queen of Tejano" *see* Selena
"Queen of Tejano Music" *see* Canales, Laura
Que Pasa, USA? (TV show) **7**:123
Quevedo, Eduardo **7**:89
Quinn, Anthony **7**:18–19
Quintana, Ismael "Pat" **7**:20
Quintana, Leroy V. **7**:21
Quintero, José **7**:22
Quinto Sol Publications **7**:77
Quinto Sol (publishing house) **4**:103, **5**:93

R

radio
  Radio Martí **6**:129
  Spanish-language **4**:106, **5**:94–95, **6**:15
Rage Against the Machine **3**:34
railroad, Texas-Mexican **8**:48
Rainbow Coalition **2**:109
Ramirez, Manny **7**:23
Ramírez, Martin **7**:24
Ramírez, Sara Estela **7**:25
Ramona (book) **2**:132, **3**:47
Ramón y Cajal, Santiago **6**:73, 74
Ramos, Basilio **7**:26
Ramos, Jorge **7**:27, 102
Ramos, Tab **7**:28
Rangel, Irma **7**:29

rap
  Latin **4**:107
  West Coast **6**:40
Raza Unida Party (RUP) **1**:13, **2**:109, **3**:10, **4**:73, 74, **6**:127
  Corky Gonzales and **4**:49
  María Latigo Hernández and **4**:88
  Ramsey Muñiz and **6**:26
Reagan, Ronald **5**:13–14
Rebirth of Our Nationality, The (mural) **8**:36
Rebozo, Charles **7**:30
Rechy, John **7**:31–32
"Recovering the Hispanic Literary Heritage of the United States" **5**:6
Red Robber of the Rio Grande *see* Cortina, Juan Nepomuceno
Reform, War of **8**:131–132
Regeneración (journal) **3**:124, 125
reggaeton **3**:21, 83, **4**:107, **6**:40
  Ivy Queen and **7**:17
Regidor, El (newspaper) **3**:14
Relacion de Cabeza de Vaca, La (book) **6**:65
Related Group of Florida **6**:111
religion **7**:33–38
  mariachi and **6**:36
  see also Catholicism
Resaca, La (book) **5**:16
retablos **1**:107, **7**:37
Reto en el Paraíso (book) **6**:12
Return of Felix Nogara, The (book) **5**:100
Return to Forever (RTF) **2**:125–126
Revisita Areíto (magazine) **2**:56
Revolt of the Cockroach People, The (book) **1**:8
"Rey de Bajo, El" *see* Valentín, Bobby
Reyes, Bernardo **2**:84
Reyes, Guillermo **7**:39
Reyes, Senen **3**:19
Reyna, María Torres **7**:40
Richardson, Bill **7**:41–42
Ride, The (album) **5**:46
Rio Grande **2**:7
Rio Piedras Massacre **1**:31
Rios, Alberto **7**:43
Rivera, Angel **4**:105
Rivera, Chita **7**:44
Rivera, Diego **3**:43, **5**:120
Rivera, Geraldo **7**:45
Rivera, Ismael **4**:126
Rivera, Mon **2**:120
Rivera, Pete **5**:130
Rivera, Tito **3**:79
Rivera, Tomás **4**:103, **7**:46–47
Rivero, Horacio **5**:113
Roback, David **7**:118
Robin Hood of El Dorado (Joaquín Murrieta) **6**:34
Robles, Belén **7**:48
Roche-Rabell, Arnaldo **7**:49
Rodriguez, Abraham, Jr. **7**:50
Rodríguez, Albita **7**:51
Rodriguez, Alex **7**:52–53
Rodríguez, Arsenio **7**:54–55
Rodríguez, Arturo S. **5**:13, **7**:56
Rodriguez, Chi Chi **7**:57
Rodriguez, Cleto **7**:58
Rodriguez, Eddie **7**:53
Rodriguez, Eloy **7**:59
Rodriguez, Ivan "Pudge" **7**:60
Rodriguez, Jennifer **7**:61

Rodriguez, Johnny **7**:62
Rodriguez, Josefa "Chipita" **7**:63
Rodriguez, Linda Chavez **7**:56
Rodriguez, Luis J. **7**:64–65
Rodriguez, Michelle **7**:66
Rodriguez, Narciso **7**:67
Rodriguez, Paul **1**:83, **7**:68
Rodriguez, Paul, Jr. **7**:68
Rodríguez, Pellín **7**:69
Rodriguez, Richard **7**:70
Rodriguez, Robert **4**:77, 78, 105, 109, **7**:71–72
  Cheech Marin and **5**:58
Rodriguez, Tito **3**:103, **5**:51, **6**:38, 39
Rodríguez de Tió, Lola **7**:73
Rodríguez-Díaz, Angel **7**:74
Roland, Gilbert **7**:75
Roman, Phil **7**:76
Roman Catholicism *see* Catholicism
Romano, Octavio **7**:77
Romero, Anthony D. **7**:78–79
Romero, Cesar **7**:80
Romero, Chan **6**:38–39
Romero, Frank **7**:81
Romero, Trinidad **7**:82
Romero-Barceló, Carlos **7**:83
Ronstadt, Linda **7**:84
Roosevelt, Franklin D.
  Good Neighbor Policy **4**:108, 127
  New Deal **1**:21, 105
Rosado del Valle, Julio **7**:85
Rosa, Robi **5**:66
Ros-Lehtinen, Ileana **3**:67, **7**:86–87
Ross, Fred **2**:89, **4**:113, 114
Rosselló, Pedro **2**:24, **7**:88
Rowland, Sherwood **5**:126
Royal Expedition **2**:129–130
Roybal, Edward **6**:132
Roybal-Allard, Lucille **7**:89, 90–91
Rubio, Eurípides **7**:92
Ruiz, John **7**:93
Ruiz de Burton, María Amparo **7**:94
Rulfo, Juan **2**:91
rumba **6**:38

S

Sáenz, Ben **7**:95
Sáenz, José de la Luz **7**:96
"Safe and Free" campaign **7**:79
Sagasta, Praxedas Mateo **6**:32
Saint Augustine, Florida, Pedro Menendez de Avilés and **5**:108
Salas, Albert **7**:98
Salas, Eddy **7**:98
Salas, Floyd **7**:97–98
Salazar, Alberto **7**:99
Salazar, Rubén **3**:90, **5**:96, **7**:100, **8**:28
Saldívar, Yolanda **8**:5
Salinas, Luis Omar **7**:101
Salinas, María Elena **7**:102
Salinas, Porfirio **7**:103
salsa **3**:100, 101, **6**:39, 98
  La India and **5**:17
  Machito quoted on **5**:51
  Marc Anthony and **5**:54
Salt Lake City, Utah **8**:27
Salvatierra v. Del Rio Independent School District (1930) **4**:45
Samaniego, Mariano **7**:104
Samba (book) **4**:72

sambas, Carmen Miranda and **5**:117, 118
Samora, Julián **7**:105
San Antonio, Texas
  founded **3**:24
  La Liga Pro-Defensa Escolar **4**:88
  pecan shellers' strike (1938) **5**:11, **8**:15, 41
  Tejano-Conjunto festival **8**:50
Sánchez, David **7**:106
Sanchez, George Isidore **7**:107
Sánchez, Loretta and Linda **7**:108
Sánchez, Luis Rafael **7**:109
Sanchez, Poncho **7**:110
Sánchez, Ricardo **7**:111
Sanchez, Ricardo S. **5**:111, 114, **7**:112–113
Sanchez, Roger **7**:114
Sanchez, Salvador **4**:37, **8**:72
Sánchez Vilella, Roberto **4**:91, **7**:115
Sandburg, Carl **2**:104
Sandoval, Arturo **3**:93, **6**:40, **7**:116
Sandoval, Hope **7**:118
Sandoval, Humberto **4**:4
San Francisco Poster Workshop **4**:18
San Jacinto, Battle of **7**:133, 134, **8**:43
San Joaquin Valley, cotton pickers' strike (1933) **5**:11
San Patricios, Los **8**:44
Santa Anna, Antonio López de **3**:58, **6**:49, **7**:132, 133, 134, **8**:24, 26, 43, 131
Santa Evita (book) **5**:82
Santa Fe, New Mexico **8**:23
Santa Fe Expedition **6**:49
Santa Fe Ring **2**:85
Santaliz Avila, Pedro **7**:119
Santamária, Mongo **6**:39
Santana (band) **7**:120
Santana, Carlos **3**:88, **4**:107, **6**:39, **7**:16, 120–121
Santayana, George **7**:122
Santeiro, Luis **7**:123
Santería **7**:37
Santiago, Herman **7**:124
Santos, Daniel **7**:125
Santos, Rolando H. **7**:126
Saralegui, Cristina **7**:127
Savage, John **7**:63
Saxon, Johnny **5**:8
Schifrin, Lalo **8**:128–129
Schomburg, Arturo Alfonso **7**:130
Schulz, Charles M. **7**:76
Scott, Winfield **4**:66, **8**:25
Secada, Jon **7**:131
segregation in education **2**:106–107, **3**:72, 73, **6**:107, 126–127, **8**:33
  Gustavo C. Garcia and **4**:10, 94
  John J. Herrera and **4**:94
  Manuel C. Gonzales and **4**:45
  see also Lemon Grove case
Seguín, Erasmo **7**:132, 133, **8**:24
Seguín, Juan N. **7**:132, 133–134, **8**:24
Selena **5**:38, **8**:4–5, 48
Sen Dog **4**:107
September 11th terrorist attacks **4**:124
Serra, Junípero **2**:86, **8**:6, 23
Serra, Richard **8**:7

Serrano, José **8**:*8*
Serrano, Samuel **8**:*9*
Sesame Street (TV show) **5**:*53*, **7**:123
settlement, U.S. *see* Southwest, U.S. settlement in the
Shadow of a Man (play) **6**:11
Shakespeare, William **1**:39
Shaman (album) **7**:*121*
shamans **2**:62, 63
Sheen, Charlie **3**:97, **8**:*10*, 12
Sheen, Martin **3**:97, **8**:*10*, *11*–12
Sheila E. **8**:*13*
Short Eyes (play) **6**:122
Show de Cristina, El (TV show) **7**:*127*
Siembra (album) **1**:133
Silva, France **5**:112
Silvera, Juan **7**:63
Silver Cloud Café, The (book) **8**:*97*
Sketches of the Valley and Other Works (book) **4**:103
Sleepy Lagoon trial **3**:74
Slidell, John **8**:25, 43
Smits, Jimmy **2**:*52*, **8**:*14*
social zoning **3**:73–74
sociedades mutualistas **4**:22
Solar Montoya (book) **5**:15
Solís Sager, Manuela **8**:15
Somohano, Arturo **8**:16
son, Arsenio Rodríguez and **7**:54, 55
son guaguancó **7**:55
son montuno **7**:55
Sonoma, California **8**:88
Sons of America, Order of **4**:21
Sorting Metaphors (poems) **6**:105
Sosa, Lionel **8**:*17*
Sosa, Sammy **8**:*18*–19
Soto, Gary **7**:101, **8**:*20*–21
Soto, Hernando de **3**:*53*–54
South Texas Agricultural Workers' Union (STAWU) **8**:15
Southwest, settlement in the **8**:*22–27*
Southwest Council of La Raza (SWCLR) **7**:105, **8**:128
Southwest Voter Registration Education Project (SVREP) **4**:52, **5**:85, **8**:102
Spanglish **8**:48
Spanish American League Against Discrimination (SALAD) **3**:*72*–73
Spanish International Network (SIN) **4**:109
Spanish language *see* language
Squatter and the Don, The (book) **7**:94
stereotypes **3**:72, **4**:104, 108, **6**:23, 83
Good Neighbor Policy and **4**:127
Student Nonviolent Coordinating Committee (SNCC) **5**:69
Suárez, Ray **8**:*28*
Suárez, Xavier L. **8**:*29*–30
subatomic particles **1**:54, 55, **4**:12
Sullo, Salvatore **2**:126
Sun Mad (picture) **4**:83
Supernatural (album) **7**:*121*
Super Orchestra Tropicana **5**:130
Supreme Court **8**:*31–34*

T

Tafoya, José Piedad **8**:35
Taft-Hartley Act (1947) **5**:13
Tanguma, Leo **8**:36
Tan, Luisa **5**:126
Tapia, Luis **8**:*37*
Tapia y Rivera, Alejandro **8**:38
Tavárez, Manuel G. **2**:30
Teachings of Don Juan, The (book) **2**:62
Teatro Campesino, El **8**:*81*–82
Teenagers, The **7**:*124*
Teissonnière, Gerardo **8**:39
tejano music **8**:5
tejanos, culture *see* Tex-Mex culture
Telemundo **4**:109, **5**:97
television
Spanish-language **5**:96–97
TV Martí **6**:129
Telles, Raymond **8**:40
Telling to Live: Latina Feminist Testimonios (book) **5**:27
Tenayuca, Emma **5**:11, **8**:15, *41*
Terrazo (book) **3**:65
Terror Squad **8**:107
Terry, Clark **5**:48
Texas War of Independence **6**:49
Texas
colonias **8**:26
Hispanic population **8**:47
see also Tex-Mex culture
Texas, history of **8**:*42*–47
American settlement (1820s) **2**:5, **8**:42
annexation to the United States **8**:25, 43
Casas Revolt **7**:132
Caucasian Race Resolution **8**:47
in the Civil War **8**:45
Manifest Destiny in **8**:45
Manuel Guerra and **4**:69
Republic of Texas **7**:132, **8**:24, 43
Rosa María Hinojosa de Ballí and **4**:101
see also Texas Revolution
Texas Council on Human Relations **8**:47
Texas Declaration of Independence (1836) **3**:58, **6**:49
Texas Farm Workers Union (TFWU) **6**:84
Texas International Airlines **5**:44
Texas Rangers **8**:49
and Jacinto Treviño **8**:67
Texas Revolution **2**:5, **8**:43
Carlos de la Garza and **3**:29
José Antonio Valdez and **8**:80
José María Jesús Carbajal and **2**:42
Placido Benavides and **1**:116
Texas Tornados **8**:50
Tex-Mex culture **8**:*48–51*
food **8**:*50–51*
music **5**:46, **6**:39, **8**:49–50
Thalía **8**:*52*
Thee Midniters **6**:39
thiarubrin **7**:59
Thomas, Piri **8**:*53*–54
Thompson, Hunter S. **1**:8
Thoreau, David **8**:45
Tiant, Luis **8**:55
Tico Records **6**:38, 39
Tienda, Marta **8**:56
"Tie a Yellow Ribbon Round the Old Oak Tree" (song) **6**:85

Tijerina, Felix **8**:*57*
Tijerina, Pete **8**:*58*
Tijerina, Réies López **1**:12, **2**:108, **6**:125–126, *128*, **8**:*59–60*
Tilted Arc (sculpture) **8**:7
Tizol, Juan **8**:*61*
Tjader, Cal **7**:110
Tomás Rivera Policy Institute (TRPI) **7**:47
Tonatiuh Quinto Sol **7**:77
Tony G **4**:107
Toraño, Maria Elena **8**:62
Torres, Edwin **8**:63
Torres, Esteban E. **8**:64
Torres, José **8**:65
Torres, Luis Lloréns **2**:34, **8**:66
Tortilla Soup (film) **6**:109
Traffic (film) **3**:45, 46
"Tragedia del 29 de Agosto, La" (song) **4**:71
transnationalism **1**:82
treasurers, U.S. **6**:87
Trejo, Ernesto **7**:101
Treviño, Jacinto **8**:67
Treviño, Jesús **8**:68
Trevino, Lee **8**:*69*–70
Trini (book) **7**:8
Trinidad, Felix **3**:32, **8**:*71*–72, 90
Trinidad, Felix, Sr. **8**:72
Trio Imperial **4**:70
Trío Los Panchos **1**:29
Trío San Juan **1**:29
Trist, Nicholas P. **4**:66
Triumph of the Spirit (film) **6**:81
Truan, Carlos **8**:*73*
Trujillo, Severino **8**:74
Truman, Harry S., assassination attempt on **1**:13
Tucson, Arizona
Leopoldo Carrillo and **2**:*54*
Mariano Samaniego and **7**:104
Tudor, Antony **1**:45
Turlington, Christy **8**:*75*

U

Unanue, Joseph **8**:*76*
Unión de Trabajadores del Valle Imperiale, La **5**:11
Unión Federal Mexicanos **5**:10
Union of Mine, Mill, and Smelter Workers **5**:12
United Cannery Agricultural Packing and Allied Workers of America (UCAPAWA) **2**:106, **6**:21
United Farm Workers (UFW) **1**:12–13, 22, 23, **4**:113, **5**:13, **6**:44
Antonio Orendain and **6**:84
Arturo S. Rodriguez and **7**:56
César Chávez and **2**:88, 89
and Delano grape strike **5**:13
Dolores Huerta and **4**:113
lapel badge **1**:*19*
United Farm Workers Organizing Committee (UFWOC) **5**:13
United Press International (UPI) **6**:57–58
United States, settlement in **8**:*22–27*
United States v. Sandoval (1897) **8**:26
Univision **5**:96–97
Urrea, Luis Alberto **8**:*77*
Urrea, Teresa **8**:*78*
novel about **8**:77
USA PATRIOT Act (2001) **7**:79

U.S. Hispanic Chamber of Commerce (USHCC) **6**:43, 44
U.S. Latino Issues (book) **1**:15
U.S.-Mexico border *see* border, Mexico-United States
U.S.-Mexico War *see* Mexican War

V

Valdés, Gilberto **6**:94
Valdés, Jesús "Chucho" **3**:79
Valdés, Miguelito **7**:9
Valdés, Vicentico **6**:39
Valdes-Rodriguez, Alisa **8**:*79*
Valdez, José Antonio **8**:80
Valdez, Luis M. **4**:*104*, 109, **6**:82, **8**:*81–82*
Valdez, Patssi **4**:4
Valens, Ritchie **4**:107, **6**:38, **8**:82, *83–84*
Valentín, Bobby **8**:85
Valentino, Rudolph **4**:108
Valenzuela, Fernando **8**:86
Valenzuela, José Luis **3**:*107*, **8**:*87*
Vallejo, Mariano Guadalupe **8**:32, 88
Valley of Peace **8**:59
Valverde, Antonio **5**:96
Vanidades (magazine) **7**:*127*
Varela, Maria **5**:69
Vargas, Diego de **3**:*55*, **8**:23
Vargas, Elizabeth **8**:89
Vargas, Fernando **8**:*90*
Felix Trinidad and **8**:*71–72*, 90
Vargas, Jay R. **8**:*91*
Vargas, Kathy **8**:92
Vargas, Miguel "Mike" **4**:109
Vasconcelos, José **4**:21, 106
Vasquez, Richard **8**:93
Vasquez, Tiburcio **3**:120, **8**:*94*
Vasquez Villalpando, Catalina **8**:*95*–96
Vatican, The **7**: 34, 36, 37
Véa, Alfredo, Jr. **8**:*97*
"Vedette of America" *see* Chacón, Iris
Vega, Bernardo **8**:98
Vega, "Little" Louie **5**:17, **8**:*99*
Vega Yunqué, Edgardo **8**:*100*
Velasco, Treaties of (1836) **7**:132, **8**:43
Velasquez, Baldemar **8**:*101*
Velásquez, Willie **8**:*102*
Velazquez, Loreta Janeta **8**:*103*
Velázquez, Nydia M. **8**:*104*–105
Vélez, Lauren **8**:*106*
Velez, Lupe **4**:*108*, **8**:*107*
Venegas, Juan E. **8**:108
Victoria, Texas **3**:39, 40
Vieques **2**:24, **6**:128
Vietnam War **5**:113
Alfredo Cantu Gonzalez and **4**:51
Euripides Rubio and **7**:92
Jay R. Vargas and **8**:*91*
opposition to **1**:94, **4**:76, **7**:100
Richard E. Cavazos and **2**:75
Roy P. Benavidez and **1**:118
Vigil, Donaciano **8**:*109*
Vilar, Irene **5**:24
Villa, Beto **8**:*110*
Villa, Francisco "Pancho" **4**:49
Villalpando, Catalina Vásquez **8**:*101*
Villanueva, Alma Luz **8**:*111*
Villanueva, Tino **8**:*112*
Villaraigosa, Antonio **6**:*133*, **8**:*113–114*

Set Index

Villaraigosa, Natalia **8**:114
Villarreal, José Antonio
8:*115*–116
Villarreal, Luis **8**:*117*
Villaseñor, Victor **8**:118
Viramontes, Helena Maria **7**:59,
8:*119*
Virgil, Donaciano **1**:67
Víspera del Hombre, La (book)
5:62
Vivir (album) **4**:118
voting **3**:73, **6**:*130*, 131
see also political
representation
Voting Rights Act Amendments
(1975) **3**:73, **5**:85
Voz de las Americas (program)
4:87
Voz del Pueblo, La (newspaper)
5:73

W

Wagner Act *see* National Labor
Relations Act
Walt Disney Productions,
Manuel Gonzales and **4**:44
Warren, Earl **8**:33, 34
Washington, Terry **4**:42
Watergate scandal **7**:30
Wedding, The (book) **6**:134

We Fed Them Cactus (book)
2:20
Weir, Bob **4**:14
Welch, Raquel **8**:*120*–121
Western Federation of Miners
(WFM) **5**:10–11
West Side Story (film and stage
show) **4**:109, **6**:22, 23,
7:44
see also Operation Wetback
Whispering to Fool The Wind
(book) **7**:43
white flight **3**:74
Whitney, John Hay **4**:108
"Why Do Fools Fall in Love?"
(song) **7**:124
Williams, Elena **8**:122, 123
Williams, William Carlos
8:*122*–123
With His Pistol in His Hand
(book) **6**:103
Woman in Battle, The (book)
8:103
*Women Who Run With the
Wolves* (book) **3**:94, 95
Wonder Woman **2**:55
World News Tonight (TV
program) **8**:89
World War I **5**:112
Latinos in **7**:96

need for agricultural and
industrial laborers **4**:122
World War II **2**:107, **5**:112, *113*,
8:46
Cleto Rodriguez and **7**:58
Edward Hidalgo and **4**:97
Felix Longoria and **2**:107,
5:33–34
José M. López and **5**:40
Joseph Unanue and **8**:76
Macario García and **4**:17
need for agricultural and
industrial laborers
2:7–8, **4**:121, 122,
5:12–13, **8**:27, 46
Raul Morin and **6**:24
Silvestre Herrera and **4**:95
Vicente Ximenes and **8**:124

X

Ximenes, Vicente **6**:132, **8**:124

Y

Yahweh ben Yahweh **8**:29
Y'Barbo, Antonio Gil **8**:125
Yglesias, José **8**:*126*
Yo Soy Joaquin (film) **4**:109
"Yo Soy Joaquin" (poem)
4:49
Young, Robert M. **6**:81

Young Citizens for Community
Action (YCCA) **3**:90
Young Lords **2**:109, 110, **6**:128,
7:45
Your Show of Shows (TV series)
2:114–115
yo-yos **3**:*122*
Yzaguirre, Raúl **8**:*127*–128

Z

Zamora, Bernice **8**:129
Zapata, Carmen **8**:*130*
Zapata, Emiliano **4**:49
Zapatistas **1**:24
Zaragoza, Ignacio **8**:*131*–132
Zeno Gandía, Manuel **8**:133
zoopharmacognosy **7**:59
Zoot Suit (play and film) **3**:107,
4:*71*, *104*, **6**:81, 82–83,
8:*81*, 82
zoot suits **4**:104
Zúñiga, Martha **8**:*134*
Zygmund, Antoni **2**:22

Picture Credits

c = centre, t = top, b = bottom.